Morality and Socially Constructed Norms

Morality and Socially Constructed Norms

LAURA VALENTINI

Great Clarendon Street, Oxford, OX2 6DP,
United Kingdom

Oxford University Press is a department of the University of Oxford.
It furthers the University's objective of excellence in research, scholarship,
and education by publishing worldwide. Oxford is a registered trade mark of
Oxford University Press in the UK and in certain other countries

© Laura Valentini 2023

The moral rights of the author have been asserted

All rights reserved. No part of this publication may be reproduced, stored in
a retrieval system, or transmitted, in any form or by any means, without the
prior permission in writing of Oxford University Press, or as expressly permitted
by law, by licence or under terms agreed with the appropriate reprographics
rights organization. Enquiries concerning reproduction outside the scope of the
above should be sent to the Rights Department, Oxford University Press, at the
address above

You must not circulate this work in any other form
and you must impose this same condition on any acquirer

Published in the United States of America by Oxford University Press
198 Madison Avenue, New York, NY 10016, United States of America

British Library Cataloguing in Publication Data

Data available

Library of Congress Control Number: 2023938538

ISBN 9780192845795

DOI: 10.1093/9780191938115.001.0001

Printed and bound in the UK by
Clays Ltd, Elcograf S.p.A.

Links to third party websites are provided by Oxford in good faith and
for information only. Oxford disclaims any responsibility for the materials
contained in any third party website referenced in this work.

Contents

Acknowledgements	vii
Introduction	1
1. Why the Moral Force of Socially Constructed Norms?	2
2. Our Topic in Focus	5
3. Desiderata	7
4. The Agency-Respect View	9
5. Implications	12
6. Ambitions and Limitations	15
7. Methodology	15
1. What Are Socially Constructed Norms?	17
1. Norms: Moral versus Socially Constructed	19
2. Socially Constructed Norms: The Agential-Investment Account	22
3. Why the Agential-Investment Account?	31
4. Intentions and Socially Constructed Norms	39
5. Distinguishing Socially Constructed Norms from Related Phenomena	41
6. Varieties of Socially Constructed Norms	43
7. Socially Constructed Norms and Moral Reactive Attitudes	48
8. Conclusion	51
2. Grounding the Moral Force of Socially Constructed Norms	52
1. The Deflationary View and Its Attractions	53
2. The Limitations of the Deflationary View	55
3. Vindicating the Moral Force of Socially Constructed Norms	60
4. The Principle of Established Practices	62
5. The Conventionalist View	65
6. The Normative-Interests View	69
7. The Joint-Commitments View	75
8. Conclusion	79
3. The Agency-Respect View	81
1. Desiderata	83
2. Respecting Normative Worlds	86
3. Principle P: The Agency-Respect Principle	89
4. Empirical Fact F: Socially Constructed Norms and People's Commitments	94
5. Action Required: The Obligation to Obey Socially Constructed Norms	97
6. The Explanatory Power of the Agency-Respect View	101
7. How the Agency-Respect View Fits the Evidence	103
8. Objections	105
9. Conclusion	118

vi CONTENTS

4. Grounding Moral Rights 119
   1. Two Types of Rights: Rights as Inviolability and Rights as Control 120
   2. Rights as Control 123
   3. Normative Powers, Publicity, and Socially Constructed Norms 126
   4. Linguistic Conventions, Speech Acts, and Normative Powers 128
   5. Intentions and Normative Powers 134
   6. Demanding and Waiving Unintentionally 136
   7. De Facto Powers, Moral Powers, and Socially Constructed Norms 138
   8. From De Facto to Moral Powers 141
   9. Rights and Wrongings 145
  10. Conclusion 149

5. Grounding Political Obligation 150
   1. The Political-Obligation Debate: Terminology and Significance 152
   2. The Difficulties with Existing Views 157
   3. Democratic Theory 163
   4. The Agency-Respect View 167
   5. The Agency-Respect View and Civil Disobedience 172
   6. Between Anarchism and Legal Normativism 176
   7. Conclusion 178

6. Explaining the Wrong of Sovereignty Violations 179
   1. Defining Sovereignty 181
   2. The Sovereignty-Violation Trilemma 185
   3. Giving Up Normative Individualism 188
   4. Giving Up the Wrong of Sovereignty Violations 189
   5. Contesting That Individuals' Legitimate Interests Are Not
     Undermined 190
   6. The Agency-Respect View 198
   7. Back to Our Three Cases 202
   8. Concerns 203
   9. Conclusion 207

Conclusion 208
   1. Conformity, Obedience, and the Deflationary View 208
   2. Agency Respect 210
   3. Who Is Wronged by Breaches of Socially Constructed Norms? 214
   4. When in Rome Do as the Romans Do 216

References 219
Index 231

Acknowledgements

I started to think about the central theme of this book in 2014. Since then, I've accumulated a massive debt of gratitude to people and institutions who have supported me along the way. I cannot do justice to all of them in the limited space available here, but I'll do my best. Profuse apologies in advance to those I might inadvertently forget.

Let me start with two colleagues whose encouragement has been a great source of motivation: Cécile Laborde and Nic Southwood. Cécile heard me give a talk on the morality of socially constructed norms, at a time when no book was planned, and she concluded that I should write a book on this topic. She was so persuasive that I spent the following week thinking about possible book architectures! Nic saw a draft paper containing what turned out to be the book's central idea and, unbeknownst to me, mentioned it to OUP's Peter Momtchiloff. Peter then got in touch with me to explore the possibility of a book on this topic. Cécile's and Nic's belief in my project gave me the confidence to commit to pursuing it. Furthermore, they both provided very generous written feedback on the manuscript. As will be apparent from the book itself, Nic's own work on norms has been an inspiration to me.

Throughout the entire writing process, I benefitted from the input of several colleagues, who generously read and commented on (parts) of the book and/or spent time with me discussing its central ideas. They include Arash Abizadeh, Sara Amighetti, Eric Beerbohm, Susanne Burri, Kimberley Brownlee, Samuel Bruce, Zsuzsanna Chappell, Rowan Cruft, David Enoch, Guy Fletcher, Rainer Forst, Charles Girard, Andrew Gold, Richard Holton, Jakob Huber, Renée Jorgensen, George Klosko, Rae Langton, Seth Lazar, Jeffrey Lenowitz, Catherine Lu, Steven Macedo, Aaron Maltais, Simon May, Liam Murphy, Temitayo Ogunye, Florian Ostmann, Avia Pasternak, Philip Pettit, Felix Pinkert, Massimo Renzo, Miriam Ronzoni, Richard Rowland, Andrea Sangiovanni, Samuel Scheffler, Liam Shields, Laurie Shrage, Thomas Sinclair, Kai Spiekermann, Lucas Stanczyk, Daniel Statman, Anna Stilz, Daniel Viehoff, Gerard Vong, Leif Wenar, Caleb Yong, and Lea Ypi. I am very grateful to them all.

Over the past few years, I presented ideas from the book at a variety of conferences, workshops, and seminars. I would like to thank the audiences at these events for their attention, questions, and comments. I am especially grateful to the participants in the Montreal Political Theory Manuscript Workshop (a one-day workshop devoted to my book manuscript) and particularly to those who commented on individual chapters—Peter Dietsch, Pablo Gilabert, Stephanie

viii ACKNOWLEDGEMENTS

Leary, Pierre Minn, Victor Muñiz-Fraticelli, and Natalie Stoljar—and to Arash Abizadeh, for organizing it all and for his hugely helpful feedback on the project.

Peter Momtchiloff at OUP has been a great editor: supportive, efficient, helpful, and very patient! I would like to thank him and the entire OUP production team for their assistance with all aspects of the publishing process. I am also greatly indebted to three anonymous reviewers for the press, who have provided extensive, perceptive, and constructive comments on the manuscript.

Work on this book has been supported by a variety of institutions, which I would like to acknowledge. These are: The Leverhulme Trust (Philip Leverhulme Prize), the Franco-Swedish Programme in Economics and Philosophy, and the Forschungskolleg Humanwissenschaften at the Goethe Universität in Frankfurt. While conducting research related to the themes of this book, I was fortunate to visit the Swedish Collegium for Advanced Study in Uppsala, the Government Department at Harvard University, and the Centre Justitia Amplificata (Frankfurt University), all of which provided wonderful, supportive, and stimulating working environments.

Parts of the book—especially Chapter 3—draw on my previously published paper "Respect for Persons and the Moral Force of Socially Constructed Norms", *Noûs*, 55 (2) (2021). I am grateful to Wiley Blackwell for granting me a permission to reprint material from the article.

Finally, I would like to thank my family. I am grateful to my mother, Annamaria, my parents-in-law, Jürgen and Barbara, as well as our aunts, uncles, and cousins, for always being there for us. The years immediately prior to the completion of this book were quite eventful: the arrival of two children, a pandemic, a parent's death, and a move to a different country (from the UK to Germany). Without the support of our families, I'm not sure how we could have done it. My mother, in particular, deserves special thanks for being so strong and holding it all together after my father's passing. Sono molto orgogliosa di te, mamma.

I also wish to thank our daughters: Gaia (three) and Clelia (one). They have made our lives richer, happier, higher-energy, and just a little more exhausting… than I ever imagined they could be. They have also made the process of getting any work done much harder than it previously was. I am grateful to them, for this, too. Every day, they teach me to accept imperfection without guilt. (I haven't learnt yet, but I like to believe I'm improving.) And looking forward to spending time with them is the best incentive to getting things done efficiently!

My biggest thank you goes to my husband, Christian, without whom I am certain this book would not exist. This is no overstatement. At various stages of planning and writing, I lost confidence in the project—or, more accurately, in myself—but Christian's continuous encouragement made me keep at it. And his substantive advice was no less valuable. Christian read multiple drafts of the book and discussed many of its central ideas with me. I am immensely grateful for his generosity, acumen, understanding, unfailing support, and patience. (I have pestered him so much with this topic that he would have reason to enforce a norm in our household banning all talk of socially constructed norms!) I am so lucky to share my personal and professional life with him.

As already briefly mentioned, my father, Alfredo Valentini, passed away in the summer of 2020. He was the best father, and words cannot begin to express how grateful I am to him for everything, really. He was a free spirit and, ironically, he didn't have much patience for socially constructed norms—or any kinds of constraints on his agency. Even though I fear he'd disagree with much of the book's content (scusa papà), I dedicate this book to his memory. I know he'd very much treasure the dedication for content-independent reasons.

Introduction

Socially constructed norms—the formal and informal norms that regulate our interpersonal, social, and political lives—are all around us: from the "ladies first" custom to the practice of queuing, from the religious norm that prescribes chastity before marriage all the way to the complex demands that legal systems place on us.[1] A constant presence in our lives, socially constructed norms elicit mixed reactions. On the one hand, we feel their moral pull. We hold one another accountable relative to those norms and respond to their violation with moral emotions such as resentment, disappointment, blame, and guilt.[2] On the other hand, we look at them with suspicion: even ostensibly innocuous norms may reflect problematic imbalances of power and contribute to injustice. In light of this ambivalence, it would be helpful to have a criterion telling us when, if ever, we are morally bound by socially constructed norms and when we should instead disregard them.

This book seeks to develop such a criterion. Its contribution is twofold. In Part 1, it provides a framework explaining *when* and *why* the fact that socially constructed norms require or forbid some course of action places us under corresponding moral obligations. In Part 2, it applies this framework to questions in moral, legal, and political philosophy, namely: (i) what grounds moral rights, (ii) what, if anything, grounds the obligation to obey the law, and (iii) why even seemingly harmless violations of a political collective's sovereignty are wrongful.

This introductory chapter offers a broad overview of the book and presents the motivations behind it, its limitations, and its methodology. To get started, in Section 1, I describe a personal anecdote that sparked my interest in the present topic, and which I expect readers will be able to relate to. The philosophical significance of my inquiry and the book's core claims will be elucidated shortly

---

[1] By "socially constructed norms" I mean norms whose existence depends on the *actual* actions and dispositions of individuals. I contrast socially constructed norms with "valid" or "critical" moral norms (Hart 1963: 20). The latter, I assume, exist independently of individuals' *actual* behaviour and dispositions, and may be legitimately employed to evaluate them. For instance, the norm that slavery is impermissible is a valid moral norm even in a slave society, namely a society that fails to *recognize* the validity of that moral norm (Perry 2006: 1176). Note also that the category of socially constructed norms is broader than that of "informal social norms", as understood in the philosophy of social science. Socially constructed norms, on my view, also include formal legal norms. For an influential account of social norms, developed from a game-theoretic perspective, see Bicchieri (2006). These definitional matters will be addressed at greater length in Chapter 1.

[2] Later on, I will introduce the more technical notion of "reactive attitudes", in line with P. F. Strawson's (1962) influential work.

2 INTRODUCTION

thereafter. In Section 2, I explain what it is for socially constructed norms to have moral normativity. In Section 3, I outline two desiderata that any plausible account of the moral normativity of socially constructed norms should satisfy. In Section 4, I sketch the argument developed in Part 1 of the book and anticipate how it meets the relevant desiderata. In Section 5, I offer an overview of the arguments in Part 2 of the book, concerning moral rights, political obligation, and sovereignty. In Section 6, I discuss the book's ambitions and limitations. Section 7 concludes with some reflections on methodology.

1. Why the Moral Force of Socially Constructed Norms?

At the age of 17, I was sent to the UK on a study holiday. I attended a language school in Bristol, together with my good friend Marta. We decided that, one weekend, we should make a trip to London. We chose to travel by bus. On the designated day, we reached the bus stop and stood there for a few minutes, waiting for our National Express to arrive. When the bus arrived, Marta and I immediately approached the front doors. A few seconds later, we realized that virtually everyone was looking at us disapprovingly. A couple of people even shouted a few words at us, which our then-rather-basic knowledge of the English language didn't allow us to understand. Still, it was clear to us that they were not words of encouragement. We looked around, trying to figure out what was going on, but we were at a loss for a few seconds, until the word "line" or "queue" was mentioned. (Probably "queue", since we were in England.) There was our sin: we had skipped the queue! The fact is, of course, that we had not even realized there was one. In Italy, where Marta and I come from, people do not queue at the bus stop; they gather around it in inchoate fashion. This may appear like an uncivilized custom to some, but I assure you, it works. If you are having trouble imagining such behaviour, think about people waiting for the train or the tube in the UK: they are dispersed along the platform, they do not queue.

At any rate, once I realized that we had breached a local norm, I felt rather embarrassed, almost guilty. I knew I had not violated some fundamental moral requirement—let's face it, "Thou shalt not skip the queue" is not among the Ten Commandments—but I did feel like I had done something mildly wrong, for which an apology was in order. I had (unintentionally, to be sure) breached a harmless local norm, and that didn't seem right to me.

Although this is my first vivid memory of finding myself in this type of situation—i.e., of local-norm breach—there have been countless others. I suspect that I am in good company here. For example, upon returning from trips to Germany, friends have recounted anecdotes involving faux pas with streetlights. The typical scenario features someone crossing an *empty* road on a red light, yet being the target of visible disapproval from the locals, who dutifully wait for the light to turn green. In all likelihood, I have also been guilty of this kind of misstep, only not in recent years. Being married to a German—and, ironically, having moved to Germany shortly before completing this book—I have become familiar with the local customs. But if I did safely cross on a red light in Germany, I know I would be at least mildly embarrassed. I would tell myself "you shouldn't have done that!" and feel the need to apologize to those around me. But why? After all, crossing on a red light when there is no traffic is perfectly fine both in Italy—where I am from—and in London—where I lived most of my adult life.[3] I never feel guilty or embarrassed when I do it in these other places. How could a mere change in location affect the moral quality of what is essentially the same behaviour? Am I just reacting to social pressure, or is there something genuinely morally problematic in breaching local norms?

The moral importance of local norms was brought home to me even more strongly in response to an episode that occurred at the start of my time as a faculty member at a previous university at which I worked. The then-head of the university had authorized the launch of a particular initiative without having the official power to do so: some crucial committee approvals were missing. His reason for acting in this way was a plausible one: one could predict that the committees would have approved the initiative, and a delayed launch might have cost the university the opportunity for some funding. Perhaps, all things considered, the university head did the right thing: in the circumstances, it may have been in the university's best interest to go ahead. Yet I and several others felt that his conduct involved a pro tanto—though perhaps not an all-things-considered—wrong: a form of action ultra vires that required acknowledgement as well as an apology. But why did we feel like this?

Let's assume, for the sake of argument, that the university head had done the right thing. Moreover, the norms he breached were, in some sense, arbitrary: the rules governing the university's decision-making could have been different; other universities are organized differently. It's not that the university head had breached some independent, fundamental moral principle. Yet my sense that something had been done for which an apology was owed wasn't diminished by my awareness of the fact that the alleged wrong consisted in the breach of a "socially constructed" norm: a contingent human creation. The intellectual challenge was justifying this intuitive sense to myself: what plausible moral principle could explain this apparent wrong? Was it defensible to react to this norm breach with judgements and emotions akin to those appropriate in cases of moral violations?

These are all examples of circumstances in which the question of the moral normativity of socially constructed norms arose for me, in my personal life. The same question also came up in my academic life. This happened when I started

---

[3] Unless there are small children around, in which case one shouldn't model potentially dangerous behaviour.

4 INTRODUCTION

working on the age-old problem of political authority and obligation.[4] Do we have a moral obligation to obey the law because it is the law? And if we do, what grounds it? Could we be morally obligated to obey democratically approved laws, even if these are somewhat unjust? Of course, there is an ongoing debate on these questions. But what matters here is what the debate is *about*. When legal and political philosophers speak of the obligation to obey the law, or of the authority of law, they refer to the following (alleged) phenomenon: the fact that a law—i.e., a particular type of socially constructed norm—requires us to act in certain ways places us under a moral obligation to comply.[5] Even in legal and political philosophy, then, the question of the moral normativity of socially constructed norms has a central role to play. It is just that the debate is focused on one class of norms only: legal ones.

By putting together the already existing literature on this topic and my own personal experiences, the idea for this book took shape. Legal and political philosophers have, for a long time, tried to explain the moral normativity of legal norms in particular. But the phenomenon of interest, which calls for an explanation, is much broader than that. We not only feel the moral pull of legal norms, but of *all kinds* of socially constructed norms, including informal ones. In fact, sometimes, informal norms have even greater purchase on us than legal ones. I, for one, don't feel that crossing an empty street on a red light in Germany is any more wrong than skipping the queue in the UK. The legal status of the norm breached in the former case makes no difference to my personal sense of wrongdoing. And I can think of cases where breaching an entrenched custom would strike me as considerably worse—morally speaking—than breaching a little-known law. If these considerations seem plausible, then we should ask when and why, if ever, socially constructed norms—no matter their pedigree—have moral normativity.

I take it that this question is of interest independently of whether one shares my intuitions about particular cases of norm-breaches. You may find it peculiar that I'd feel guilty about crossing on a red light in Germany (in fact, I am certain many of you do!), and you may think that my university head had nothing to apologize for. But unless you are *never* in the grip of any of the norms—legal or otherwise—that you encounter in your environment, this book should have something to say to you too.

---

[4] The problem really is age-old. For instance, it is famously discussed in Plato's *Crito*, which describes events taking place in 399 BCE.

[5] I am assuming a positivist account of the nature of law—i.e., one according to which the content of law is given by social facts, as opposed to evaluative considerations about its goodness or moral merits. I take such an account to be broadly in line with our common-sense views about the nature of law. For general discussion of legal positivism, see Green (2009). I shall return to this matter in Chapter 5.

Moreover, even though the present question has not been directly explored in the philosophical literature—at least not in such general terms—it is of considerable philosophical significance. Some major dichotomies in contemporary moral, legal, and political philosophy presuppose competing answers to it. In moral philosophy, for example, universalists are reluctant to ascribe inherent moral force to local norms, while relativists see them as valid sources of moral normativity. In legal philosophy, anarchists insist that legal norms have no moral status, while advocates of the obligation to obey the law see legal imperatives as morally binding. In political philosophy, liberals insist on the value of the individual over and above the norms governing her community, while communitarians attach great importance to the practices shaping particular social contexts.

Each side of these well-known divides has something important to say: this is why the divides are so persistent. But each side also fails to do justice to the complexity of the relationship between morality and socially constructed norms, or so I will suggest. That relationship, I argue in this book, is not an all-or-nothing affair. It is not that socially constructed norms either always have moral import or never do. In our practical deliberations—i.e., when we are deciding what to do—we have reason to sometimes defer to socially constructed norms and to sometimes distrust them. The challenge is to identify a criterion telling us when and why we should defer rather than distrust, and vice versa. This is the task I set myself in Part 1 of the book. As I will show in Part 2, with this criterion in hand, we can make some progress in relation to long-standing and important debates in moral, legal, and political philosophy.

2. Our Topic in Focus

This book is concerned with identifying the grounds and limits of the moral normativity of socially constructed norms. It seeks to uncover when and why the fact that an action is mandated (or forbidden) by a socially constructed norm renders that action at least pro tanto morally obligatory (or forbidden). This phenomenon calls for an explanation because socially constructed norms alone cannot bring moral obligations into existence, or at least so I shall assume. One cannot derive "an ought from an is".[6] Only moral principles can generate moral obligations. The search for the grounds of the moral normativity of socially constructed norms is thus the search for a moral principle P that explains when and why *the fact that* a certain action is required or prohibited by socially constructed norms makes a difference to its moral status.

---

[6] For critical perspectives on this widely accepted "dogma", see, e.g., Anscombe (1958) and Searle (1964).

6   INTRODUCTION

To be sure, there are several ways in which socially constructed norms, coupled with familiar moral principles, make a difference to what we ought to do. For instance, the norm that one should drive on the left, coupled with the principle that "one should not cause needless harm", results in our obligation to drive on the left. Alternatively, the social norm, prevalent in certain countries, that one should tip waiters, coupled with the principle that "one should not frustrate legitimate expectations", results in our obligation to leave at tip at the end of our meal.[7] What is more, faced with the questions "Why ought you to drive on the left?" and "Why ought you to tip waiters?", it is natural to respond: "Because local norms require that I do".

We might thus be led to believe that the "no needless harm principle" and the "legitimate expectations principle" are two candidate grounds for the moral normativity of socially constructed norms. In just one paragraph, we already seem to have made progress towards answering our question. Isn't that great?

Unfortunately, things are more complicated than they seem. Neither the driving nor the tipping examples offer an illustration of the phenomenon I am after. In both cases, socially constructed norms *contingently cause* certain empirical facts—i.e., people driving on the left, waiters forming certain expectations—and this, in turn, activates the demands of independent moral principles. The demands of said principles are not triggered by the fact that driving on the left and tipping are norm-mandated activities. If people just happened to drive on the left, without this being prescribed by a socially constructed norm, the obligation to drive on the left on harm-avoidance grounds would kick in all the same. Similarly, if legitimate expectations were caused by something other than the operation of a norm, the obligation to satisfy them would continue to exist. In other words, these examples do not illustrate the moral significance *of socially constructed norms*, but show that the contingent causal effects of such norms may activate moral demands.

When speaking of the moral normativity of socially constructed norms, I have something else in mind: our being under obligations to perform certain actions *because* those actions are mandated by socially constructed norms, not because such norms have certain causal effects. To get a better sense of what this means, consider again our driving and tipping examples. Suppose we find ourselves on a completely empty street, with no witnesses and no risk of any vehicle turning up in the next five minutes. In such a situation, whether we drive on the left or on the right makes no difference to anyone's safety. Still, a socially constructed norm mandates that we drive on the left. By virtue of what principle (if any) does this very fact—independently of its causal effects—morally obligate us to keep driving on the left? Or suppose Bob is a regular customer at a restaurant where you're a

---

[7] For general discussion of legitimate expectations, see Meyer et al. (2017).

waiter. Bob is known for never tipping. Consequently, as Bob is paying his bill, you form no expectation that he will leave you a tip. The legitimate-expectations principle is thereby disabled. Does Bob nonetheless do something wrong by violating the requirements of an existing norm (cf. Southwood and Friedrich 2009: 272)?[8]

These are the kinds of questions I wish to address. Answering them in the affirmative requires finding a moral principle P capable of explaining why the very fact that local norms mandate or prohibit certain actions matters morally.

3. Desiderata

We have seen that grounding the moral normativity of socially constructed norms requires identifying a suitable moral principle P. But what, exactly, would make a candidate principle P a good one? Throughout the book, I assume that two basic, familiar desiderata have to be satisfied: explanatory power and fit.

Explanatory power: the explanation is powerful, which means that it makes the phenomenon in question less surprising.[9]

Explanatory power is a familiar desideratum for any theoretical or scientific enterprise. A candidate principle P will satisfy it by showing that the moral normativity of socially constructed norms does not magically spring out of empirical facts, but follows from familiar moral commitments. In doing so, P will take away the surprise element from our phenomenon of interest.

To see how an explanation can be more or less powerful in this sense, consider this simple example. I find my window open upon returning home from a quick trip to the supermarket. This is surprising: I was expecting it to be closed. What could possibly explain this? Here are some candidate explanations: (i) I forgot to close the window before leaving the apartment; (ii) strong wind opened the window; (iii) a burglar broke in; and (iv) the secret services were spying on me and left abruptly when they heard I was coming back. Suppose today is a calm, sunny day, with no wind. And suppose that the burglar alarm (which is very reliable) did not go off and indicate a break in; nor is there any evidence of theft. Finally suppose—though there's not much need to suppose here—that I lead a very inconspicuous life: none of my activities are of any interest to the secret services. Given all this, explanations (ii) and (iii) are more or

---

[8] Southwood and Friedrich discuss the ethics of promising, but offer an example that has inspired my own here.

[9] Explanatory power is a topic much debated in the philosophy of science. I am here drawing on the notion proposed by Schupbach and Sprenger (2011: 108).

8 INTRODUCTION

less ruled out, and although explanation (iv) might remain logically consistent with the explanandum, it appears extremely far-fetched; it would be a conspiracy theory. The occurrence of (iv) would be *more* surprising than the event we are trying to explain. Its explanatory power is therefore minimal. Explanation (i) is clearly superior. It points to a familiar phenomenon, namely accidentally forgetting to close a window, which is straightforwardly connected to the explanandum: the window being open.

By the same token, to meet the explanatory-power desideratum, our principle *P* should be independently plausible and familiar, so as to make an apparently mysterious phenomenon—i.e., the moral normativity of socially constructed norms—a simple consequence of our already held moral views. Let me now turn to our second desideratum:

Fit: the explanation fits the available evidence.

Once again, this desideratum is familiar from scientific endeavours. A good scientific explanation of an empirical phenomenon must fit the observed data. Since here we are focusing on moral, rather than empirical, facts, our target explanation should fit the appropriate data: our judgements about the moral bindingness of socially constructed norms. I mentioned at the outset that these norms elicit mixed reactions: sometimes we feel their moral pull, other times we find them pernicious. Principle *P* should vindicate the moral force of those socially constructed norms we intuitively think of as binding, while not conferring any such force on those we find problematic. This is not to say that a candidate principle *P* would have to be discarded right away if it were unable to account for some of our judgements. After all, some such judgements may be unreliable, the product of habituation, and we may have independent theoretical reasons for discounting them.[10] All I am suggesting is that a principle that requires us to revise too many of those judgements, without providing a convincing theoretical backing for such revisions, would be unsatisfactory. In other words, the principle should fit "the judgements that matter".

Principle *P* should not only fit our judgements about whether norm-breaches are wrongful or not. It should also match our judgements about the *gravity* of the wrongs involved, as well as their *direction*. By "gravity" I mean the seriousness of the moral breach perpetrated by violating a norm. Intuitively, some norm-violations are much more serious than others. Failing to stop at red lights even when the street is empty may seem—at least to some—mildly wrong, but it is certainly a much less serious wrong than shouting insults and swearwords in sacred places. Principle *P* should account for such differences.

Let us now turn to direction. Some instances of norm-breaches may appear wrong simpliciter, rather than wronging some individuals in particular. Take a

---

[10] As is well known, in the process of reflective equilibrium (Rawls 1999a), some considered judgements may have to be revised. I say more about methodology in the final section of this introduction.

social or legal norm that prohibits the consumption of alcohol in public places. Breaching that norm, one *may* think, is wrongful, but does not wrong any individual in particular. At most, it results in a diffuse wrong "against the community". By contrast, violations of property norms have a specific target, an individual who is *wronged* by the breach in question: the owner. Again, in order to satisfy the "fit" desideratum fully, our principle *P* should enable us to account for these variations in considered judgements.

With these desiderata in hand, I now turn to sketching the view I defend in this book and which, I believe, meets them.

4. The Agency-Respect View

The book's main argument rests on two key premises, one ontological, the other normative.

4.1 The ontological premise

The first, ontological premise sets out a particular view about the existence conditions of socially constructed norms. I call it the "agential-investment account" and articulate it in Chapter 1. I argue that a socially constructed norm to φ exists in a given context whenever a general requirement to φ is widely and publicly accepted in that context. Acceptance of a requirement, in turn, involves both a *belief* in that requirement and a *commitment* to it as a general standard of behaviour.

To give this thought some intuitive plausibility, consider the queuing norm. Those who support the norm believe that one ought to queue and are committed to queuing as a general standard of conduct. This can be observed in their own queuing behaviour as well as in their dispositions to sanction and criticize those who fail to comply. What supporters of the queuing norm want to see happen is general compliance with the norm, not merely personal compliance. This, I argue, distinguishes a norm from a private standard of behaviour. Moreover, supporters of the queuing norm are commonly aware of one another's beliefs and dispositions in this regard: their acceptance of the norm is thus "public". Throughout the book, when talking about socially constructed norms, I shall have this type of phenomenon in mind. Let me now turn to the second, normative premise.

4.2 The normative premise

The second premise of my argument sets out my preferred principle *P*. This is a familiar principle in contemporary moral and political philosophy, one that lies at the heart of the liberal tradition. I call it the "agency-respect principle" and

10   INTRODUCTION

discuss it at length in Chapter 3, after critically examining alternative explanations of the moral normativity of socially constructed norms in Chapter 2. This principle states that we have a pro tanto (i.e., overridable) moral obligation to respect other people's authentic and morally permissible commitments, provided this is not too costly to us.

The principle is reminiscent of the Rawlsian-Kantian injunction to give others the freedom and means to pursue their ends and goals, compatibly with our equal right to do the same. It offers an articulation of the popular idea that individuals are owed respect qua agents capable of self-direction. Their autonomy, in turn, manifests itself through their authentically formed commitments, namely commitments not vitiated by brainwashing, coercion, or other forms of undue pressure. Authentic commitments reflect a person's agency, her "true" self (cf. Taylor 1985). Provided those commitments fall within the bounds of morality, and provided respecting them is not excessively burdensome, they generate pro tanto moral demands.

4.3 Combining the premises

If we take the agency-respect principle and combine it with my ontological premise about the existence conditions of socially constructed norms, we can make a respect-based case for the moral normativity of those norms. The agency-respect principle says that, under specified conditions, we ought to respect people's commitments. Socially constructed norms, in turn, are constituted by public commitments of a certain sort. Provided those norms satisfy the conditions specified by P—namely authenticity, permissibility, and reasonable costs—they place moral demands on us on agency-respect grounds. I call the resulting view the "agency-respect view" of the moral normativity of socially constructed norms.

On this view, the agency-respect principle explains why the fact that socially constructed norms require us to do something matters morally, quite independently of its contingent consequences. The explanation is, simply, that respecting the norms is necessary to respect their supporters' authentic commitments. If we didn't respect those norms—of course, assuming they are permissible and there are no overriding costs considerations—we would fail to give people the "agency respect" that they are owed.

No doubt readers will have many questions about this argument strategy, and about the two premises I have just outlined. I will seek to address those questions and concerns in the chapters that follow. This introduction is not the place to discuss them. I do, however, wish to briefly anticipate how the agency-respect view satisfies the desiderata sketched in the previous section.

Consider *explanatory power* first. My proposed explanation of the moral normativity of socially constructed norms relies on a principle, namely the agency-respect principle, that is already familiar from influential works in moral and political philosophy. The principle is not proposed as an ad hoc attempt to explain the phenomenon of interest. Instead, it is one that many of us already accept. If I am indeed right that this principle grounds the moral normativity of socially constructed norms, then this normativity should come as no surprise: it follows from a well-known liberal tenet.

The agency-respect explanation also presents a good level of *fit* with our considered moral judgements. Agency respect only grounds the moral normativity of socially constructed norms that are constituted by morally permissible commitments. Morally abhorrent norms, which reproduce injustice and are vehicles of power abuses, have no moral force on this account. Furthermore, the agency-respect view gives us a straightforward way of accommodating the different strengths of the obligation to obey socially constructed norms in different cases. The more the commitments underpinning the norms are central to agents' plans of life and sense of self—i.e., the more their agency is invested in the norms—the weightier our obligation to act as those norms require. This is why swearing in a sacred place is a graver moral breach than jaywalking, for example, at least to the extent that religious commitments are more central to the lives of those who hold them than commitments to the normativity of traffic rules.

Finally, the agency-respect explanation tallies with our judgements about the direction of the wrong involved in norm-breaches. When a norm prohibiting alcohol consumption in public is violated, we can plausibly say that the wrong (if it is a wrong) is a general, diffused one against the community. The individuals belonging to the community are agency-disrespected by the breach. But in cases where the breach involves the violation of, say, someone's property rights or someone's place in the queue, we can say that, in addition to there being a diffuse wrong against the community, this particular individual has been wronged. This is because the relevant social norms *mark that individual out* as a right-holder, and, consequently, make him or her distinctively connected to the wrong in question.

This is, in a nutshell, the argument I set out in Part 1 of the book. Even optimistically supposing that, by the end of Part 1, readers find my account of the moral normativity of socially constructed norms persuasive, they may still wonder how far-reaching, or modest, its implications are. After all, up to this point I have referred to examples of relatively unimportant norm-breaches, such as queue-jumping, jaywalking, swearing, and actions ultra vires on the part of university officials. It may be good to have a solid account of why all of these norm-breaches are in fact morally problematic. But the philosophical relevance of this finding would be limited if all the finding could do is explain why certain actions are mildly wrong. What I suggest, however, is that the present account can also allow us to make some progress on long-standing debates within normative areas of philosophy. This is what I set out to explain in Part 2 of the book. I outline its core claims in the next section.

12 INTRODUCTION

5. Implications

Part 2 of the book is devoted to showcasing the potential of the framework developed in Part 1 for some important questions in moral, legal, and political philosophy: the grounding of moral rights, the obligation to obey the law, and the wrong of sovereignty violations. The choice of these three topics may seem somewhat disparate, so let me give some motivation for it, before anticipating my main claims. First, the debates I shall discuss in Part 2 are important and ongoing in the relevant fields of philosophy, and therefore of interest in their own right. Second, these debates are each situated in a specific subfield of so-called practical, as opposed to theoretical, philosophy. Showing the relevance of my framework for each of them, then, proves the point that examining the moral normativity of socially constructed norms has implications that cross the boundaries between these three subfields. Third, while much of Part 1 focuses on norms issuing prescriptions or prohibitions, the debates addressed in Part 2 allow me to extend my analysis to a different class of norms: power-conferring ones (see Hart 1961: Ch. 3). This is because questions about the grounds of moral rights, the grounds of political obligation, and the explanation of the wrong of sovereignty violations all concern *normative powers*.

Normative powers—by way of first approximation—are powers to change our own or others' normative situation at will. These powers are typically exercised through appropriate speech acts. Familiar examples include the power to bind oneself through promises, the power to release others from obligations through consent, the power to obligate others through commands, and so forth (for discussion, see, e.g., Owens 2012; Raz 1972; Watson 2009).

On a prominent understanding, which will take centre stage in my discussion, *rights* involve the normative power to control others' duties, by either demanding their performance or waiving them. Similarly, *political obligation* is often characterized as the normative power of the law, or the state, to place obligations on us through its say so. Finally, a state's *sovereignty* consists in its normative power to make binding decisions within its jurisdiction, free from external interference. Taken together, the three chapters help us better understand the nature and function of normative powers, across several issue-domains. If I am right, a particular class of socially constructed norms is key to the existence and functioning of those powers (cf. Owens 2012).

But what, more specifically, does my approach imply for each debate? I briefly anticipate my answer below.

5.1 The grounds of moral rights

In Chapter 4, I take up the controversy surrounding the grounding of moral rights. Do we possess moral rights by nature alone, or are socially constructed norms necessary existence conditions of moral rights? The majority of contemporary authors—at least those with a deontological orientation—lean towards the view that human beings possess moral rights independently of social practices and conventions (see, e.g., Feinberg 1970; Hart 1955; Kamm 2002; Nagel 1995). This idea has become particularly popular over the past few decades, in the context of the debate on the moral foundations of human rights. That said, not everyone subscribes to this "natural-rights view".

Some theorists have argued that the existence of rights, including moral rights, depends on social recognition, social practices, or social norms (see, e.g., Darby 2009; Nieswandt 2016; cf. Sumner 1987). Even the literature on human rights has recently seen the development of approaches—sometimes referred to as "political" or "practice-based"—which challenge the notion that we could possess human rights as a matter of pure natural morality (e.g., Rawls 1999b; Beitz 2009; Raz 2010).

In Chapter 4, I develop and defend a view that steers a middle course between the positions advocated by natural-rights theorists and their critics. I distinguish between two understandings of rights: "rights as inviolability" and "rights as control". The former designate fundamental moral protections that accrue to individuals qua ultimate units of moral concern. The latter refer to specific normative powers—i.e., the powers to demand the performance of certain actions and the power to waive obligations to perform them. I argue that rights as control include "power-conferring" socially constructed norms among their existence conditions, while rights as inviolability do not. Central to my argument is the claim that the exercise of normative powers must meet a publicity condition, and that such a condition can only be met if socially constructed norms specify what counts as the exercise of any particular such power, in any given circumstance. The disagreement between advocates of natural rights and their opponents, I suggest, ultimately depends on ambiguities concerning what, exactly, rights are, and—on one understanding of rights—socially constructed norms play a key part in grounding them. The final sections of the chapter pinpoint the role of the agency-respect principle in lending moral normativity to power-conferring socially constructed norms.

5.2 The obligation to obey the law

In Chapter 5, I take up the issue of political obligation. An age-old debate in legal and political philosophy concerns the question of whether we have a moral obligation to obey the law because it is the law. Philosophical anarchists answer in the negative. They accept that we often ought to act *in conformity with* the law, because doing so brings all kinds of benefits, but deny our obligation to *obey* it, to act as the law commands *because* the law commands it (e.g., Simmons 1979; Wolff 1970; cf. Klosko 2011). Advocates of political authority, by contrast, invoke

14 INTRODUCTION

a variety of different grounds in support of the view that we do, in fact, have an obligation to obey the law. The grounds in question range from (i) consent, to (ii) the democratic pedigree of the law, (iii) the fact that we gain benefits from others' obedience, benefits which we are under a fairness-based obligation to reciprocate, (iv) the associative obligations that allegedly arise from living in a law-governed political community, and (v) our duties of justice to support reasonably just institutions, to name a few (for overviews, see Christiano 2013; Dagger and Lefkowitz 2014).

Chapter 5 brings the framework developed in Part 1 to bear on this question. I first suggest that many attempts to defend the obligation to obey the law in fact only succeed in justifying an obligation to act in conformity with it (Klosko 2011; Valentini 2018). I then show that, on the agency-respect view, we can make a case for political obligation, while remaining sensitive to anarchist concerns. Provided legal norms are morally permissible, people's commitments to them are authentic, and adhering to them isn't too costly, they place pro tanto obligations on us on agency-respect grounds. Contrary to what advocates of the obligation to obey the law often imply, however, that obligation is potentially rather weak—it all depends on the strength of the agential commitments sustaining the rule of law. Moreover, when formal legal norms clash with informal social norms, on the agency-respect view it does not automatically follow that the former take priority over the latter. To that extent, the agency-respect view sides with anarchists in holding that the law is not morally special.

5.3 The wrong of sovereignty violations

Finally, Chapter 6 takes up the question of what, if anything, accounts for the wrong of violating the sovereignty of political collectives, such as states. There are, of course, many familiar wrongs that often accompany such violations: bodily harm, theft, oppression, and exploitation. But the question is at its most philosophically interesting when we consider examples of *pure sovereignty violations*, where a collective's sovereignty is disregarded—i.e., the collective's binding will is ignored—yet no harms appear to befall individuals. Peaceful (hypothetical) unilateral annexations are a case in point (e.g., Altman and Wellman 2009: 14; Stilz 2019: Chs 4–5). What is striking about pure sovereignty violations is that, *at first sight*, accounting for their intuitive wrongness requires abandoning the widely held, plausible view that wrongdoing always stems from the violation of individuals' legitimate interests. I consider different avenues for making sense of the wrong of pure sovereignty violations, with a particular focus on those that trace it to the impact they have on the autonomy of individuals (contrary to the appearance that such violations do not affect individuals' interests). After raising some concerns about existing views, I bring the agency-respect framework to bear on this matter. Pure sovereignty violations, I argue, are wrongful to the extent that they frustrate the authentic and permissible commitments of those who sustain domestic and international sovereignty norms.

6. Ambitions and Limitations

No doubt, readers will have noticed that this book is ambitious. Readers will also have noticed, in picking it up, that it is not a big tome. With a few exceptions, it seems to me that ambition and brevity seldom go together. How, a reader might wonder, can one write a book discussing the moral normativity of socially constructed norms, and then address debates about the grounding of moral rights, the obligation to obey the law, and the nature of sovereignty in about 200 pages? Surely, each of these topics would deserve a book in and of itself, each of which should be well above 200 pages long!

While I do not disagree that some of the topics discussed in this book could be the object—in fact, have been the object—of much lengthier discussions, there is a reason for the book's relative brevity, beyond its author's exhaustion. The book's main contribution is set out in Part 1: it consists in asking a question which, so far, the literature has not devoted much attention to (i.e., what grounds the moral normativity of socially constructed norms) and in offering what I hope is a plausible answer to it.[11] That answer takes the form of a general *framework*—which I call the agency-respect view—some aspects of which, as will become clear in the subsequent discussion, are modular and open-ended.

In Part 2, I then *sketch* the implications of this framework, and of taking socially constructed norms seriously, for some long-standing philosophical debates. My aim is to show that, when brought to bear on these debates, the framework points us in fruitful and hitherto unexplored directions. Emphatically, I do not aspire to demonstrate that the positions I take about rights, political obligation, and sovereignty are superior to everything that has already been said about these subjects. Nor do I seek to offer a complete treatment of these topics, even as they relate to the agency-respect view. This would be a hubristic ambition destined to be frustrated. Instead, I want to illustrate how approaching these subjects from the perspective of the moral normativity of socially constructed norms yields interesting insights. This more realistic ambition can be fulfilled, I believe, in a medium-length book.

7. Methodology

This is a book in analytic moral, legal, and political philosophy, and relies upon the methodologies that are typical of these areas. What I have to say about them

---

[11] Owens (2022) focuses on the moral normativity of convention, and it is the only recent book-length treatment of this topic I am aware of.

16 INTRODUCTION

isn't particularly original, so readers familiar with said methodologies may well prefer to go straight to Chapter 1. For those not put off by the admittedly unexciting content of this section, here is a brief overview of my methodological choices and commitments. My discussions will mostly involve (a) conceptual analysis and (b) the development of general principles aimed at explaining and illuminating our "considered moral judgements"—namely those moral judgements we hold most confidently and upon consideration.

Conceptual analysis will be key to providing characterizations of contested notions, such as "rights" (Chapter 4) and "socially constructed norms" (Chapter 1). In developing definitions of these notions, I shall strive to remain faithful to our pre-theoretic, ordinary-language use of them, while at the same time making sure that the definitions I provide capture interesting and important phenomena. My view is that there is no such thing as the correct definition of a concept. Concepts are like "mental filing systems", and definitions can therefore be more or less useful, depending on the purposes for which we wish to use a particular concept (List and Valentini 2016).

Regarding the development of general principles, I follow the widely employed Rawlsian method of "reflective equilibrium" (Rawls 1999a). According to this method, our considered moral judgements are to be treated as defeasible evidence. In searching for principles capable of explaining this evidence, we move back and forth between candidate principles and those judgements, sometimes revising the former, other times the latter, until an equilibrium is reached between the general theory and the evidence (considered judgements) which the theory is meant to explain (for discussion, see Daniels 2013). While, of course, the evidence provided by considered judgements is defeasible, it goes without saying that if a candidate principle is at odds with too many and too significant such judgements, we have reason to doubt its plausibility, unless there are compelling countervailing theoretical considerations. This test was in fact already articulated in the criterion of "fit" outlined earlier in Section 2.

There is a question about whether the considered judgements we systematize via reflective equilibrium really capture some independent moral reality. For present purposes, I need not take a stand on this matter. Readers who are moral realists and trust intuitions can see the development of principles via reflective equilibrium as attempts to explain what true morality requires. By contrast, those who are sceptical about the reliability of intuitions as trackers of the moral truth can at least accept that our considered moral judgements happen to encode the morality we subscribe to from our vantage point. To that extent, the present book can be seen as offering a systematization of *that* morality, one that enables us to see the principles that underpin our moral sensitivities in a clear and coherent fashion. If I succeeded in that less ambitious task, I would already feel quite satisfied with my efforts.

Morality and Socially Constructed Norms. Laura Valentini, Oxford University Press. © Laura Valentini 2023.
DOI: 10.1093/9780191938115.003.0001

1

What Are Socially Constructed Norms?

We are likely to have encountered the notion of a social norm and its "cousins"—e.g., a social rule, a social convention, a positive norm—in many contexts. These notions are routinely used to describe familiar phenomena, such as queuing, tipping, taking one's shoes off when entering someone's home, offering one's seat to the elderly on public transport, not chewing with one's mouth open, stopping at red lights, and so forth. All of these activities, it is often said, are governed by norms or conventions or social rules—what I will collectively refer to as "socially constructed norms".[1]

While we all have a rough sense of what socially constructed norms are, scholarly accounts of such norms vary widely. Such variation is partly accounted for by the fact that socially constructed norms are studied in a multiplicity of disciplines—including law, social psychology, sociology, economics, and philosophy. To the extent that the concerns animating these disciplines differ, it is unsurprising that each discipline has offered a definition of socially constructed norms suited for its own purposes.

For instance, in the rational choice and economics tradition, socially constructed norms have been characterized as *equilibrium solutions* to coordination problems. The norm that one should greet people by extending one's right hand is a case in point: the norm solves a coordination problem, and once it is in place, individuals have no incentive to deviate from it (Burke and Young 2011: 313–14). More broadly, some see socially constructed norms as "voluntary *behaviour* that is prevalent within a given reference group" (Interis 2011: 425, my emphasis). Others think of socially constructed norms as constituted by widespread *conditional preferences* for compliance with certain principles (Bicchieri 2006). Others still regard them as clusters of *normative attitudes* held by a large enough number of individuals in a given context. The attitudes in question include, for example, beliefs that a given conduct is obligatory, dispositions to criticize and sanction non-compliers, guilt and shame in response to norm-breaches, and so forth (Brennan et al. 2013; cf. Hart 1961).[2] The list of examples could continue.

---

[1] I use the label "socially constructed norms" instead of "social norms" or "conventional norms", since the latter two expressions are often associated with particular accounts of what these norms are, and can thus lead to confusion. The broader label "socially constructed norms" strikes me as more neutral, and therefore less susceptible to misinterpretation.

[2] "Brennan et al." stands for Brennan, Eriksson, Goodin, and Southwood.

18 WHAT ARE SOCIALLY CONSTRUCTED NORMS?

My aim in this chapter is not to determine which notion of a socially constructed norm, among the many so far proposed in the scholarly literature, is correct. In fact, I am not sure this question is even meaningful.[3] How we define socially constructed norms partly depends on the function we wish this notion to play within our broader theoretical endeavour. Different literatures may use the label "socially constructed norms" to designate different phenomena, each of which has a role to play in explanatory social science or normative theory. Quarrelling about who defines socially constructed norms correctly simpliciter, therefore, seems like a fruitless exercise.

In line with these observations, in this chapter I propose an account of socially constructed norms that I believe is well suited to my purposes. My overall aim in this book is to explain when and why socially constructed norms are morally binding. When they are, we may appropriately hold one another accountable by reference to their demands. Those who avoidably fail to comply with those demands become legitimate targets of blame, criticism, and sanctions. The account of socially constructed norms I offer must be fit for this particular theoretical task. This involves satisfying two desiderata.

On the one hand, socially constructed norms should be characterized as objects for which my guiding question can be meaningfully asked. From the perspective of this desideratum, for instance, counting privately held rules of conduct, which cannot be known to others, among socially constructed norms would be problematic. It makes little sense to *even ask* whether we should hold others responsible for violating such rules. If the rules can't be known to them—i.e., if they aren't in some sense *public*—violations cannot ordinarily be candidates for eliciting reactive attitudes such as blame or resentment.

On the other hand, the account of socially constructed norms I develop should not already imply a particular answer to the question I pose. That is, it should not be gerrymandered in such a way as to be ad hoc. For example, a moralized understanding of socially constructed norms, such as one that involved reference to justice, would fail to meet this desideratum. On the assumption that obeying just norms is morally obligatory, the account would make the moral bindingness of such norms true by definitional fiat. To escape this gerrymandering problem, my account should be broadly consistent with our ordinary-language notion of a socially constructed norm, and capture at least core, uncontroversial instances of such norms. It should pick out a relevant social phenomenon, for which the label "socially constructed norm" seems fitting.

With a view to fulfilling these desiderata, the chapter proceeds as follows. In Section 1, I introduce the notion of a norm, and distinguish between valid moral

---

[3] As Christian List and I (2016) have argued elsewhere, definitions cannot be, strictly speaking, true or false. Instead, they can be more or less useful, more or less well suited to the theoretical task at hand.

norms and socially constructed ones. In Section 2, I focus on socially constructed norms specifically, and offer an account of the existence conditions of such norms: I call it the "agential-investment account". I propose that a socially constructed norm exists in a given context C whenever a general requirement is widely and publicly accepted among C's inhabitants. I explain that accepting a requirement involves (i) believing its content and (ii) being committed to it as a general standard of behaviour. In Section 3, I motivate the agential-investment account by comparing it with alternative accounts of the existence conditions of socially constructed norms. In Section 4, I say more about the kinds of commitments that, on the agential-investment account, underpin socially constructed norms. As we will see in subsequent chapters, it is precisely those commitments that contribute to lending moral normativity to such norms. In Section 5, I distinguish socially constructed norms from other, related phenomena, such as personal policies, habits, and conventions. In Section 6, I consider the differences between formal and informal socially constructed norms, and between directive (or prescriptive) and power-conferring ones. In Section 7, I zoom in on the types of socially constructed norms that will be of particular interest to us: norms whose breaches trigger particular reactive attitudes, associated with moral violations. Section 8 concludes.

Let me clarify that, in this chapter, I am solely concerned with the question of what socially constructed norms are. I will have nothing to say about their emergence and evolution (on this see, e.g., Ullmann-Margalit 1977; Skyrms 1996; Bicchieri et al. 1997; Sugden 2004; Young 2015). Albeit interesting, this is a social-scientific question that falls outside the scope of my inquiry. Furthermore, since my account of socially constructed norms is developed with a particular purpose in mind, I will not devote much space to outlining and criticizing other scholars' accounts. While I have learnt from those accounts, and will refer to some of them along the way—especially those that are closest to mine—they are designed to fulfil different theoretical tasks, so that discussing them at length would be somewhat beside the point (see, e.g., Hart 1961; Elster 1989; Bicchieri 2006; Brennan et al. 2013).

1. Norms: Moral versus Socially Constructed

Let me begin by listing some norms. Even prior to offering a precise definition of what a norm is, we can identify countless uncontroversial instances of norms—instances that any plausible definition should be able to account for. Here is a brief selection.

- "People ought not to litter when walking on the street".
- "People ought to pay their taxes".

20   WHAT ARE SOCIALLY CONSTRUCTED NORMS?

- "Men ought to take their hats off upon entering a church".
- "Young people ought to offer their bus seats to the elderly".
- "Dinner party guests ought to arrive a few minutes later than the official start-time of the party".
- "Ladies ought to be served first".
- "Students' essays ought to be marked and returned within two weeks of submission".
- "Doctoral students ought to attend the doctoral workshop".
- "Drivers ought to stop at red lights".
- "One ought not to harm innocent others".
- "One ought not to use others' property without their consent".

The above list contains a number of familiar norms and illustrates their typical structure. Norms, as I understand them here following Brennan et al., are general rules of conduct.[4] They take this canonical form: "Every A, in C, ought (not) to/ may φ", where A is an agent-type, C is a context-type, and φ is an action-type (Brennan et al. 2013: 3). Norms are *normative* insofar as they are expressed by propositions containing normative (or deontic) operators such as "ought", "must", and "may".[5] They set out what counts as permissible, required, or forbidden behaviour for certain classes of agents in given situations. For example, adult men (A) are required to take their hats off (φ) upon entering a church (C); young people (A) are required to offer their seats to the elderly (φ) when on the bus (C); everyone (A) is forbidden from littering (φ) when walking on the street (C); everyone (A) is forbidden from harming innocent others (φ) across the board (C); and so forth.

While this is the canonical form that norms take, there exist multiple types of norms, and taxonomies of norms vary depending on the particular dimensions they focus on. Such dimensions include: scope (i.e., who is subject to the norms), content-type (i.e., which domain of human life the norms govern), source of

---

[4] Of course, the notion of a norm can also be employed in a different manner. For example, "natural norms" in Philippa Foot's (2001: 32–3) work designate standards of goodness for particular species. It is a norm in this sense that male peacocks have a colourful tail; the absence of a colourful tail for a male peacock would be a defect (and not merely statistically unusual), since it would put that individual animal at a reproductive disadvantage. Or else, norms may designate statistical regularities: what is standard behaviour in certain contexts. For example, one could say that the "normal" breakfast in Italy consists of a cappuccino and a croissant. This is what Italians typically eat for breakfast, but there's no norm in Italy requiring that one consumes a particular type of breakfast. Finally, the notion of "norms" may be used to designate rules that are not deontic, such as perhaps mathematical or logical norms. I set these other understandings of the notion of a norm aside for present purposes.

[5] Throughout the chapter, I shall focus on norms that prescribe or forbid certain conduct, and say relatively little about permissibility norms. Such norms, however, also exist, and count as normative just as much as prescriptive norms do. Moreover, as I shall explain in Section 6 of this chapter, and further discuss in Chapter 4, power-conferring norms, namely norms that confer on individuals the power to alter their own or others' normative situation, also fall within the scope of my analysis, since they are "normative" in the required sense.

authoritativeness (i.e., what, in the eyes of norm-followers, grounds the normativity of the norms), function (e.g., solving coordination problems, creating accountability, etc.), and several others (O'Neill 2017).

For present purposes, I wish to highlight a particular distinction: that between *socially constructed norms* and *valid moral norms* (see, e.g., Brennan et al. 2013: 5ff.). These two classes of norms can be distinguished by reference to their existence conditions: the facts by virtue of which these norms exist. Socially constructed norms exist whenever a general rule of conduct, such as those previously enumerated, is widely and publicly accepted in a given context (Hart 1961: 55). That is, socially constructed norms have "social existence conditions" (Perry 2006: 1174). Their existence depends on things like the *actual* attitudes, thoughts, beliefs, and behaviour of individuals. I will elaborate on the relevant social existence conditions in the next section.

Valid moral norms, at least in the eyes of most professional moral philosophers as well as members of the public, exist independently of what individuals or groups actually happen to accept, believe, or do.[6] What exactly the existence conditions of valid moral norms are is a complex question, with which meta-ethicists concern themselves (for an overview, see Sayre-McCord 2014). For our purposes, we need not subscribe to a particular meta-ethical view about the existence of valid moral norms. All we need to point out is that, unless one embraces "status-quo conventionalism" about valid moral norms—according to which the existence conditions of valid moral norms coincide with the existence conditions of socially constructed ones—the two classes of norms come apart.

This is fully in line with ordinary moral thinking. For instance, the existence of a valid moral norm prohibiting slavery seems to be altogether independent of the existence of socially constructed norms prohibiting slavery. Slavery is morally wrong, and thus morally prohibited, independently of whether a given society happens to accept and recognize this truth (Perry 2006: 1176).

The difference between socially constructed norms and valid moral norms is further confirmed by the common practice of appealing to the latter to criticize and change the former.[7] For example, it is customary to criticize existing socially constructed norms that prescribe a gendered division of labour—e.g., "women are responsible for the household" and "men are breadwinners"—by appeal to the valid moral norm that men and women ought to be treated as equals, and thus ought to have equal opportunities.

The aim of this book is to explore the relationship between valid moral norms—or what I shall call "principles"—and socially constructed ones. As explained in the

---

[6] That said, valid moral norms may depend on the dispositions individuals would have or the actions they would perform under suitable hypothetical conditions.

[7] See H. L. A. Hart's (1963: 20) distinction between "critical" morality and "positive" or de facto morality.

book's Introduction, I wish to examine whether and, if so, under what conditions, socially constructed norms gain *moral* normativity. That is, I wish to establish whether, sometimes, the fact that a socially constructed norm requires us to φ places us under a moral—and not merely a social—obligation to φ.[8]

Before embarking upon this task, though, a more in-depth analysis of socially constructed norms is required. We need to gain a clearer sense of what it takes for such norms to exist. This is what I turn to in the next section. (From now on, unless otherwise stated, whenever I use the term "norm", I mean "socially constructed norm".)

2. Socially Constructed Norms: The Agential-Investment Account

I said that socially constructed norms exist when a general action-guiding rule is widely and publicly accepted in a given context. This formulation of the existence conditions of socially constructed norms needs further unpacking. In particular, I must clarify what it is for a rule to be "accepted" (2.1), and to be accepted both "widely" (2.2) and "publicly" (2.3). Doing so will lead me to propose a particular account of the existence conditions of socially constructed norms, which I call the "agential-investment account". On my view, socially constructed norms come into being when individuals "put their intentional agency behind" certain general requirements: when they make an agential investment in them.[9] And when they do so widely and publicly, a socially constructed norm exists.

Let me say from the start, however, that the account I propose is meant to be *modular.* I offer a particular interpretation of what it is for a general requirement to be widely and publicly accepted, but readers may not fully agree with this interpretation. They may then wish to fill out the relevant parameters (i.e.,

---

[8] The literature sometimes draws a distinction between "moral" and "conventional" norms *internal* to the category of socially constructed norms. For example, the norm that one should not needlessly harm innocent others is socially constructed, to the extent that it is widely and publicly accepted by large sets of individuals in multiple contexts. Similarly, the norm that one should not chew with one's mouth open is socially constructed. However, the former norm is often classified as a socially constructed *moral* norm, and the latter as a *conventional* one. How the distinction is drawn varies from author to author (see O'Neill 2017, for discussion). Often-invoked rationales include: (i) violations of moral socially constructed norms are more seriously wrongful than violations of conventional ones, (ii) moral socially constructed norms are universally valid, unlike conventional ones, which are context-specific, (iii) in the eyes of norm-followers, the authoritativeness of moral socially constructed norms stems from some objective moral principle, and not from tradition or social advantage. No matter what the particular rationale invoked, moral norms so understood differ from what, in the main text, I have called *valid* moral norms. The latter are not a sub-class of socially constructed norms, but altogether different types of norms. For discussion of the "moral vs conventional" distinction, see Southwood (2011). For discussion of socially constructed norms with "moral connotations", see Section 7 of this chapter.

[9] I owe the expression "putting one's agency behind something" to Ruth Chang (2013b), who uses it in a different context, for different purposes.

wide acceptance, publicity) somewhat differently. While I do think that the interpretation I offer is fitting for my purposes, even those who disagree with aspects of it need not come to the conclusion that the rest of the book has nothing to offer to them. Much of what I say about the moral normativity of socially constructed norms in later chapters would continue to apply under different accounts of the existence conditions of those norms, provided the accounts in question overlap sufficiently with the one I offer here. Given that accounts of the existence conditions of socially constructed norms are bound to overlap somewhat—after all, they concern the same subject matter—I am reasonably hopeful that disagreement with the present one wouldn't greatly undermine the significance of the conclusions reached in the rest of the book.

2.1 Accepting a general rule

I begin by specifying what I mean by the acceptance of a general rule or requirement.[10] I interpret this notion as involving: (i) a cognitive state, namely, *a belief*, and (ii) an appropriate action-guiding attitude, namely, *a commitment*.

First of all, to accept a general requirement that p, with p being the proposition expressing the requirement—e.g., that men and women ought to share household tasks equally—I must believe that p, namely that men and women ought to share household tasks equally. Similarly, acceptance of the general requirements that people ought to pay their taxes, that one ought to follow a particular dress code at graduation ceremonies, that one ought not to skip the queue, etc., necessitates corresponding ought-beliefs. Complying with a requirement without corresponding ought-beliefs—e.g., queuing at the bus stop out of conformism but without believing than one ought to queue—does not amount to accepting that requirement. The person who queues but does not care cannot be said to accept the demands of the queuing norm: she just unreflectively goes along with what others do.

Although—I hope—intuitive, the claim that normative beliefs are necessary for accepting a requirement may be doubted. I say more to motivate the indispensability of such beliefs, at least for my purposes, in Section 3.1, below. Now I turn to the question of whether normative beliefs *suffice* for acceptance of a general requirement. To answer this question, we need to bear in mind that, since socially constructed norms are meant to be action guiding, the propositional attitudes underpinning them must be able to move people to act. Normative beliefs—i.e., beliefs about what we ought to do—can thus suffice for acceptance of a general requirement only if they are capable of motivating action (Bicchieri 2006: 10).

---

[10] Since I will be using examples involving prescriptive rules, I will use the notions of "rule" and "requirement" interchangeably.

24 WHAT ARE SOCIALLY CONSTRUCTED NORMS?

The motivating power of normative beliefs is a matter of philosophical controversy. On one picture of moral motivation—often called anti-Humean—normative beliefs can motivate by themselves, without requiring appeal to familiar action-guiding attitudes such as desires, commitments, or preferences (for general discussion, see Rosati 2016). From this perspective, the belief that one ought not to kill the innocent can suffice to move one to refrain from killing the innocent. No corresponding desire or commitment to so refrain is required. On this picture of moral motivation, the presence of normative beliefs whose content matches general requirements is therefore both necessary and sufficient for acceptance of those requirements.

On an alternative—so-called Humean—picture, beliefs alone, including moral beliefs, cannot motivate. This conviction stems from the very nature of beliefs as propositional attitudes. Beliefs are attitudes with a "mind-to-world" direction of fit (cf. Anscombe 1957: 56). They *represent* what we take the world to be like and, by themselves, they cannot prompt us to act. For example, when I believe the proposition "grass is green", my corresponding mental state represents the grass as being green: a feature I ascribe to the world. My mind, thus, seeks to "fit" the world. Only an attitude with a "world-to-mind" direction of fit—that is an attitude the aim of which is to modify the world rather than to represent it—can move us to act in particular ways (see also Smith 1987). Such an attitude could be a desire, a preference, an intention, a commitment, etc. For instance, when I desire that I eat an ice-cream, my corresponding mental state aims to make the world conform to the object of my desire: to make it the case that the truth conditions of the proposition "I eat an ice-cream" be satisfied. From this Humean perspective, while accepting a general requirement could involve an appropriate ought-belief, the ought-belief would not be sufficient for it. It would have to be coupled with a relevant action-guiding attitude.

Adjudicating the controversy between these competing accounts of motivation is well beyond the scope of the present discussion. I will instead explicitly assume the Humean picture, and thus regard acceptance of a general requirement as dependent on the presence of *both* a representational attitude—a belief—*and* an action-guiding one. (The reasons behind my sympathy for this picture are briefly outlined in this footnote.[11])

---

[11] I am aware that this picture has been challenged (e.g., Korsgaard 1986). I do, however, find it generally compelling for two reasons. First, this Humean "belief-desire" model is the picture of motivation implicit in much explanatory social and natural science. Its success at explaining and predicting the behaviour of both human and non-human animals thus counts in its favour. Second, the model does not require us to draw a sharp, and arguably mysterious line between beliefs about empirical facts and beliefs about normative facts. Beliefs about empirical facts—e.g., the belief that grass is green, that punching someone hurts them, that vaccinations protect one from illnesses, etc.—are not, *by themselves*, action-guiding or capable of motivating. If we were to posit that beliefs about normative facts can indeed motivate, we would thereby imply that such beliefs are not in fact *the same types* of propositional attitudes as what we ordinarily call beliefs about the "non-normative". Normative beliefs

SOCIALLY CONSTRUCTED NORMS   25

That said, let me flag that my subscribing to the Humean account of motivation does not make the rest of my discussion irrelevant to readers with anti-Humean sympathies. These readers can simply proceed on the assumption that the action-guiding attitude I consider necessary for acceptance of a general requirement—i.e., what I call "commitment", more on which in a moment—is in fact *entailed* by normative beliefs. Not much of substance will change if we keep the notions of a normative belief and of a commitment separate (as I will do), or if we hold that one automatically implies the other.[12]

But what is a commitment?[13] I understand this notion broadly, as a distinctive pro-attitude towards particular objects. Possible objects of commitment include goals (e.g., losing weight), practices or actions (e.g., going to church on Sundays), values (e.g., sincerity), people (e.g., one's friend or partner), and norms or principles (e.g., "one ought to show respect to the elderly"). Three features of commitments are worth emphasizing.

First, I follow Cheshire Calhoun (2009: 618) in regarding a commitment as a particular type of intention.[14] Intentions are pro-attitudes distinct from desires and not reducible to them (Bratman 1984). More specifically, intentions involve an agential investment that ordinary desires lack. We can desire to φ, without having settled on whether to φ. But once we have formed the intention to φ, the question of whether to φ is no longer an open one: we have already answered it in the affirmative (Bratman 1981: 256, fn. 5).[15]

Commitments are to be understood as specific *types* of intentions, namely *robust* ones. Intentions that are easy to abandon, such as the intention to pick up an umbrella before going to the office or of eating an ice-cream after dinner, hardly qualify as commitments proper (Calhoun 2009: 618–19).[16] To take the latter example, after finishing my main course at a restaurant I may announce that I intend to order dessert. Upon reading the menu, however, I realize that nothing on offer inspires me. With some disappointment, I change my mind, and order a coffee instead. While we can certainly say that I had intended to order dessert—in fact, I had already partly embarked upon the relevant action by looking at the menu—it would be odd to say that I was *committed* to ordering it. My original intention was not robust enough; it was too easily revisable. Commitments

---

would possess a further property that beliefs about empirical facts lack. This is why I feel myself pulled in the direction of the Humean picture.

[12] Thanks to Christian List for discussion.

[13] As will become apparent, I do not have in mind here interpersonal commitments *to* other people, like promises or contracts.

[14] The link between commitment and intention is familiar from the literature. See, e.g., Hieronymi (2005: 450). For a different account of commitment, understood as the exercise of a normative power, see Chang (2013a).

[15] There is also a complex philosophical debate on the precise nature of intention, which I won't be reviewing here. For an overview and discussion, see Setiya (2015).

[16] I am agnostic about how much robustness is enough. Different specifications of this parameter are compatible with the broad view I am presenting here.

proper, by contrast, tend to persist despite temptations to give them up, and those who are committed often make active efforts to see to it that their intentions not dissipate too quickly.

Second, commitments can be formed in different ways. People sometimes make commitments consciously, for instance, when they decide to convert to a particular religion or to pursue a certain career. Alternatively, people may grow into commitments over time—e.g., to a particular hobby, institution, person, or principle—without explicitly making a decision to so commit (Chang 2013a: 75). In both cases, as Calhoun points out, commitments are active: they are something that we author. What differs is simply the time-horizon and level of awareness with which this authorial process takes place. Commitments therefore further differ from desires or urges that simply arise in us, and over which we seem to have no agential control (Calhoun 2009: 617; see also Chang 2013a: 92).

Third, commitments can be differently motivated or caused. One may commit for all sorts of reasons, some of which will strike us as more noble or genuine than others. For instance, a woman may commit to losing weight to improve her health or to pursue a distorted ideal of female beauty popularized by the media. One may commit for moral reasons or for prudential ones. I may be committed to not injuring innocent others because I believe it would be wrong to do so, or I may be so committed simply because of fear of sanctions. A teenager may be committed to doing extremely well at school either because she herself genuinely cares about her education or because her parents have been so pushy and ambitious that she has been "beaten into submission". In all these cases, commitments exist: the agents in question have formed a robust intention to direct their agency towards a particular goal. Yet the significance—moral or otherwise—of the relevant commitments varies depending on how they came into being. (The latter point will be elaborated on in Chapter 3.)

Having clarified what I mean by a "commitment", I must now link this notion back to socially constructed norms. I said that the existence of a norm depends on people's acceptance of a corresponding general rule. I propose that such acceptance involves not only a belief in, but also a commitment to, that rule, namely a robust intention that the rule function as a general standard of behaviour: an authoritative guide for one's own and others' actions. With respect to any given norm N, *norm-supporters* are those individuals who believe the content of N and are committed to N as a general standard of behaviour.

To see how this account of acceptance fits ordinary cases of socially constructed norms, consider the following simple example. What is it for the inhabitants of a small village to accept the general rule that one should queue up when waiting for the bus? It is for them to believe the content of the rule and to be committed to it, i.e., to robustly intend that the rule function as a general standard of behaviour. This is apparent in the villagers' adherence to the queuing rule, and in their disposition to criticize, disapprove of, and sanction one another for breaches of it (cf. Hart 1961: 55–7). The intention involved must be sufficiently robust: one does not really accept the rule that one ought to queue for the bus if, as soon as following it becomes costly—e.g., one arrives last—one's intention that it function as a standard of behaviour for oneself and others evaporates.

Importantly, all that is needed for the acceptance of a rule, on my account, is a belief coupled with a commitment: an action-guiding attitude, not a piece of behaviour (Bicchieri 2006: 8). A norm can thus exist even when the commitment remains, occasionally, unfulfilled. To see this, suppose that, one morning, the villagers wake up to the shocking news that a terrorist attack has taken place near their local church. Distressed and distracted, they pay little attention to what they do, inadvertently breach the queuing norm, and fail to criticize one another for it. Does this mean that the villagers have temporarily stopped accepting the queuing requirement, hence that the corresponding norm has temporarily ceased to exist? It seems not. The norm—and the villagers' acceptance of its demands—is still there, even if the villagers fail to comply with it. If an observer were to make the villagers aware of their norm-breaches, they would apologize for them. They still *robustly intend* for the queuing requirement to function as a general standard of behaviour—i.e., they are still committed to it—they just contingently fail to act on their intentions. Of course, if those intentions were *never* acted upon, then we would have reason to doubt the existence of a norm. But we should not take the absence of behavioural manifestations as conclusive evidence that no norm exists.

This should not surprise us. It is intuitively plausible to suppose that socially constructed norms may exist and yet not be widely complied with (Brennan et al. 2013: 21). Consider the following example. Experiments have shown that people are far more likely to wash their hands in public toilets when there are witnesses (see the discussion in Brennan and Pettit 2004: 32). A study carried out in a public female toilet reports that while only 39 per cent of users washed their hands when nobody else was around, the percentage rose to almost 80 per cent when others were present.[17] From this, we can infer that, in all likelihood, the requirement to wash one's hands is not generally observed in private contexts. Yet, this need not invalidate the claim that "[w]ashing one's hands after using toilet facilities is a social norm in our culture" (Munger and Harris 1989: 733). Evidence that this norm exists, non-compliance notwithstanding, is offered by the fact that people who fail to wash their hands after toilet use in the presence of others may receive disapproving looks, be thought badly of, or even be criticized and reminded of basic hygiene practices. Furthermore, they may themselves feel a little guilty and embarrassed, knowing that their conduct contravenes sensible hygiene standards. When this is so, people believe they ought to wash their hands and are committed to this requirement as a general standard of behaviour. Their

---

[17] For the original study, see Munger and Harris (1989).

28   WHAT ARE SOCIALLY CONSTRUCTED NORMS?

intention to treat the "washing one's hands" rule as such a standard is robust in that it persists across a wide range of scenarios. That said, in some such scenarios several people fail to act on their intentions out of laziness, weakness of will, or simply because they are distracted. The risk of being negatively judged, though, often helps them overcome their reluctance or distraction and follow through with their commitments.

Far from being psychologically far-fetched, this phenomenon is rather familiar. Take, for example, the case of the "committed but unsuccessful dieter". This is someone who, every Monday at 7 a.m., consistently resolves to begin a diet, only to lapse into eating unhealthy food by dinner time. The unsuccessful dieter clearly appears committed to dieting: he persistently intends to eat healthily, but equally persistently fails to honour his own commitment. One way in which the dieter can help himself honour his commitment is by joining a dieting programme, whereby, on a weekly basis, his progress is monitored together with that of others who are also in need of losing a few pounds. The prospect of public failure can be a strong motivator, helping him overcome his weakness of will.

To sum up, acceptance of a general rule or requirement involves a belief in the content of the requirement, coupled with a commitment to the requirement functioning as a general standard of behaviour. For a norm to exist, however, the relevant commitment need not always result in corresponding compliant behaviour.

2.2 Widespread acceptance

I have stated that, for a socially constructed norm to exist in a given context C, acceptance of the corresponding rule must be *widespread*: that is, a sufficiently large number of individuals within the context under consideration must possess the right kinds of beliefs and commitments. What proportion of individuals must accept a general rule of conduct for there to be a socially constructed norm is a vague matter, just like the question of how many grains of sand it takes for there to be a heap (Brennan et al. 2013: 30; Hart 1961: 55). In many cases, the existence of a norm will be clear-cut. In others, it will be unclear whether a norm exists: different specifications of the "sufficiently large number" parameter will give us different verdicts. Throughout, I shall be referring to norms the existence of which is reasonably beyond doubt. How to deal with vagueness—a topic much discussed in the philosophy of language—need not concern us here (for general discussion, see Sorensen 2018).

2.3 Public acceptance

For a norm to exist, the corresponding rule must be *publicly* accepted. By this I mean that, within the context under consideration, individuals are aware of each other's acceptance of the relevant rule of conduct. This is what makes the norm *socially*, as opposed to privately, *constructed*. To see this, consider the following example.

Suppose I am at a social gathering involving several guests from different countries and cultures. I myself come from a culture characterized by the following personal-space rule (call it R): "One ought not to stand too close to one's interlocutor". I accept this rule, that is, I believe its content and am committed to it as a general standard of behaviour. However, I do not know whether other guests at the gathering share the same beliefs and commitments. They, in turn, are in the exact same situation: they are ignorant as to everyone else's beliefs and commitments in relation to R. As it happens, all guests are privately committed to rule R as a general standard of behaviour. Still, in such circumstances, no *socially* constructed personal-space norm appears to exist. Acceptance of the rule is not public: it is a purely private matter (cf. Brennan et al. 2013: 30–1).

One might wonder why I treat publicity as an *existence condition* of socially constructed norms, and not merely as necessary for the *ascertainability* of the existence of those norms. I have two reasons for doing so. First, we need to distinguish between the general rules to which an individual subscribes and the general rules a community or group sustains. Intuitively, socially constructed norms belong to the latter, rather than the former, category. A random group of individuals who happen to accept the same general rules of conduct are not as yet a *community* sustaining those norms: they lack common awareness that the rules are generally supported. If a norm has to be socially constructed—as opposed to individually constructed—it must be meaningful for those who accept the corresponding rule to say "*we* accept such-and-such rule in this context" or "this is our norm here". Without the publicity condition, such we-statements would be unavailable. In other words, the attitudes that make up socially constructed norms—i.e., beliefs and commitments, on my account—must be *common* among a group of people.

"Common attitudes" lie somewhere in between what List (2014) calls merely "aggregate attitudes" and "corporate attitudes". Aggregate attitudes are simply summaries of individual attitudes; the most clear-cut case is one in which all individuals hold attitudes with the same content. Corporate attitudes are the attitudes of a group agent: a state, a commercial corporation, a university, and so forth. Common attitudes, instead, involve a group of individuals whose attitudes have the same content *and* who are also mutually aware of one another's attitudes: each is aware that the others hold the attitudes, each is aware that the others are aware that the attitudes are held, and so on. What distinguishes common attitudes from merely widely held individual ones is this common awareness. This, I suggest, is what makes socially constructed norms, precisely, *social*.

There is also a second, and probably more important, reason for including publicity among the existence conditions of socially constructed norms. This is that, as explained by Brennan et al. (2013: sec. 2.4), socially constructed norms, as public standards of behaviour, allow us to be *accountable to one another*. If the publicity requirement wasn't met, this accountability function could not be fulfilled. From the perspective of a broader project aimed at examining the moral normativity of socially constructed norms, this accountability function appears crucial.

If socially constructed norms have moral normativity, breaching them is wrongful in a way that typically warrants "accountability responses", such as blame, resentment, requests for justification or explanation, and the like (Shoemaker 2013; Strawson 1962). But if the norms were not in some way public, if their presence was not transparent to those who are to be held accountable by their standards, we would be faced with an uncomfortable hiatus between claims about the wrong involved in breaching those norms (assuming such wrong exists) and appropriate accountability responses (Darwall 2006: 313–14).

If widely but not publicly held standards of behaviour sufficed for the existence of socially constructed norms, breaches of such norms "qua norms" would give rise, at most, to blameless wrongdoing. A community could not criticize or sanction—in a morally defensible way—individuals who fail to abide by the norms for "failing to abide by *our* norms", both because the norms wouldn't properly qualify as "theirs" and because this fact would make it unreasonable to expect those who do not independently subscribe to those norms to abide by them. How could they be expected to follow the norms, given that they are not accessible to them?

In sum, we have good reasons for including a publicity requirement among the existence conditions of socially constructed norms, and, as explained above, I interpret publicity in terms of common awareness. This concludes my exposition of the agential-investment account, an overview of which is offered in Figure 1 below. In the next section, I try to motivate the account by comparing it to possible alternatives.

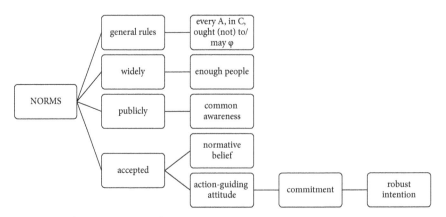

Figure 1 The modularity of the agential-investment account

3. Why the Agential-Investment Account?

I have argued that accepting a general requirement involves (i) a belief in the content of the requirement and (ii) a commitment to the requirement as a general standard of behaviour. These two conditions are central to the agential-investment account. Each, however, might be subject to criticisms and questions. For example: Is the mental state "belief" really necessary for the existence of norms? And why should commitments be the relevant action-guiding attitudes rather than, say, desires? In what follows, I address these and other, related questions.

3.1 Why are beliefs necessary for the existence of norms?

An objector might suggest that socially constructed norms exist even when nobody believes the propositions expressing the content of those norms. To support this claim, the objector may offer some alleged counterexamples to the view that normative beliefs are necessary for there to be norms.

First, the objector might say, consider a young man who sees a sixty-year-old woman wearing a teenage girl's outfit and instinctively forms an attitude of disapproval.[18] Just a split-second later, however, the man disavows this normative attitude, believing in fact that people are free to wear whatever they like and that the rule "one ought to wear age-appropriate clothes" is mistaken. Here, the objector might continue, our observer accepts a rule—as evidenced by his instinctive reaction—without possessing corresponding normative beliefs. This being so, our observer counts as a norm-supporter. If sufficiently many others share his reactions, and this is a matter of common awareness, we can say that an "age-appropriate dressing norm" exists in the relevant context.

I find the claim that the observer accepts a certain dressing rule debatable. In fact, he explicitly disavows it. He does have an instinctive disapproving reaction, but it is a reaction he does not endorse. It may very well be that, in the society in which he lives, most people do in fact believe that one should dress age-appropriately, and that this contributes to the existence of a norm that he may have, somewhat subconsciously, internalized. But it would be hard to imagine a society in which a socially constructed norm about age-appropriate clothing exists and yet *nobody* believes that one ought to wear age-appropriate clothes. They just instinctively disapprove of elderly people who wear revealing outfits, while immediately regretting their disapproval and feeling guilty as a result. This strikes me as a rather unrealistic limiting case, which is too marginal to invalidate the definition I have offered.

---

[18] I thank Nic Southwood for suggesting this example to me.

On my view, our scenario is best interpreted as involving a young man who accepts the rule that one ought *not* to judge other people based on their clothes and has the appropriate feelings of unease when he deviates from that rule. Consequently, he *rejects* the rule that "one ought to wear age-appropriate clothing", even though, partly through habituation, he instinctively shares some of the attitudes of those who accept it. But if enough people in his society thought and felt the way he does, the norm that one ought to wear age-appropriate clothes would not exist.

In response to this diagnosis of the scenario just presented, the objector may invite us to consider a different, less far-fetched phenomenon, much discussed in social psychology: pluralistic ignorance. This occurs when individuals mistakenly believe that their own judgements are different from those of others. Take the following rule: "one ought to be comfortable consuming large amounts of alcohol". Studies have shown that many students on college campuses do not subscribe to this rule: they do not believe that one ought to be comfortable with significant alcohol consumption. Yet, students also mistakenly attribute beliefs about the appropriateness of high alcohol consumption to their peers. Eager to conform and fit in, they publicly behave as if they endorsed the relevant rule, showing themselves more comfortable with alcohol consumption than they actually are. This, in turn, reinforces the generalized misattribution of the relevant normative beliefs (Prentice and Miller 1993).

It might be argued that this case demonstrates that a norm can exist—e.g., a norm about alcohol consumption—in the absence of corresponding normative beliefs. After all, all the behavioural manifestations that characterize the existence of a norm are present: students pressure one another into alcohol consumption, they publicly shun or mock those who "stay away from booze", they feel compelled to drink, and so forth (see, e.g., Bicchieri 2006: 186ff.).

I want to, again, resist this reading of the situation. This case is more aptly described as one in which individuals incorrectly believe that there exists a certain socially constructed norm (Brennan et al. 2013: 35). The norm is "illusory", even if, from an external point of view, there are plenty of cues suggesting that a norm is there (Prentice and Miller 1993: 254).

The distinction between genuine norms and perceived ones is worth drawing for two reasons. First, the behaviours associated with genuine and perceived norms can be changed or eliminated in very different ways. A perceived norm would quickly cease to exist if people's true beliefs were publicly exposed (List 2014: 1613–14). Nobody accepts the relevant normative proposition—e.g., "one ought to feel comfortable consuming plenty of alcohol"—they just pretend to. If the need to pretend were removed, the non-existence of the relevant norm would be revealed.

Second, perceived norms are not accompanied by the normative attitudes and accountability responses typical of genuine ones. If the "heavy alcohol consumption" norm is illusory, then low alcohol consumption is not met with genuine disapproval, or a sense of guilt or agential inadequacy. There is only "fake disapproval". When college students mock or criticize their more judicious peers for drinking too little, they do not, in fact, believe that the behaviour they are mocking or criticizing is wrong. They act merely out of prudential considerations and conformism. They may even feel some cognitive dissonance, sanctioning their peers who prefer sobriety while knowing deep down that such sanctions are unwarranted. High alcohol consumption, in other words, does not matter to them. It is not something they care about independently of social pressure. And, in the context of an exploration of socially constructed norms aimed at studying their moral normativity, distinguishing between rules that individuals genuinely endorse and rules that they follow only out of mistaken beliefs about others' beliefs seems important. Only the former—which are accompanied by normative beliefs—I suggest, should qualify as socially constructed norms proper, *given* the aims of the present inquiry. Of course, if our inquiry had a different goal—e.g., understanding norms as explanations of human behaviour—we would probably draw conceptual boundaries differently.

Faced with these remarks, an objector may flag an odd implication of the claim that the existence of socially constructed norms depends on the presence of corresponding normative beliefs. This is that if it turned out that non-cognitivism about the normative is true, hence that there do not exist normative facts that our beliefs can represent, there would also be no socially constructed norms.[19]

This is an astute observation, to which four responses seem available. I begin by outlining them, and then explain which one(s) I am inclined to adopt. The first is to affirm one's belief in normative cognitivism, and thus to consider the bizarre implication not genuinely worrisome. The second is to bite the bullet and concede that, were normative non-cognitivism true, socially constructed norms in the sense relevant to the present inquiry would not exist. Of course, this would not be to deny the existence of such norms *simpliciter*. As I have already noted, definitions of socially constructed norms that make no reference to normative beliefs might be suited to other purposes. The third response abandons the belief condition and regards commitments as the sole constituents of socially constructed norms. This, of course, carries the implication that such norms exist even in cases of pluralistic ignorance. The fourth response involves enriching the notion of commitment so that the function played by beliefs in my account can be "outsourced" to commitments. For example, we may distinguish between "sincere" commitments and "fake" commitments, whereby violations of the former trigger genuine reactive attitudes, while violations of the latter trigger behaviour that *appears* underpinned by such attitudes but in fact is not. Then the question becomes what features make a commitment sincere or fake. Presumably we can

---

[19] I thank an anonymous reader for raising this concern.

remain agnostic about this, while still affirming that the commitments existing in cases of pluralistic ignorance are qualitatively different from those characterizing circumstances not marked by mistaken beliefs about others' commitments. And we can then insist that, for present purposes, only the latter kinds of commitments give rise to norms proper.

Which avenue to take here? Since I find a broadly cognitivist stance about the normative domain common-sensical and plausible, I am inclined to stick to the claim that socially constructed norms require normative beliefs, thereby making myself vulnerable to the objector's odd implication—without, however, being too concerned about it. That said, a great deal of what I have to say in this book is not dependent on this inclination of mine. In other words, readers who are sceptical about normative cognitivism may abandon the belief condition altogether, or rely on a notion of commitment nuanced enough to do the job that the belief-condition was supposed to perform. In the former case, the set of what count as socially constructed norms will be somewhat larger than under my account; in the latter case, the sets will coincide, despite being identified on the basis of slightly different rationales. Most of my arguments about the moral normativity of socially constructed norms, though, would still apply, since—as we shall see in Chapter 3—they focus on the role played by commitments (not beliefs) in constituting such norms.

3.2 Why commitments and not desires?

I have argued that socially constructed norms exist in the presence of an appropriate action-guiding attitude: a commitment, understood as a robust intention. Readers, however, might wonder why I have focused on intention instead of a different attitude, one that is key to the Humean account of motivation briefly mentioned above, namely desire. Desires, after all, have the right direction of fit: world-to-mind. They aim to make the world conform to their content. When I desire to φ—e.g., to eat an ice-cream—I aim for the world to conform to the content of my mental state: to be such that I eat an ice-cream. Action, from this broadly Humean perspective, involves intervening in the world on the basis of one's desires, in light of one's beliefs. Furthermore, common sense tells us that the fulfilment of our desires is something we take pleasure in, or at least feel positively towards.[20] It would seem odd to say: "I desire to eat an ice-cream, but I don't feel like eating an ice-cream: I wouldn't enjoy it".

---

[20] There is, of course, much debate about what a desire is. Some theories hold that a desire that X is a disposition to act to see to it that X be realized. This definition, however, seems too broad. After all, desires are not the only possible action-guiding attitudes. Here, I seek to offer a characterization of desire that both is in line with common sense and allows us to distinguish desires from other action-guiding attitudes. For a very helpful overview of the literature on desire, see Schroeder (2020).

Why not argue that a person accepts a general requirement R when she "robustly *desires*" that the requirement function as a standard of behaviour? I have two reasons for preferring a commitment-based account to a desire-based one. First, desire seems too weak an action-guiding attitude: too removed from action. The traditional Humean model has been influentially updated by Michael Bratman (1987), who pointed out the importance of a third mental state, in addition to beliefs and desires, to explain rational action: intention. Since Bratman, the Belief-Desire-Intention model of agency (or BDI model) has become a popular explanatory tool, including in disciplines such as computer science. In a nutshell, the idea is that action involves three types of mental states and corresponding attitudes, namely: informational states (beliefs), motivational states (desires), and deliberative states (intentions) (Rao and Georgeff 1995). The latter, deliberative states, engage our will and set us on course for a particular action. They, in a sense, commit us—provisionally—to act in one way rather than another. Once we have formed an intention to act in a particular way, we are "closer" to that action than when we simply desire to act in that way.

The presence of desires, even when coupled with beliefs, appears insufficient for there to be socially constructed norms. Consider, for instance, a hypothetical rule requiring that individuals pollute only minimally, and forbidding pollution above a pretty strict threshold. Imagine a society where the majority of people believe that individuals ought to pollute no more than minimally, desire that this rule function as a standard of behaviour, and are mutually aware of these facts. Yet, most continue to drive SUVs and consume considerable amounts of electricity. When they do so, nobody criticizes or disapproves of them. Nobody sanctions them for their pollution-heavy lifestyle. In such circumstances, it seems that no socially constructed norm prohibiting high levels of pollution exists: it is just that several people within society *wish* such a norm existed (cf. Brennan et al. 2013: 25).[21]

It may be thought that this scenario is somewhat incoherent: how can these beliefs and desires be present, without any corresponding behavioural or

---

[21] A cousin of a purely desire-based account of socially constructed norms is Bicchieri's (2006) influential, preference-based one (though Bicchieri's discussion explicitly excludes legal norms, so the scope of her analysis is narrower than mine). On Bicchieri's view—somewhat roughly stated—a social norm exists when, within a given population, enough individuals know that a corresponding rule exists, and have a preference for conformity with it, on condition that they (i) believe that the rule is generally complied with and (ii) believe either that others expect them to comply or that others think they ought to comply and might sanction them in case of non-compliance (Bicchieri 2006: 11). Bicchieri's account of norms is, somewhat oddly, non-normative: none of the attitudes she invokes as existence conditions of norms contains deontic operators such as "oughts". We are simply dealing with preferences—which Bicchieri (2006: 6) understands as "dispositions to act"—conditional on expectations (Maher 2007: 140). While what Bicchieri calls social norms may be an interesting social phenomenon, their lack of normativity makes them unsuited for the task at hand, which consists in asking whether and, if so, why the moral reactive attitudes typically triggered by the violation of socially constructed norms are justified. For critical discussion of Bicchieri's view, which informs some of the points made in this section and from which I have learnt, see Brennan et al. (2013: 23–6).

36 WHAT ARE SOCIALLY CONSTRUCTED NORMS?

attitudinal manifestation? There may, indeed, be something incoherent about holding this package of attitudes, but this is in fact what often happens in reality. Consider the situation in many developed societies today. If asked, most people would declare a belief that they and others ought to pollute much less, and may even desire that this rule were made into an effective standard of behaviour. Yet, observation suggests that, unfortunately, we are far from this wish for stricter rules being turned into a social reality, accompanied by formal or informal sanctions in cases of violation.

Second, the connection between desires and pleasure—or positive feelings more generally—is at odds with the phenomenology of norm-compliance. Many of the norms we are guided by are, in fact, not ones we desire to act on. For instance, when I was a child in Italy, there was a pretty strong social norm, among the Catholic majority, that fellow Catholics ought to go to church on Sundays. Not doing so was met with disapproval. In this context, imagine someone, call him Luigi, who believes he should go to church on Sundays, always does, and quietly disapproves of others who do not go. As it happens, however, Luigi does not *desire* to go to church; deep down, he finds it boring and dreads going. Still, he is committed to going and treats the rule that one should attend church on Sundays as a general standard of behaviour. The character depicted in this example—Luigi—strikes me as perfectly coherent, and his case illustrates how a socially constructed norm could exist in the absence of corresponding desires, provided the relevant commitments are there (see the example in Brennan et al. 2013: 27, which parallels this line of reasoning).

In sum, as action-guiding attitudes, desires appear unsuited to underpin socially constructed norms.

3.3 Why commitments and not behaviour?

In light of the foregoing observations, it might be tempting for readers to wonder why acceptance of a general rule requires only commitments and not *compliant behaviour* instead.

As I hope my earlier discussion of the norm requiring handwashing after toilet use shows, while a focus on desires would be too weak, a focus on behaviour would be too demanding. This is because we want to leave room for the possibility that a socially constructed norm might exist, and yet not be routinely complied with. Moreover, some norms may exist without having *any behavioural manifestation*. For instance, there may be a norm requiring people to reciprocate one another's presents. Yet, people might refrain from ever giving each other any presents in order to avoid having to reciprocate (Turnbull 1972, discussed in Bicchieri 2006: 195). Here, a norm clearly exists, and yet it is not accompanied by explicit behavioural manifestations, because the conditions for the norm's requirements to be triggered—i.e., giving presents—are deliberately never satisfied. (Of course, the existence of the norm might still help to explain why people never give each other presents.)

A focus on commitment, then, seems to allow us to capture precisely the right kind of agential investment: deeper than what would obtain with desires alone, but not "guaranteed" as in the case of behaviour.

3.4 Why commitments and not a cluster of normative attitudes?

Finally, one might suggest that, given the multifarious nature of socially constructed norms, one should not attempt to set out precise conditions for acceptance of a requirement. One should instead conclude that accepting a requirement involves a *plurality* of attitudes and behaviours. We would, in this case, be in the presence of a Wittgensteinian "family resemblance" concept of socially constructed norms.

This more flexible route has been taken by some theorists. For example, H. L. A. Hart characterizes acceptance of a rule as involving both behavioural regularities and individuals looking at "the behaviour in question as a general standard to be followed by the group as a whole" (Hart 1961: 56). This results in individuals' disposition to sanction and criticize one another for deviations from the standard, and to regard such criticisms and sanctions as justified (Hart 1961: 55–6). For instance, it seems plausible to say that the rules governing the game of tennis consist of "accepted requirements". This acceptance manifests itself in players' adherence to the rules of tennis, and in their disposition to criticize and sanction one another for breaches thereof. From Hart's perspective, then, the existence of a norm depends on a complex mix of normative attitudes and behaviours.

In a similar vein—in fact, explicitly following Hart—Brennan et al. (2013: 29–30) argue that to accept a rule is for the individuals involved to have a cluster of normative attitudes that match the content and normative force of that rule. These include "(a) normative beliefs, judgements, and other cognitive states, (b) normative expectations, (c) reactive attitudes and dispositions to have such attitudes, and (d) any other attitudes that entail (a), (b), or (c)" (Brennan et al. 2013: 29).[22] Consider, for example, the rule that one should wear modest clothes when entering a church. Individuals can be said to accept that rule, on this account, when they, for example, believe that one ought to wear modest clothes in church, or disapprove of or sanction those who deviate from the relevant rule, and so forth.

---

[22] In fact, Brennan et al. (2013: Ch. 2, n. 18) add that, if emotions and desires are thought to entail "normative cognitive states", then they also count as normative attitudes.

38 WHAT ARE SOCIALLY CONSTRUCTED NORMS?

I have learnt a great deal from these accounts. Indeed, the agential-investment account builds on them and accepts their core insight that, *without normative attitudes*, there cannot be socially constructed norms. To that extent, I see my account as very much indebted to, and in line with, those discussed in this sub-section.

That said, while the accounts developed by Hart and Brennan et al. have the obvious advantage of being sufficiently flexible to allow us to capture a broad set of social phenomena we may plausibly call socially constructed norms, they lack precision. They point to the fact that accepting a rule often involves a cluster of attitudes—specifically, normative ones—without specifying whether any of them is strictly speaking *necessary or sufficient* for there to be norms. This open-endedness makes their account vulnerable to the charge of over-inclusiveness.

For Brennan et al., for instance, shared disapproval of a given behaviour not accompanied by a belief in the wrongness of said behaviour—as in the case of the "age-appropriate dressing" norm discussed earlier—may suffice for the existence of a socially constructed norm. But as I have suggested, a mere split-second normative attitude of disapproval, not accompanied by corresponding beliefs and characterized by a lack of robustness, seems insufficient to give rise to a socially constructed norm.

Similarly, for Brennan et al. a shared normative belief not accompanied by a relevant action-guiding attitude may be sufficient for the existence of socially constructed norms. Yet, to the extent that those norms are meant to be action-guiding, it seems somewhat implausible to suggest that shared normative beliefs *alone* could suffice for such norms to exist—unless one also held the view that beliefs can motivate. Again, think about the belief that people ought not to pollute above a certain threshold. The existence of that belief, among a large enough group of people, even as a matter of common awareness, does not appear sufficient for the existence of a socially constructed norm if nobody in fact ever takes steps to act on that belief.[23]

So, even if family resemblance accounts have the resources to allow them to fit a large class of phenomena we may wish to call "socially constructed norms", they come with some counter-intuitive implications. In particular, they may end up being over-inclusive: detecting socially constructed norms even where none is, arguably, in play.

The agential-investment account overcomes some of the difficulties with these more capacious accounts at very little cost. It gives a precise characterization of what it takes to accept a general requirement, and it does so in a way that fits

---

[23] Brennan et al. (2013: 33) consider the objection that "if norms are clusters of normative attitudes, it seems to follow that they are motivationally impotent". Their response is that, even if normative attitudes do not themselves motivate, desires (hence action-guiding attitudes) often accompany them in practice.

many of our pre-theoretical judgements about what counts as a norm and what doesn't. The greater precision of this account, as will be shown in subsequent chapters, will help us better pinpoint where the *moral* normativity of socially constructed norms comes from, while avoiding the problem of over-inclusiveness.

4. Intentions and Socially Constructed Norms

I have, so far, offered some reasons in defence of the view that accepting a rule involves believing its content and committing to it as a general standard of behaviour. A commitment, in turn, has been fleshed out in terms of a robust intention. A rule functions as a general standard of behaviour in a given context when it is generally (though not necessarily always) complied with, and violations elicit criticisms, disapproval, and sanctions (Hart 1961: 55–7). This means that, on my account, whether the object of norm-constituting intentions is realized does not depend merely on one's own actions. Whether a requirement functions as a standard of behaviour depends on *others* adhering to it too.

Specifically, the agents who accept the general requirements making up socially constructed norms do not intend to treat those requirements as standards of behaviour in a purely self-regarding manner. Treating a requirement as a personal standard of behaviour means striving to conform to it, and developing the appropriate attitudes of guilt or failure when one fails to live up to that standard. It does not, however, involve disapproving of others, sanctioning them in case of non-compliance, trying to get them to comply through the imposition of sanctions (informal or formal), and so forth. This is precisely what characterizes socially constructed norms. Others' violations of such norms trigger negative responses in norm-supporters. This, however, presupposes that norm-supporters possess action-guiding attitudes that range over other people's conduct too, not merely their own. On my account, then, the object of one's intentions can also include the actions of others.

This notion of intention is broader than the standard notion, discussed in the philosophy of action, which is assumed to range over one's own actions alone. The thought behind this standard assumption is that forming an intention partly *settles* the question of what to do. Once I have formed an intention to φ, I have, as it were, at least provisionally settled on φ-ing. However, so the argument goes, we can plausibly settle on certain actions being done only when these actions are our own (Velleman 1997). On this picture of intention, I cannot "intend that such and such be the case", if whether such and such is the case is not entirely within my power.

In my view, this notion of intention is too restrictive. We can meaningfully define intention—a distinctive action-guiding attitude, not reducible to desires— as having objects the fulfilment of which is not entirely up to the agent who

40 WHAT ARE SOCIALLY CONSTRUCTED NORMS?

intends. First, such an understanding of intention is familiar from ordinary language and experience. As Wayne A. Davis (1984: 48) points out: "We often intend other people to do things, and as a result make, help or let them do it". For example, I may intend that my friend help me out with some errands and consequently act in ways aimed at making him do so. After a day spent helping me out, my friend might reveal that, in order to assist me, he had to abandon his plan to meet his girlfriend. It would not seem inappropriate for me to react saying: "I did not intend for you to make such a big sacrifice". My intention, when I insistently asked my friend for some help, was for him to help me assuming this would come at little cost to him, *not* for him to help me at the cost of neglecting his girlfriend.

When we intend something, we direct our actions towards that particular object. We, in a way, commit—more or less intensely—to the realization of that object, *even if* its realization is not entirely up to us, but may depend on others' cooperation. Of course, it would seem irrational to intend the *impossible*, but it seems perfectly plausible to intend goals that are possible but not entirely within our control. I can "intend to make something happen" even if I know that whether something will happen is not entirely up to me. For example, I can intend to catch the bus, even if whether I catch it may depend on whether the driver sees me running after the vehicle and stops as a result. Importantly, intending to catch the bus involves a firmer commitment to acting than just wishing or desiring to catch it. This, I think, is core to intention, even if in many cases we may intend the achievement of goals that are not, strictly speaking, within our control.[24]

The idea—proposed here—that intentions may range not only over one's own actions but also over those of others, is familiar from the work of Michael Bratman (1999) on shared intentionality. Bratman has argued that the individual intentions that make up shared intentions take the form "I intend that *we j*" (where "*j*" stands for a joint action, such as carrying a piano upstairs together). To simplify somewhat, for Bratman (1999) joint intentions obtain within a group when (i) the members of that group each hold intentions of the form "I intend that *we j*" (where "*j*" is a joint action), (ii) each is prepared to adjust their conduct so as to *j*, and (iii) this is common knowledge among group members.[25]

---

[24] One might object that when we say "I intend to catch the bus" what we mean is something like "I intend to do everything in my power to catch the bus", such that the object of intention still only consists of things within our control. I find this explanation a little contrived. Surely, when I intend to catch the bus, what I intend is "catching the bus"—that is the aim towards which my actions are directed. If someone saw me running on the street and asked "why are you running, what are you intending to achieve in doing so?", my answer would be "catching the bus". Unless we have stronger reasons for thinking it irrational that the object of intention could include a goal the achievement of which is not entirely within our power, the proposed rephrasing seems forced.

[25] In Bratman's (1999: 121) more technical language, being prepared to adjust one's conduct means being prepared to act so that one's sub-plans of action "mesh" with those of other participants in the shared intention. We may, for instance, share an intention to paint a house together, but for us to do so, we need to be disposed to agree on a division of labour, a colour, etc. In other words, our sub-plans of action must mesh in the right way.

My account of the existence conditions of socially constructed norms, of course, does not presuppose Bratman's account of joint intentional action. But what my account of the existence conditions of norms and Bratman's account of the existence conditions of shared intentions have in common is the appeal to a broad notion of intention. For Bratman, too, intentions can range over the actions of people other than oneself. I am, therefore, in good company in wishing to understand intention more broadly than it is typically understood within the philosophy of action. This broader use of the notion of intention should therefore not unduly threaten the plausibility of my account of socially constructed norms.

5. Distinguishing Socially Constructed Norms from Related Phenomena

To put the phenomenon of socially constructed norms into sharper focus, it is useful to distinguish it from related, but different phenomena: habits, conventions, and personal policies.

5.1 Habits

Socially constructed norms need to be distinguished from non-prescriptive behavioural regularities or "habits" (Hart 1961: 56; Southwood and Eriksson 2011). For example, a large number of Italians eat pasta for lunch. This behaviour is so common and predictable that one might think that it is explained by a socially constructed norm of the form "one ought to eat pasta for lunch". This, however, would be a mistake. Deviations from this regularity do not trigger criticisms or sanctions. Italians do not believe that one ought to eat pasta for lunch, and that there would be something wrong in eating a steak or a salad instead. To that extent, Italians have no *norm* requiring people to eat pasta for lunch. They do, however, have the *habit* of doing so. (The prohibition on drinking cappuccino while eating pizza or on putting parmesan cheese on seafood pasta is a different matter.)

5.2 Conventions

Socially constructed norms must also be distinguished from what are known as *social conventions* (Lewis 2002/1969; Schelling 1960; Southwood and Eriksson 2011). The expression "social conventions" designates established behavioural regularities that offer solutions to coordination problems. Crucially, however, "mere" conventions lack the prescriptiveness typical of norms.

42   WHAT ARE SOCIALLY CONSTRUCTED NORMS?

Consider, for instance, a swimming pool with two lanes: at the bottom of one lane stands a sign prescribing that swimmers should proceed clockwise; at the bottom of the other stands a sign for "free" swimming.[26] From time to time, users of the "free lane" spontaneously coordinate, thereby also swimming clockwise. When that happens, their behaviour is—at least temporarily—indistinguishable from that of swimmers in the adjacent, regulated lane. Yet, in the free lane, proceeding clockwise is not something that swimmers *ought* to do. There is no socially constructed norm prescribing that behaviour. It is just that, sometimes, a *convention* emerges. To be sure, when other pool frequenters break that convention, their arrival may be inconvenient for some swimmers. These inconvenienced swimmers might tell themselves, "Bad luck! The clockwise arrangement had worked so well for me!". Yet, they would not react thinking "What are these guys doing? Don't they see that they are supposed to swim clockwise!". And this is because there is no *norm* demanding clockwise swimming in the free lane: no beliefs in, and commitments to, general requirements are present. By contrast, behaviour contrary to the prescriptions applying to the regulated lane breaches a socially constructed norm, is met with disapproval, and typically corrected, either by other swimmers or by the pool attendant.

To be clear, I am not denying that norms might *emerge* from conventions: that what was initially a "mere" convention might then become a norm in the sense I have described. I am simply pointing out that, conceptually, we can distinguish between conventions on the one hand, and norms on the other.

5.3 Personal policies

Socially constructed norms must also be distinguished from what Michael Bratman (1989) and David Velleman (1989: 307–9) call personal "policies". The latter are rules of conduct we often adopt in our lives, such as "always acting politely", or "not answering emails over weekends", or "behaving with integrity", and so forth. There are two crucial differences between personal policies and socially constructed norms. First, personal policies need not be normative. I may have adopted a policy of not answering emails over weekends, without treating the policy as a binding standard of behaviour. Deviations from the policy need not trigger a sense of guilt or failure. Second, while personal policies apply to one's own behaviour, socially constructed norms are self- *and* other-regarding: they purport to prescribe a particular conduct not only for the person who accepts their requirements, but for third parties too. Socially constructed norms, as I have mentioned, are *general* rules of conduct; personal policies are not.

---

[26] Thanks to Christian List for suggesting this example.

6. Varieties of Socially Constructed Norms

It is now worth pausing to highlight the differences between different types of socially constructed norms. The examples I have offered along the way include a variety of such norms. For our purposes, the most salient distinction is that between *informal* and *formal norms,* and the related distinction between *directive* and *power-conferring norms.*

6.1 Formal and informal norms

Borrowing terminology from H. L. A. Hart, we may distinguish between "primary rules"—which directly govern individuals' conduct—and "secondary rules"—which concern how primary rules may be created, modified, eliminated, etc. (Hart 1961: Ch. 5). Formal norms, again following Hart, involve a combination of both types of rules. Informal norms, by contrast, typically consist of primary rules only.

For example, the norm that one ought to queue at the bus stop is informal, insofar as it consists of a primary rule: a rule that directly governs conduct, and there exists no "meta-rule" concerning its creation, modification, and elimination. By contrast, the norm that, say, students ought to submit their essays two weeks after the end of the module is a formal one. It is a primary rule—i.e., it prescribes a particular conduct on the part of students—but is created, modified, etc. via specific procedures. In particular, at some universities the course convenor must propose modes of assessment and deadlines well in advance. These proposals turn into formal norms only once official approval from the university's teaching committee has been obtained.

Once we understand the distinction between formal and informal norms in this way, it becomes obvious that the attitudes constituting the former are somewhat different from those typical of the latter. In characterizing these differences, I will follow the work of Brennan et al. (2013: Ch. 3). In the case of informal norms—which, as I have said, are constituted by primary rules only—the object of individuals' norm-relevant beliefs and commitments corresponds to the content of the norms in question. Consider, for instance, the norm (of etiquette) that one should chew with one's mouth closed. Acceptance of that norm involves people's beliefs that one ought to chew with one's mouth closed and commitments to this requirement as a general standard of behaviour. The object of the commitment is precisely the rule that gives the norm its content. The same goes for norms such as "One ought to queue at the bus stop", "One ought to take one's shoes off before entering someone's home", "One ought not to leave food on the plate", and so forth.

This overlap between the objects of one's beliefs and commitments and the content of the corresponding norms is often missing in the case of formal norms.

44 WHAT ARE SOCIALLY CONSTRUCTED NORMS?

In sufficiently complex formal normative systems, subjects do not know the content of all norms. For instance, in virtually all legal systems there are obscure and complex laws that will never be of direct concern to most individual members of the population, and that most of the population will never be aware of (Brennan et al. 2013: 47). These include building regulations, tax regulations, regulations to do with food and medical safety, and so forth. The same observations can be made in relation to smaller-scale systems of formal norms. Think, for example, of the rules governing a university. As an academic, I may know the content of some of them—those that apply to me directly—but not of all of them.

This feature of formal norms, it might be thought, threatens the existence conditions of socially constructed norms as I have defined them. The worry is that, if people do not know the content of the norms, they cannot possess the relevant beliefs and robustly intend for the norms' directives to function as standards of behaviour. And if a sufficiently large number of people lacks the relevant beliefs and commitments—as a matter of common awareness—then no norm can be said to exist. Legal systems, and smaller-scale systems of formal norms, would thus either not exist, or be much less rich than we take them to be, or not be constituted by socially constructed norms proper (see Brennan et al. 2013: 47–8).

This difficulty can be addressed by noting that the commitments that partly constitute the acceptance of a rule can be either *direct* or *indirect* (cf. Brennan et al. 2013: 49).[27] Consider the norm that one should stop at the red light. I may be committed *either* to the requirement to stop as a general standard of behaviour simpliciter, *or* to all requirements arrived at through a certain procedure—independently of their content—as general standards of behaviour, with the requirement to stop at the red light being in fact an output of the designated procedure. The relevant commitment, in one case, is direct: it directly refers to the content of the rule. In the other case, it is indirect: it concerns the pedigree of the rule, rather than its specific content. In both cases, however, the agent believes that the rule ought to be followed and robustly intends that it function as a general standard of behaviour, albeit for different reasons.

Generalizing from this, it is true to say that I know very little about the precise content of many of the laws that apply to my country, or even of many of the regulations that apply to my university. Moreover, if I do not find myself in situations or demographic groups to which those laws and regulations apply, I will probably never discover their content. Yet, to the extent that I believe and robustly

---

[27] In this context, Brennan et al. (2013: 49) introduce a distinction between "de dicto attitudes" and "de re attitudes". The former are attitudes directly concerning the particular prescriptions/prohibitions that constitute the content of a norm. The latter are attitudes concerning the "type" of norm under consideration: e.g., legal, social, etc. The attitudes that matter, in the case of formal norms, can be "de re": i.e., attitudes concerning a whole class of norms, such as those that count as law, in light of their procedural qualities. I take the distinction between direct and indirect acceptance to mirror that between de dicto and de re attitudes.

intend that "everything that qualifies as law" and that "every university rule established according to such and such procedure" should function as a standard of behaviour, I can be said to accept those rules too. My acceptance of those primary rules, in turn, depends on their having been produced through a set of secondary rules that I believe ought to be followed and I robustly intend should function as sources of valid standards of behaviour. From this perspective, I believe and robustly intend that any rule that has emerged from a given procedure—e.g., the legislative procedure in my country or that of my university—should function as a general standard of behaviour: an authoritative guide for my own and others' actions.

Of all formal norms, legal ones are the most familiar and, typically, the most consequential. There are, of course, rich and long-standing debates about what precisely the law is, debates that I cannot engage with in the present context. Luckily, defending a specific theory of law is unnecessary for my purposes. All that I commit to is a broad form of legal *positivism*, according to which what counts as valid law is reducible to a set of social facts. Moral considerations do not contribute to constituting valid law, unless socially constructed legal norms make reference to such considerations. Of course, the *moral* validity of legal prescriptions and prohibitions depends on their conformity with moral norms. (The moral normativity of legal norms specifically will be discussed in Chapter 5.)

Mention of the law in this context may elicit the following concern. I have argued that the existence of socially constructed norms requires both appropriate beliefs and commitments on the part of a large enough number of people in the relevant context. But we can easily imagine cases—e.g., annexation, colonialism, occupation—in which these conditions are not satisfied. Those who govern issue commands backed by the threat of sanctions, and an intricate system of rules is enforced upon the population, yet the population does not believe that those rules ought to be complied with. The population is disaffected, and stability is achieved through intimidation and coercion. On my account, it seems to follow that in circumstances such as these no legal *norms* can be said to exist; a conclusion that will surely strike several as counterintuitive.[28] There are two possible responses to this concern. The first is to follow Hart, who regards officials' attitudes in particular as key to establishing whether there exist legal norms.[29] In the cases discussed, while plausibly the majority of the population lacks the relevant beliefs and commitments, (foreign) officials probably possess them. This would in turn still allow us to conclude that in cases of colonialism, annexation, and foreign rule more generally, legal norms do exist.

---

[28] I thank Temi Ogunye for raising this concern.

[29] H. L. A. Hart (1961) famously argues that only officials' (not the wider population's) attitudes are relevant to the existence of *law* specifically.

46 WHAT ARE SOCIALLY CONSTRUCTED NORMS?

A second option, and my preferred one, is to "bite the bullet" and accept that, when in a given context the legally enforced system of rules is not underpinned by relevant beliefs and commitments on the part of the population, then those rules do not amount to *norms* proper (cf. Brennan et al. 2013: 48–9). In those contexts, the law is just a set of commands backed by the threat of sanctions, but for which the question of moral normativity, at least as I pose it here, does not arise. Accepting this conclusion though doesn't strike me as a particularly high price to pay for the following reason. The question of norms' moral normativity arises insofar as such norms are already treated as having moral valence. Their violation triggers moral reactive attitudes and is accompanied by sincere disapproval. We then want to know whether our practices of praising, blaming, and holding responsible are, in fact, justified. But when those practices are not in place, when rule-breaches are not accompanied by the relevant responses, the question we are posing does not arise in the first place. (Recall our previous discussion of pluralistic ignorance.) And this seems exactly right. Do we really need to ask whether rules that are brutally imposed upon a population, who is in fact alienated from such rules, possess *moral* normativity? The answer seems, straightforwardly, no. Excluding such rules from the set of socially constructed norms thus comes at little cost to my analysis. Having said this, a different response may be called for if our aim were a different one, say, conceptualizing norms for the purpose of explaining certain human behaviours.

6.2 Directive and power-conferring norms

Our discussion of the distinction between formal and informal norms hints at another important distinction, that between norms that directly govern our behaviour—via the imposition of obligations, prohibitions, or permissions—and norms that confer certain powers on us—namely powers to create or extinguish obligations, permissions, prohibitions, and the like. So far, my discussion has largely concentrated on the first class of norms—let us call them "directive" or "prescriptive" norms—and specifically on norms mandating or prohibiting certain forms of conduct (I have said less about permissive norms insofar as such norms are prima facie less morally controversial). But the distinction between formal and informal norms presupposes the category of power-conferring norms, of which Hart's "secondary rules" are a clear example.[30]

Let me elaborate on this category, taking secondary rules as a relevant illustration. Such rules, as we have seen, do not directly tell us how we ought to act.

---

[30] In fact, Hart (1961: Ch. 3) himself distinguishes between duty-imposing and power-conferring norms.

Instead, they specify how we might bring about, modify, or remove primary rules. Secondary rules empower us—or public officials—to modify the normative situation. Consider the rules which determine how to create valid directive laws within a certain jurisdiction. For example, in Italy, where I am originally from, an elected parliament, composed of two chambers—the "Chamber of Deputies" and the "Senate"—is responsible for legislation. A legislative proposal—which can be put forward by a variety of agents, ranging from the government, to elected representatives, to a sufficiently large number of ordinary citizens—has to be approved by both chambers and signed off by the President of the Republic in order to turn into a genuine law. This procedural rule, which I have here described in an over-simplified manner, empowers various official entities to produce legally binding norms, which then directly govern citizens' behaviour.

The law empowers not only public officials, but also private citizens. Think about the legal norms establishing what it takes to enter into a marriage or into a contract. Such norms specify the procedures that need to be followed in order for people to establish a set of directive norms applying to them. Married couples are bound by rights and obligations which do not apply to unmarried ones. Similarly, the terms of a contract regulate and constrain the behaviour of those who are party to it, but not of others.

Furthermore, there exist plenty of power-conferring norms which lack legal status, and which are not embedded into more complex structures describable as the "union of primary and secondary rules" (Hart 1961: Ch. 5). Consider, for instance, the norms regulating the practice of promising and of consent. The former specify what it takes for an individual to successfully bind herself to another—without the bond being backed by legal sanctions. The latter—at least when it comes to low-stakes interactions—establish what it takes for someone to render permissible behaviour that would otherwise be prohibited: for example, allowing a friend to borrow one's pen.

Crucially, despite having a different function than their directive counterparts, power-conferring norms are made out of the same ontological building blocks and therefore merit the "title" of norms all the same. Consider, for instance, the norm enabling promise-making. By way of approximation, this can be expressed by the following normative proposition p: "Every agent A who utters the words 'I promise to φ' directed at B, in context C, acquires an obligation to φ owed to B (i.e., she ought to φ), subject to B's uptake". The existence of this norm in any given context rests on a large enough number of people publicly accepting the content of the corresponding rule. That is, a large enough number of people must (i) believe that p and (ii) be committed to p functioning as a general standard of behaviour. This commitment is reflected in people's taking up a critical stance in relation to violations of promises. When we do not keep our promises, we are reproached, blamed, and socially sanctioned.

48 WHAT ARE SOCIALLY CONSTRUCTED NORMS?

In sum, as this and other examples show, while directive and power-conferring norms have different functions, they are each a species of the same genus: socially constructed norms.

7. Socially Constructed Norms and Moral Reactive Attitudes

I have argued that a socially constructed norm exists in a context C, whenever a general requirement is widely and publicly accepted within that context. I have then given my own interpretation of the various parameters in this definition, coming to the conclusion that socially constructed norms involve beliefs in, and commitments to, certain oughts as general standards of behaviour.

The definition of socially constructed norms offered here may seem very capacious. It may be thought to cover all sorts of norms, including linguistic norms, aesthetic norms, epistemic norms, as well as, of course, formal and informal norms of day-to-day conduct such as those I have been discussing all along.

I am not too sure about this. How broad the definition is partly depends on controversial assumptions one could make about the nature of these various types of norms. Take epistemic norms, for instance. It isn't obvious that they govern behaviour, in the way in which, say, legal norms typically do. Of course, we could speak of "mental actions" in their case, but whether such actions are on a par with physical ones is an open question (e.g., O'Brien and Soteriou 2009). Furthermore, on some views, whether we form a given belief is not something that falls within our control, and if belief-formation is not within our control, then it is not clear how we could *follow norms* for belief-formation itself—though there could be norms governing which evidence we ought to consider, how epistemically conscientious we should be, and so on (see, e.g., Alston 1989).[31]

My aim, however, is not to adjudicate such controversies, so, instead of insisting on the capaciousness or lack thereof of my account of the existence conditions of socially constructed norms, I simply restrict the scope of my analysis to a particularly prominent class of such norms. These are norms the violation of which triggers *moral reactive attitudes* (Strawson 1962). Which reactive attitudes or emotions count as moral is itself a tricky question. For my purposes, I focus on uncontroversial cases of moral emotions or reactive attitudes—such as blame, resentment, and guilt—and accept that slightly different specifications of what these are may deliver different categorizations of socially constructed norms.

No matter what we think about the nature of epistemic, linguistic, or aesthetic norms, it seems clear that, at least often enough, their violation does not trigger *those* kinds of responses. Consider, for instance, the typical reaction when one

---

[31] This is not to deny the existence of a lively debate on the ethics of belief. For an overview, see Chignell (2018).

makes a grammar mistake. The violation of grammar norms is met with a somewhat negative response, but not with moral reactive attitudes. The mistake doesn't reveal poor character, it does not signal wrongdoing—unless we assume that there is an independent moral duty to "learn one's grammar".

This could be so, say, in the case of a pupil who is supposed to do well at school. His parents' telling him off for producing homework littered with grammar mistakes could indeed involve moral reactive attitudes. But in cases where no underlying duties are presupposed, grammar mistakes activate no such attitudes. To see this, consider the following, autobiographical anecdote. When in the company of my parents-in-law, I speak German. This invariably results in me making several grammatical mistakes (thankfully, since moving to Germany, the rate at which I make such mistakes has been diminishing). My mother-in-law, a former language teacher, routinely points them out to me, in order to help me improve my linguistic competence. When this happens, I often instinctively react by saying "Entschuldigung!" (namely "sorry" in German). When I say so, I do not mean to apologize, however. I know I haven't done anything wrong. I don't feel guilty. What I do intend to say is more akin to "Silly me!". To this, my mother-in-law always responds: "You have nothing to apologize for!". In so saying, she reinforces the message that my ungrammatical sentence implies no wrongdoing. It just lacks the property of grammaticality.

Similarly, consider violations of aesthetic norms. Here too, episodes from my family life can provide helpful illustrations. My mother-in-law has robust aesthetic views. She feels strongly both about how things in her house—well, in fact, any house—should be arranged and about what my husband should wear. I have witnessed several exchanges involving my mother-in-law insisting that my husband should wear a belt, while my husband simply could not be bothered. He is, in this respect, the exact opposite of his mother: the kind of person who doesn't realize when he is wearing his jumper inside out. While "encouraging" Christian, my husband, to wear a belt, my mother-in-law used expressions such as "The trousers look terrible without a belt!" and "You give such an untidy impression!". Clearly, she was criticizing Christian, expressing indubitable aesthetic disapproval. Yet, she was not blaming Christian, nor was she resenting him for not wearing a belt. And Christian, too, I can assure you, feels no guilt at his failure to wear a belt.

In sum, making grammar mistakes can be prudentially unwise, and not wearing a belt fails to comply with my mother-in-law's aesthetic norms, but barring independent moral duties to speak grammatically, to wear belts, or to accommodate one's mother's aesthetic preferences, these actions (or omissions) are typically not accompanied by moral reactive-attitude responses, or so it seems to me.

Things are different, however, with other types of socially constructed norms. Consider, for example, the norm that one ought not to queue-jump. In contexts where the norm is operative, violations are met with reactive attitudes that are very much moral: the queue-jumper is seen as cheating, as "taking someone else's place", appropriating a spot they have no right to. Those who are committed to the norm are likely to regard the queue-jumper as doing something wrong, for which an apology would be appropriate. And the person who loses her spot in the queue would likely resent the queue-jumper.

The same types of reactions, it seems to me, are elicited by violations of politeness norms. Failing to greet someone, slouching on an airplane seat so much as to take up one's neighbour's space—to name a couple of instances—involve norm-violations that are often met with mild moral reactive attitudes. They are seen as inconsiderate behaviour, for which one should feel somewhat guilty (though not terribly so), and for which an apology would be appropriate (Buss 1999).

My focus will be norms of this kind: i.e., norms whose violation can be said to trigger moral reactive attitudes to a greater or lesser extent.[32] When I speak of the moral normativity of socially constructed norms, I only refer to *those* norms in particular. I am interested in the question of whether we are justified in attaching moral valance to the violation of norms that we *already* treat as somewhat morally significant. What I say is not meant to apply to grammatical or aesthetic or prudential norms. More precisely, what I say is not meant to apply to norm-violations that are not ordinarily accompanied by moral reactive attitudes.

A scope restriction like the one I am proposing may be acceptable, but readers may question the particular criterion on the basis of which I carry out such restriction. In particular, they may question that moral reactive attitudes are the right way of defining the scope of the socially constructed norms I am interested in, and instead suggest alternative criteria. For example, they may say that the socially constructed norms of interest should be "moral ones", but understood as involving impartial principles. Alternatively, they may believe that the relevant norms should be those that are regarded as having "universal applicability". Or, different still, they may suggest that I should focus on socially constructed norms the violation of which is *seriously* wrong (for helpful discussion, see Crisp 2018: 801–2).

These suggestions, while not implausible, would not do for my purposes. This is because they all involve substantively controversial accounts of what makes something "moral". It is a substantively open question whether morality is impartial, universal, or only deals with "seriously wrongful acts". The reactive-attitude criterion, on the other hand, allows for greater neutrality, while singling out all and only those violations of socially constructed norms which invite the kinds of responses that are apt in cases of violations of *valid* moral norms. Whether, and if

---

[32] What these norms are is, in turn, an empirical question. For instance, in a society where wearing a belt is considered a sign of respect, and not doing so of disrespect, failures to conform to the belt-norm will likely elicit moral reactive attitudes; but not in a society—like ours—where wearing a belt lacks this kind of significance.

so when and why, those reactions are justified in the case of socially constructed norms will be our topic for the rest of the book.

8. Conclusion

In this chapter I have offered an account of the existence conditions of socially constructed norms: the agential-investment account. I have argued that a norm exists in context C whenever, in C, a general requirement is widely and publicly accepted as binding. I have explained why acceptance should be understood as involving beliefs in, and commitments to, the relevant requirements. I have shown how this account of socially constructed norms captures many paradigmatic instances of such norms, and how it can distinguish between formal and informal norms, as well as between directive and power-conferring ones. As I said at the start, my aim was fairly modest. Instead of seeking to demonstrate the superiority of the agential-investment account compared to other accounts, I have tried to defend its plausibility for my specific purposes. It may very well be that this account of socially constructed norms would not be ideally suited for several explanatory purposes in the social sciences, and that alternative accounts would be superior. But I hope to have convinced readers that socially constructed norms, as I have characterized them, are an important and pervasive social phenomenon. This should suffice to motivate the investigation that follows, namely an inquiry into the *moral* normativity of such norms.

Morality and Socially Constructed Norms. Laura Valentini, Oxford University Press. © Laura Valentini 2023.
DOI: 10.1093/9780191938115.003.0002

2

Grounding the Moral Force of Socially Constructed Norms

Does the fact that a socially constructed norm requires us to φ place us under a pro tanto, namely an overridable, obligation to φ? In other words, do socially constructed norms have moral normativity? Call this the "moral normativity question".

The answer to this question has significant implications. Since our social, legal, and political lives are governed by countless norms, whether and, if so, under what conditions these are morally binding is hugely consequential for our moral rights and duties. What is more, if we answer in the affirmative, violations of socially constructed norms justifiably attract moral reactive attitudes, such as blame, guilt, shame, and resentment, and invite punishment as a legitimate response.

It is thus no surprise that this question has been addressed, more or less explicitly, in several different areas of philosophy. Legal philosophers, for instance, have long been debating whether there exists an obligation to obey the law because it is the law—i.e., whether the fact that something is demanded by law makes it morally obligatory (for an overview, see Dagger and Lefkowitz 2014). Moral philosophers have instead focused on practices such as promising and asked whether their constitutive rules can give rise to genuine moral obligations: of the promisor towards the promisee (for an overview, see Habib 2022; Heuer 2012a; 2012b). Political philosophers, in turn, have debated whether obligations of justice are, at least in part, grounded in the norms and practices of existing communities—whether they are "practice-dependent" (see, e.g., Sangiovanni 2008; Walzer 1987).

Instead of asking about the moral normativity of socially constructed norms in relation to specific norms (e.g., legal, promissory, political) and to specific types of obligations (e.g., legal obligations, obligations of justice), the aim of this chapter is to address the moral normativity question in its general form. I shall explore the most prominent answers to this question, as I have been able to identify them in the literature, and raise concerns for all of them. Identifying the difficulties with existing answers paves the way for my own answer, which I propose and defend in the next chapter.

The present chapter proceeds as follows. In Section 1, I explain what it means for norms to have moral normativity and present the "deflationary view", which asserts that socially constructed norms lack such normativity. In Section 2, I point to some limitations of the deflationary view, thereby motivating the search for a positive answer to the moral normativity question. In Section 3, I explain what it takes to develop a successful positive answer to that question. The subsequent sections consider whether four prominent answers are, in fact, successful. In Section 4, I discuss Scanlon's "principle of established practices", and suggest that, despite appearances, it collapses into a version of the deflationary view. I then turn, in Section 5, to "conventionalism" about rights and duties: the view that all rights and duties are grounded in the norms governing social practices. I argue that conventionalism, while in principle well suited to the task at hand, is problematically ad hoc. In Section 6, I focus on the "normative-interests view", according to which norms have moral normativity to the extent that they further our normative interests: i.e., our interests in possessing socially efficacious rights, duties, powers, etc. I show that, despite its considerable appeal, this view suffers from an explanatory gap. Finally, in Section 7, I discuss the "joint-commitments view". On this view, each socially constructed norm is underpinned by joint commitments, which are mutually binding for the parties involved. I argue that while this view points us in the right direction, it is only applicable to a small subset of norms, hence lacks generality. Furthermore, its explanation for the wrongness of norm-breaches is limited in one important respect. Section 8 concludes.

1. The Deflationary View and Its Attractions

We are interested in the moral normativity question: in whether *the fact that* a socially constructed norm prescribes that one should φ places one under a pro tanto moral duty to φ. Thinking about familiar norms, including those listed in the previous chapter, we might be tempted to answer in the affirmative. After all, most would agree that it is typically (at least pro tanto) wrong—hence against duty—for drivers not to stop at red lights, for young people not to offer their seats to the elderly, for one to injure innocent others, for doctoral students not to attend the PhD workshop without justification, and so forth. Violations of these norms are often met with (different degrees of) disapproval, resentment, guilt, and blame.

From this, however, it does not follow that these socially constructed norms have moral normativity.[1] In fact, the reasons we would most readily invoke to explain the wrongness of the actions in question have nothing to do with the fact that they breach existing norms. Why should we stop at red lights? Because doing so is typically safe and efficient, given that others also stop when it's red and go when it's green. The fact that a norm prescribes stopping is not part of the most

---

[1] For further discussion of this point, see also Section 2 of the book's Introduction.

54 GROUNDING THE MORAL FORCE OF SOCIALLY CONSTRUCTED NORMS

natural explanation for why we should stop. That fact only *causally* contributes to making stopping at red lights the safest option in the circumstances, since we can reliably expect people to coordinate around that norm (Klosko 2011: 512).

Similarly, consider the norms that doctoral students ought to attend the PhD workshop and that we ought not to physically harm innocent others. The obvious explanation for why the addressees of these norms ought to conform to them is that the norms *mirror independent moral principles.* Students should attend the workshop because attendance is mutually beneficial, and fairness gives all of them a duty to contribute: nobody should free ride. Similarly, one has a weighty duty not to physically harm innocent others because this is what morality independently demands (Raz 1985b: 141). By the same token, one should offer one's bus seat to the elderly in compliance with the general moral principle that one should help those in need when this is not too costly to oneself.

In all these cases, the fact that a particular action is required by a socially constructed norm does not explain why we have a pro tanto duty to perform it. These cases thus fail to support the view that such norms have moral normativity. At most, they show that we often have reasons to act as these norms prescribe, stemming from the contingent substantive merits—e.g., safety, fairness, efficiency, respect for rights—of the prescribed actions, not from the fact that those actions are prescribed by socially constructed norms.

To borrow terminology from the literature on political obligation, the obligations involved in the cases just presented are "content-dependent", rather than "content-independent". An obligation to φ is content-dependent when what grounds it is some substantive merit of φ-ing (see Hart 1982: Ch. 10; cf. Gardner 2001; Green 2012). An obligation to φ is content-independent when it is grounded in something other than the substantive merits of φ-ing. For instance, a promissory obligation to φ is paradigmatically content-independent, since it is grounded in the fact that φ-ing is the object of a promise, independently of its substantive merits (Raz 2006: 1013). I may promise to buy you chocolate cake, and thereby place myself under an obligation to do so, even if you are diabetic and buying you chocolate cake is a substantively terrible idea. In the present context, we are looking for obligations to φ that are content-independent because they are grounded *in the fact that* φ-ing is mandated by socially constructed norms, rather than in the substantive merits of φ-ing.[2]

Taking the examples of norms offered up to this point as paradigmatic, one may be tempted to accept a "deflationary view" of the moral normativity of socially constructed norms. On this view, the very fact that certain actions are required or prohibited by those norms does not affect their moral status. That is, we never have (content-independent) obligations to φ because φ-ing is

---

[2] This distinction will be picked up again in Chapter 5.

norm-mandated. It is just that we often have good independent reasons to act as socially constructed norms demand (cf. Enoch 2011: 28).

The deflationary view has much going for it: it explains why we often feel morally compelled to do what existing norms require, but it does not uncritically defer to tradition and the status quo. It helps us account for our judgements about the moral bindingness of norm-mandated action, while allowing us to avoid the thorny question of how a social fact (an "is") could give rise to a moral obligation (an "ought").

Although tempting, the deflationary view is ultimately unsatisfactory. In particular, its *explanatory power* is limited, as is its ability to *fit* some of our considered moral judgements.[3]

2. The Limitations of the Deflationary View

While our reasons for doing what existing norms prescribe often go back to the substantive merits of the actions they prescribe, this is not always so. Sometimes, the first reasons that come to mind point to the very fact that a given norm exists in the context in which we find ourselves. For instance, when I visit a foreign land I often feel I ought to φ—provided φ-ing is morally acceptable—*because* local norms prescribe that I should φ; and this is so even if I find φ-ing inconvenient. If I am entering a Hindu temple, I feel I ought to take my shoes off *because* the local norms require that I do, quite independently of the merits of the relevant action. Or, as explained in the book's Introduction, when I first visited the UK I was not familiar with the practice of queuing for the bus. Once I realized that such a practice existed, I immediately felt I ought to go along with it precisely because queuing *was the norm* in the UK.

Experience tells me that I am not alone in feeling that, at least sometimes, the reason I ought to φ is that local norms demand that I do. Treating this sense of obligation as merely epiphenomenal and ultimately justified by the contingent substantive merits of the actions prescribed by the norms—as the deflationary view does—is therefore at odds with our moral phenomenology.

A proponent of the deflationary view may insist that there exist alternative explanations for our obligations to remove our shoes in the Hindu temple and to queue for the bus in the UK. The explanations point, respectively, to hygiene in relation to removing our shoes and to fairness and efficiency in relation to queuing. Taking one's shoes off is good practice, from a hygiene point of view. And jumping the queue is wrong since it amounts to free riding. The practice of

---

[3] The desiderata of explanatory power and fit were first outlined in the book's Introduction (pp. 7–8).

queuing is mutually beneficial, and those who skip the queue seek to benefit from it without doing their part.

The trouble with this response is that, even though it still allows the deflationary view to *fit* our considered judgements in the cases just discussed, the *explanation* the deflationary view offers is unsatisfactory. The *main* reason I (and I suspect many others) take my (their) shoes off before entering a temple has little to do with hygiene, and all to do with the fact that this is what local norms require. Similarly, the reason I started queuing for the bus once I realized that this was the norm in the UK was precisely that this was the local norm. Worries about free riding do not explain why my teenage self felt bad about having inadvertently violated that norm.

In response, one might suggest that, in both cases, "property-like" considerations are in fact doing the explanatory work. Whoever owns the temple can set the rules that should be observed in it—rules that are binding on all others. Similarly, a country or a city "belongs" to its inhabitants, and the rules they accept (such as the queuing norm) are binding on all. Once again, I do not find this explanation persuasive. I doubt that most people who take off their shoes before entering a temple do so out of respect for the *legal owners* of the temple, whoever they are. I certainly do not. It is out of respect for locals more broadly, who endorse norms concerning proper behaviour in sites of religious worship, that I comply. Similar considerations apply even more strongly to the case of queuing, where the concept of ownership can only apply metaphorically. After all, it is not clear in what sense locals "own" public spaces. Here, the ownership-based explanation collapses into the claim it was meant to refute: one ought to queue because this is the norm locals support.[4]

Finally, it may be proposed that what explains our reluctance to breach local norms is the independent moral principle that one should not offend others, coupled with the fact that violating the relevant norms would result in locals taking offence.[5] Again, this explanation strikes me as unsatisfactory. When I refrain from flouting the norm requiring taking my shoes off, I do so not because, as a matter of fact, I expect locals to get offended otherwise. I do so because I believe that, were I to ignore local norms, I would give them *reason* to be offended. Suppose I am in front of a temple when nobody else is around. In that case, walking in with my shoes on would predictably cause no offence. This would not, however, change my view about the wrongness of that action. The same considerations apply

---

[4] Moreover, the "ownership explanation" proposed by the objector does not itself invoke a fundamental moral principle, but another socially constructed norm (unless one holds particular views about natural ownership rights). The question would then have to be posed again: why is one under an obligation to comply with local ownership norms? The alleged alternative explanation offered by the objector thus makes our question resurface, just at a different level.

[5] I thank Arash Abizadeh for raising this objection.

to the queuing norm. Not upsetting others may play a part in the explanation, but the bulk of it has to do with respecting local customs.

What is more, there exist intuitive cases of wrongdoing which the deflationary view cannot explain. Even at the level of *fit* with the relevant evidence, then, the view is sub-optimal. Fitting all relevant judgements requires hypothesizing that at least some socially constructed norms have moral force. To see this, consider the following three scenarios.

Traffic Light: My German father-in-law, Jürgen, was driving late at night, through a village in his home region. He came to an intersection in the road. The traffic light went red. He looked in every direction: there was no car, person, or speed camera in sight. It would have been physically impossible for anyone to get hurt if he had continued straight, ignoring the red light. Moreover, nobody would have witnessed the breach. The only outcome would have been a happy one: an earlier arrival home. Yet my father-in-law stopped at the red light.[6]

Would not stopping have been pro tanto wrong? An affirmative answer presupposes ascribing moral normativity to the norm, prevalent in rural Germany, that one ought always to stop at red lights. Nothing else could explain why failing to stop would have been wrong in the circumstances. After all, ignoring the red light would have led to no harm. In fact, it would have been the "Pareto superior" thing to do. Jürgen would have been better off—namely home sooner—at nobody else's expense.[7]

Different demographics, it is worth noting, are likely to respond differently to this scenario. Most Southern Italians would insist that there would have been nothing wrong with ignoring the red light, and that my father-in-law's refusal to do so was a manifestation of his "German rigidity". But I would also expect many Germans to insist that he did the right thing.

These observations suggest that a case like *Traffic Light* lends relatively weak support to the hypothesis that some socially constructed norms have moral normativity. Ordinary people's judgements about it are rather disparate. Furthermore, it is tempting to explain away the intuition that not stopping would be pro tanto wrong as an instinctive reaction, driven by real-life considerations: for example, not stopping is often risky and undermines an otherwise useful rule. Even if such considerations are stipulated away in the proposed scenario, our intuitions— trained to respond to real-world circumstances—may inadvertently continue to track them; or so a proponent of the deflationary view could plausibly argue.

---

[6] This is an autobiographical variant of a famous example in the "obligation to obey the law" literature. See, e.g., Smith (1973: 971).

[7] Considerations of free-riding do not apply here. Driving through *in a scenario like Traffic Light* is universalizable. If everyone did it, the provision of the benefit of road coordination/safety would not be undermined. Thanks to Massimo Renzo for discussion.

Consider a second scenario.[8]

Barbeque: You are on a camping trip. You call some friends and make plans to spend the day with them, only to return in the late evening. Your barbeque set, pots and pans are stored outside your tent. The Rossi family, whose tent is just a few metres from yours, notices your absence, and decides to make use of your grill and related accessories for an improvised barbeque feast. They celebrate during the day, but put everything back in order prior to your return. When you get back, you notice nothing.

What the Rossis did, I assume, was wrong, even if not gravely so. As in *Traffic Light*, however, nobody is made worse off, nobody's expectations are actually frustrated (since you notice nothing), and the Rossis are made better off. Furthermore, unless one subscribes to a rigid natural property rights view, the norm breached by the Rossis—i.e., "one ought not to use others' property harmlessly without consent"—does not seem independently morally mandated. Consider, for instance, an alternative norm, which includes a special provision for third-party use when this does not interfere with the owner's use (cf. Cohen 2009). This norm does not seem in principle any less morally acceptable than that breached by the Rossis. Indeed, we could even suppose that the Rossis are tourists visiting from a land where this alternative norm regulates the possession and use of resources. If an explanation for the wrongness of the Rossis' actions exists, this must rest on the fact that those actions breach the relevant de facto property norm.[9]

Consider this third and final case.

Non-proceduralist President: In the wake of the 9/11 terror attacks, President George W. Bush authorized the National Security Agency to track international calls and e-communications of people inside the US, without a court warrant

---

[8] Cf. the harmless trespass scenario discussed in Ripstein (2006).

[9] Andrea Sangiovanni has suggested to me that the wrong occurring in *Barbeque* is arguably best explained by the fact that the Rossis expose you to possible harm: i.e., in nearby possible worlds, they do break the pans, wear them down, you find out and get reasonably frightened, etc. Your interests, in other words, are not *robustly* protected by the Rossis and this is why they wrong you. I find this explanation unconvincing for the following reason. We expose each other to possible harm all the time: for example, every time I ride a bike I expose pedestrians to possible harm; every time I carry a cup of coffee I expose those near me to the possibility of getting their shirts stained, etc. Yet, none of these actions appear morally wrong. We thus need to distinguish between instances of exposure to possible harm that count as wrongful and instances that do not. One option may be to focus on the magnitude of the possible harm in question, but clearly this won't help us with *Barbeque*, since the possible harm there is minimal—i.e., a few dirty pans—and certainly lesser than in the case of responsible bike riding or car driving, both of which involve no wrongdoing. Appeal to exposure to possible harm, without mentioning that such exposure violates your property rights, then, doesn't seem able to explain why the Rossis wrong you. But then the question of the moral significance of contingent property-rights norms arises again.

(Risen and Lichtblau 2005). Once this became known, the President was criticized for acting ultra vires, in violation of the 1978 Foreign Intelligence Surveillance Act (FISA), which prohibits warrantless domestic electronic surveillance. In an open letter to Congress, published in the *New York Review of Books*, a group of leading legal scholars and former government officials insisted that, to be lawful, such surveillance would need to be authorized by Congress, through legislative amendment (Dworkin et al. 2006).

Let us assume that the President's critics are right: he did act ultra vires. Let us further assume, for the sake of argument, that: (i) domestic warrantless surveillance was indispensable to avert serious terrorist threats and (ii) this legal breach was a one-off occurrence, necessitated by exceptional circumstances. Even so, the President's violation of a socially constructed (legal) norm appears pro tanto wrong. A head of government acting in this manner would seem to owe its citizens an explanation, if not an apology, for the breach, even on the assumption that, all things considered, he did the right thing.

Crucially for our purposes, the pro tanto wrong in question is contingent on the US Constitution and US law more generally having the content that they do. If the Constitution had given the President greater discretion, or if the original provisions in the 1978 FISA had been different, the President's actions would not have involved any wrongful procedural breach. And it would seem implausible to suggest that the precise details of US law are independently morally mandated. We can imagine a morally permissible, but different, democratic setup under which the president has greater discretion, or under which the 1978 FISA has slightly different content. In short, the pro tanto wrong involved in *Non-proceduralist President* cannot be explained satisfactorily unless we assume that a certain act being prohibited by existing norms makes a difference to its status: it makes its performance pro tanto wrong.[10]

---

[10] Nic Southwood has pointed out to me that the President's actions may seem wrongful because they set back people's interests in privacy. But whether a setback of interests is wrongful depends on the balance of interests at stake, and in this case, *ex hypothesi*, individuals' privacy interests are outweighed by the public interest in safety. So, while the setback may be harmful, it is not wrongful. It may also be suggested that the source of the moral normativity of the 1978 FISA is obvious: its democratic pedigree. I do not think this settles the matter, insofar as there are many different ways of instantiating democracy. Why does the particular instantiation of democracy found in the United States, then, have moral normativity, such that an unconstitutional shift to a different, but equally democratic, system would strike us as wrongful? An appeal to the democratic credentials of the existing system will not do in answering this further question. What we need is an account of the moral normativity of already existing (i.e., positive) democratic norms in the US. This matter will be further discussed in Chapter 5. Finally, Andrew Gold has suggested that the President's wrongdoing may seem akin to a breach of promise, insofar as US Presidents swear to "preserve, protect and defend" the Constitution upon taking office. This explanation, I think, does not fully capture the nature of the wrong in question. Our reactions to the case would likely remain the same even if we assumed that no such oath of office took place; just like our intuitions about the obligation to obey the law in general tend to be unaffected by whether those subjected to the law have in fact consented to obeying it.

60   GROUNDING THE MORAL FORCE OF SOCIALLY CONSTRUCTED NORMS

Non-proceduralist President and, arguably to a lesser extent, *Barbeque* and *Traffic Light* provide some motivation for the hypothesis that socially constructed norms have moral normativity. But can this hypothesis be systematically vindicated? I believe that it can, and I will present and defend my preferred vindication of it in the next chapter. Before doing so, however, I need to (i) explain what a successful vindication requires and (ii) explore some of the most prominent existing attempts to vindicate the moral normativity of socially constructed norms. Only if they are not satisfactory will it make sense to look for a new theory. I proceed to carry out tasks (i) and (ii) in subsequent sections.

3. Vindicating the Moral Force of Socially Constructed Norms

Is it ever the case that we ought to φ *because* φ-ing is required by a socially constructed norm? That is, can the fact that φ-ing is required by a socially constructed norm *ground* our being under a moral obligation to φ? Grounding, as I understand it here, is an explanatory relation holding between facts (which can be expressed by propositions). In the words of Kit Fine (2001: 15, original emphases), "if the truth of [a proposition] is grounded in other truths, then they *account* for its truth; [the proposition's] being the case holds *in virtue of* the other truths' being the case".[11] Such grounding relations can be of different kinds: metaphysical, natural, or normative (K. Fine 2012: 38–39).[12] Which type of grounding relation is of interest to us depends on the domain in which we are operating: metaphysical, scientific, or ethical/moral.

Here, we are interested in normative grounding, since what we are looking to ground is a moral fact: the fact that someone is under a moral obligation to φ. More specifically, we are asking whether an *empirical fact* (i.e., "being mandated by a socially constructed norm") can ground a *moral fact* (i.e., "being under a moral obligation").

The question, one might think, is ill-posed. After all, it is widely—though not universally—accepted that one cannot derive an ought from an is.[13] Or, to put it in the words of G. A. Cohen (2003: 214, emphases omitted), "a [moral] principle can reflect or respond to a fact only because it is also a response to a principle that is not a response to a fact".[14] The "responding" Cohen talks about here refers to a grounding relation. Cohen's point is that empirical facts, per se, cannot ground

---

[11] Grounding relations also obtain between the facts that make given propositions true or false.

[12] Much has been said about grounding in the literature on metaphysics, and we need not examine that debate in detail here. For classic discussions, see Correia and Schneider (2012), Rosen (2010), and Schaffer (2009).

[13] But see, e.g., Searle (1964).

[14] While I am relying on Cohen's argument, there are aspects of it with which I disagree (but which are not relevant to the matter under analysis here). See Ronzoni and Valentini (2008). For further discussion, see Sangiovanni (2016).

VINDICATING THE MORAL FORCE OF SOCIALLY CONSTRUCTED NORMS   61

moral requirements or principles, namely moral facts. Instead, whenever an empirical fact is invoked as the ground of a moral fact (e.g., a moral duty), there must be a further moral fact (e.g., a moral principle), that explains why the empirical fact counts as the relevant ground.

Let me offer a simple example. Consider the following moral fact "one ought to be polite to people" and the following empirical fact "being polite to people makes people happy". Suppose, further, that this empirical fact is presented as a ground for the moral one, such that: "One ought to be polite to people *because* being polite to people makes people happy". Our explanation for why we should act politely cannot end here. The fact that being polite to people makes them happy, per se, does not suffice to explain why we ought to be polite to people. A satisfactory explanation must invoke a further moral fact, namely the principle that "one ought to make people happy". That principle, in turn, explains why the empirical fact that behaving politely makes people happy grounds an obligation to be polite.

More schematically put, in Cohen's framework the grounding relations between empirical and moral facts take the following form.

Grounding sequence
- <u>Action required (moral fact)</u>: You ought to φ (φ = be polite to people).
- By virtue of what ought I to φ?
- <u>Empirical fact</u>: Because being polite to people makes them happy.
- By virtue of what does the fact that being polite to people makes them happy ground my obligation to φ?
- <u>General moral principle (moral fact)</u>: Because one ought to make people happy.

I believe that Cohen's logic here is spot-on. An empirical fact, per se, cannot ground a normative one.[15] This, however, does not imply that the question about the moral normativity of socially constructed norms is ill posed. Instead, it means that vindicating their moral normativity requires identifying a moral principle P (i.e., a normative fact[16]) that explains why an empirical fact (i.e., φ-ing is required by a socially constructed norm) can ground a moral obligation (i.e., one ought to φ). Not any principle will do for this purpose, of course. What we need is a principle that singles out "being mandated by a socially constructed norm" as a morally relevant attribute of a given action φ-ing.

To see this, it might be worth directly comparing and contrasting—in a stylized form—how a deflationary view would ground the obligation to, say, stop at a red light, and how a view that successfully vindicates the moral normativity of

---

[15] Even if some disagree with this claim, it doesn't seem to be contested by the proponents of the views I shall be discussing in this chapter.
[16] Strictly speaking, a principle is not a normative *fact*. I use this terminology as shorthand for "the normative fact that one ought to do what P requires".

socially constructed norms would ground that same obligation. I first outline a model deflationary grounding sequence, and then outline our target grounding sequence—i.e., the type of sequence that would successfully vindicate the moral normativity of a socially constructed norm (e.g., that one should stop at the red light).

Deflationary grounding sequence
- Action required: You ought to φ (φ = stop at the red light).
- By virtue of what ought I to φ?
- Empirical fact: Because stopping at the red light minimizes the risk of harming others.
- By virtue of what does the fact that stopping at the red light minimizes the risk of harming others ground my obligation to φ?
- General moral principle: Because one ought to minimize the risk of harming others.

Here, we have a fact invoked as a ground for a particular requirement to φ. But the fact in question is not that φ-ing is mandated by a socially constructed norm. Instead, the fact in question refers to a different (substantive) attribute of φ-ing, i.e., it minimizes the risk of harming others. In turn, a further normative demand—i.e., to act in ways that minimize the risk of harming others—explains why the fact that φ-ing minimizes the risk of harming others grounds the requirement to φ. Now consider this alternative explanation for our obligation to φ.

Target grounding sequence
- Action required: You ought to φ (φ = stop at the red light).
- By virtue of what ought I to φ?
- Empirical fact: Because a socially constructed norm requires you to φ.
- By virtue of what does the fact that φ-ing is required by a socially constructed norm ground my obligation to φ?
- Target general moral principle: Because *P*.

The challenge of grounding the moral normativity of socially constructed norms involves identifying an *independently plausible principle* (*P*) that can play the right grounding or explanatory role. This must be a principle which, when placed at the bottom of the target grounding sequence, allows us to reach the conclusion that φ-ing is morally required because it is mandated by a socially constructed norm.

4. The Principle of Established Practices

The first principle I shall consider is T. M. Scanlon's "principle of established practices", which reads as follows:

THE PRINCIPLE OF ESTABLISHED PRACTICES   63

[When] there is a need for some principle to govern a particular kind of activity, but there are a number of different principles that would do this in a way that no one could reasonably reject…then if one of these (nonrejectable) principles is generally (it need not be unanimously) accepted in a given community, then it is wrong to violate it simply because this suits one's convenience.

(Scanlon 1998: 339)

In Scanlon's view, if there are multiple reasonable principles that could govern a beneficial practice—e.g., think of a system of property rights or traffic regulation—widespread de facto acceptance of one such principle serves as a "selection criterion": the accepted principle becomes binding on all. Making bindingness conditional on unanimous acceptance, Scanlon notes, would be unreasonable, since it would render effective regulation of the relevant practice virtually impossible, thereby forcing us to forego its benefits.

More recently, Scanlon has restated this principle in a somewhat more concise, and I think more effective, form. According to this reformulation, one ought to "go along with established practices that promote important social goals in non-objectionable ways" (Scanlon 2013: 405). This is why, for example, we have obligations to pay taxes (provided the tax system is reasonably fair), to separate our trash, to follow traffic norms, and so forth.

To examine the suitability of the principle of established practices as a ground for the moral normativity of socially constructed norms, let us plug it into our grounding sequence, focusing once again on the practice of traffic regulation.

- <u>Action required</u>: You ought to φ (φ = stop at the red light).
- By virtue of what ought I to φ?
- <u>Empirical fact</u>: Because stopping at the red light is part of an established practice that promotes important social goals in non-objectionable ways.
- By virtue of what does the fact that stopping at the red light is part of an established practice that promotes important social goals in non-objectionable ways ground my obligation to φ?
- <u>Target general moral principle</u>: Because one ought to "go along with established practices that promote important social goals in non-objectionable ways".

There are two difficulties with the principle of established practices as a candidate principle P. First, the principle only vindicates obligations to go along with norms governing practices that promote important social goals. Practices that we may regard as "socially optional", which do not help us secure important goods, are excluded from the domain of application of the principle. Yet, many socially constructed norms precisely regulate practices of this optional kind: think of practices of courtesy, etiquette, or non-necessary coordination practices, such as queuing. Ideally, we would want our principle P to range over those practices too, and not be limited to practices that promote important social goals.

64   GROUNDING THE MORAL FORCE OF SOCIALLY CONSTRUCTED NORMS

Second, and more importantly, the rationale underpinning Scanlon's principle is, ultimately, an instrumental one. The reason why it would be unreasonable not to go along with established practices is that deviation from such practices would result in the practices no longer delivering their distinctive goods ("important social goals"). Take again traffic rules: if people were to deviate from them for personal convenience, the goods of road safety and fluid traffic would cease to exist. Or else, if due to personal convenience people refrained from paying their taxes, the array of public services funded by taxation would no longer be available. In other words, the principle of established practices is not "ultimate", but itself grounded in a further, instrumental principle, requiring us to contribute (our fair share) to promoting important social goals in non-objectionable ways. The point can be illustrated by enriching our original grounding sequence as follows.

- <u>Action required</u>: You ought to φ (φ = stop at the red light).
- By virtue of what ought I to φ?
- <u>Empirical fact</u>: Because stopping at the red light is part of an established practice that promotes important social goals in non-objectionable ways.
- By virtue of what does the fact that stopping at the red light is part of an established practice that promotes important social goals in non-objectionable ways ground my obligation to φ?
- <u>Principle of established practices</u>: Because one ought to "go along with established practices that promote important social goals in non-objectionable ways".
- By virtue of what ought one to "go along with established practices that promote important social goals in non-objectionable ways"?
- <u>Empirical fact</u>: Because going along with established practices that promote important social goals in non-objectionable ways is necessary to promote the relevant social goals.
- By virtue of what does the fact that "going along with established practices that promote important social goals in non-objectionable ways is necessary to promote the relevant social goals" ground our obligation to go along with said established practices?
- <u>Target general moral principle</u>: Because we have an obligation to act in ways that promote important social goals in non-objectionable ways.

As this enriched grounding sequence shows, it is ultimately an instrumental concern with the promotion of important social goals that grounds the principle of established practices. But, as we have seen in our discussion of the deflationary view, instrumental justifications for complying with socially constructed norms cannot explain why *the fact that* certain actions are mandated or prohibited by those norms matters morally. Instrumental justifications cannot account for why deviation from existing socially constructed norms remains wrongful even when it *does not* undermine the realization of important social goals. The cases I offered earlier—i.e., *Traffic Light, Barbeque*, and *Non-proceduralist President*—are illustrations of this difficulty.[17]

In fact, looking at our enriched grounding sequence, it turns out that the principle of established practices is actually superfluous. The most immediate reason why one ought to stop at the red light is that doing so promotes important social goals in non-objectionable ways, the goals being road safety and fluid traffic. The fact that stopping at red lights is part of an established practice only causally explains why stopping contributes to road safety.

In sum, the rationale behind the principle of established practices doesn't pick out the fact that an action is mandated or prohibited by a socially constructed norm as the explanation for its moral obligatoriness or impermissibility. Instead, the action's moral status stems from its norm-independent merits—i.e., its contributing to the delivery of some important goods—merits that are causally explained by the fact that the action is part of a generally accepted system of socially constructed norms. Despite appearances, the principle of established practices belongs to the "deflationary" family and, for that reason, it is not a suitable candidate for our target principle *P*.

5. The Conventionalist View

An alternative candidate for *P* has been recently proposed by Katharina Nieswandt (2018) in the context of her analysis of conventionalism about rights and duties. This analysis, in turn, draws on Elizabeth Anscombe's work (1978).[18] True conventionalism, Nieswandt argues, grounds rights and duties in facts that exist *within* practices. In particular, if a practice is justified—which, for Nieswandt (2018: 27), means "binding" or "obligatory"—then practice-internal duties are grounded in the facts that the practice's rules designate as obligation-generating.

---

[17] It may be argued that the principle of established practices is motivated not only by instrumental considerations, but also by considerations of fairness. In that case, the principle would allow us to condemn deviations from the practice even when these do not prevent it from delivering its distinctive benefits, since such deviations would be unfair: a matter of free-riding. In this case too, however, the principle would collapse into a version of the deflationary view, since it would not pick out the fact that certain actions are mandated by socially constructed norms as morally relevant, but the fact that failing to perform said actions would be unfair. There would then only be a contingent connection between the unfairness of the actions and the actions being mandated by socially constructed norms. In several cases, such as *Traffic Light, Barbeque*, and *Non-Proceduralist President*, deviations from the norm do not seem to trigger fairness considerations—such deviations are universalizable without this undermining the benefits provided by the norms—and yet they are arguably still morally problematic. For discussion of this reading of Scanlon's principle, see Owens (2022: 26ff.). For further discussion of fairness considerations in the context of vindicating the moral normativity of (legal) norms, see Chapter 5.

[18] See, e.g., Nieswandt's (2017) reconstruction of Anscombe's account of how practices or conventions can be sources of normativity. Anscombe's work is, in turn, inspired by David Hume's.

66 GROUNDING THE MORAL FORCE OF SOCIALLY CONSTRUCTED NORMS

As she puts it: "If the rules of [a] practice...say that X must φ given fact F, and [the practice is justified], then, given F, X must φ because of F" (Nieswandt 2018: 17).[19]

For instance, take the practice of promising, on which Nieswandt focuses her analysis.[20] This practice is justified in the sense that it is the kind of practice we ought to have in order to further certain important human goods: for example, mutual trust, assurance, and broader social utility. The rules of the practice, roughly stated, say that: "Whenever someone utters the words 'I promise to φ', they thereby bind themselves to another party to φ (subject to the other party's uptake)". A conventionalist view, for Nieswandt, holds that the ground of my obligation to φ is the *fact* that I promised (by saying "I promise"). The rules of the practice of promising give this fact obligation-generating power. And this obligation-generating power is real—not bogus, or simply perceived—because the practice of promising is itself justified: it furthers important human goods. It is a practice we ought to have. In other words, promise-based obligations are not mere social obligations, but genuine moral ones.

Nieswandt is careful to distinguish this view from what she calls "pseudo" or "superficial" conventionalism. Pseudo-conventionalists mistakenly ground practice-internal duties not in the facts that a practice's rules designate as obligation-generating, but in the considerations that justify the practice in the first place. So, a pseudo-conventionalist would argue that breaching a promise is wrong *because* it undermines a practice that is conducive to important human goods.

The difficulty with such pseudo-conventionalism—famously discussed by Scanlon (1990)—is that it gives the "wrong kinds of reasons" for promise-based duties. When I violate a promise, it looks like I wrong—and possibly harm—the promisee, not the world at large or everyone who sustains the practice of promising. Breaking a promise is wrong because of what it does *to the promisee*, not because of what it does to the practice, hence the greater good of humanity.

Unlike pseudo-conventionalist views, which conflate the grounds of the moral normativity of a practice with the grounds of the duties that exist within a given practice, genuine conventionalism is not guilty of this mistake. This, according to Nieswandt, makes it a particularly appealing view about the grounds of our moral rights and duties.

Nieswandt's conventionalism is relevant to our discussion insofar as it appears to offer precisely the target principle *P* we are looking for. To see this, let me reproduce the grounding sequence, placing the conventionalist principle she proposes at the bottom of it.

---

[19] In her text, Nieswandt names the practice "P" for short. To avoid confusion with *P* as understood here—namely as the target principle that grounds the moral normativity of socially constructed norms—I have removed references to P in Nieswandt's quotation and replaced them with references to "the practice".

[20] She is explicit, though, that her analysis can be applied to many other practices.

Conventionalist grounding sequence
- <u>Action required</u>: You ought to φ (φ = stop).
- By virtue of what ought I to φ?
- <u>Empirical fact</u>: Because the light is red.
- By virtue of what does the fact that the light is red ground my obligation to φ?
- <u>Target general moral principle</u>: Because "If the rules of a practice say that X must φ given fact F, and the practice is justified, then, given F, X must φ because of F".

The target moral principle states precisely the general formula of Nieswandt's conventionalism. This principle offers a clear ground for the norm-based obligation to φ. It says that, if a practice is justified, its governing norms can lend obligation-generating power to facts: i.e., they have moral normativity. The fact that there exists a justified practice whose rules require that one should stop given that the light is red makes it true that one should stop given that the light is red. Manifestly, the practice of "traffic regulation" is justified. On this view, if we ask "Why should I stop at the red light?" the answer is "Because the rules of a justified practice demand that, given that the light is red, you do so".

I find Nieswandt's analysis of conventionalism helpful and illuminating. I am, however, unpersuaded that her conventionalist principle offers a convincing ground for the moral normativity of socially constructed norms. Let me explain why. The principle tells us that the rules of a justified practice generate genuine obligations.[21] But it denies that what, in turn, gives those rules moral bindingness *also* grounds the relevant practice-generated obligations. The justification of a practice is a "background condition" for the validity of practice-generated obligations, but not itself their ground (Nieswandt 2018: 17). In the case of the practice of "regulated traffic", this means that the values of safety and efficiency which, plausibly, justify the practice, are background conditions for its moral bindingness but do not ground practice-internal duties.

The obvious question to raise, in this context, is: why should this be so? That is, why should we believe that what ultimately grounds the moral normativity of a practice is not also what grounds the moral normativity of practice-internal duties—the duties corresponding to the demands of the norms structuring the practice? Of course, we have seen that, in the case of promissory obligations—for instance—pointing to the broader values that justify a practice makes one susceptible to the wrong reasons problem. But if conventionalism (of the non-pseudo

---

[21] Nieswandt (2018: 27) argues that those obligations are "binding", but also seems to think that nothing much hinges on whether we call them "moral". That said, her language throughout suggests that she in fact thinks of them as moral obligations. After all, promissory obligations—which are her main example—are a paradigmatic instance of moral obligations.

variety) were solely motivated by a desire to avoid the wrong reasons problem, we would have to be concerned about its ad hoc nature. Its rigid separation between what justifies a practice and what grounds practice-internal duties would be a stipulation made with the sole aim of avoiding an unpalatable implication of an otherwise perfectly sensible view.

Nieswandt thinks that there is more to genuine conventionalism. In particular, she holds that the conflation between (i) what justifies (i.e., grounds the binding-ness of) a practice and (ii) what grounds practice-internal duties is tempting but fallacious *in general*. It is not simply an ad hoc move the conventionalist must resort to in order to avoid the wrong reasons problem. To make the point, she offers an interesting example, focusing on the practice of football, and claiming that the lessons learnt from it extend to moral cases as well.

Nieswandt (2018: 25–26) notes that the "offside rule" was introduced within the practice of football to make the game livelier. This is why the rule was adopted. However, if we ask why a football player is forbidden from scoring a goal offside, answering that scoring offside makes the game less lively seems to get the explan-ation completely wrong. The reason why an offside goal is invalid has all to do with the rules of football. In fact, there may be instances in which allowing an offside goal would make matches livelier, by evening out the score. So, the infer-ence from what explains why we should adopt a certain rule to what grounds rule-based duties is fallacious.

I am not persuaded by this argument. While I am fully prepared to believe that the reason why the offside rule was added to the practice of football had to do with how it would make football more entertaining, this seems to me irrelevant to what makes the practice of football "justified" in the sense of its rules being *mor-ally binding* for those participating in it. The practice of football, with or without the offside rule, is certainly morally permissible, since it violates no moral impera-tives. But its rules, it seems to me, become binding on participants only when, and because, they *agree* to play *football*. When they do, they bind themselves to each other to play precisely that game. Consequently, allowing an offside goal to count as valid would be tantamount to no longer playing football proper—given football's rules. And if we agree to play football, but one party, or even the referee, starts enforcing the rules of a different game, an agreement has been breached. This is why it is wrong to allow a valid goal to be scored offside. And this is why, when this happens, moral reactive attitudes are activated. Players and spectators speak of cheating and unfairness.

In sum, what explains the (moral) bindingness of the offside rule is the implicit agreement between participants: it is the familiar moral principle that one ought not to breach agreements. If we appeal to this principle—rather than to the greater entertainment value of a game with the offside rule—to explain why it is wrong to score a goal offside, what Nieswandt described as a fallacy no longer seems one. There appears to be nothing odd in asserting that the reason why allowing a goal to be scored offside is wrong is that participants agreed—in advance—that such goals would be treated as invalid. But in doing so, we are precisely explaining the wrongness of violating a practice-based rule by appeal to the considerations that lend moral bindingness to the practice.

The football example is not an isolated case. Similar conclusions can be reached in relation to what justifies the practice of regulated traffic and the grounds of the duties internal to this practice. For a conventionalist, recall, our duty to stop at a red light is grounded as follows.

Conventionalism about traffic regulations: The rules of the practice of traffic regulation say that drivers must stop given that the light is red. Traffic regulation is a morally justified (in fact, mandated) practice, since we have an obligation to act in ways that minimize the risk of harm to others, and traffic regulation allows us to do just that. In light of this, given that the light is red, drivers must stop *because* the light is red (cf. Nieswandt 2018: 17).

Let us see whether it is really fallacious to ground the obligation to stop at the red light in the considerations that justify the relevant practice (i.e., which make it morally binding). Here, we have (i) the practice-internal obligation to stop at the red light and (ii) the practice-justifying obligation to act in ways that minimize the risk of harm to others. But there appears to be absolutely nothing wrong or fallacious in the suggestion that one ought to stop at the red light because, and insofar as, doing so minimizes the risk of harm to others. In fact, it seems artificial to keep the two separate.

Of course, this line of reasoning brings us back to the deflationary view. Yet that view cannot be defeated by asserting what it denies. Unfortunately, this is what conventionalism—with its stipulated separation between what justifies a practice and what grounds practice-internal duties—does.

In sum, pure conventionalism does not provide a satisfactory candidate for our principle *P*. While its general structure does allow for practice-generated obligations, it asserts the existence of those obligations without offering a convincing story as to where they come from. Perhaps a convincing story could be provided— I am not categorically excluding this possibility—but, as it stands, conventionalism is explanatorily unsatisfactory.

6. The Normative-Interests View

Another view, developed by David Owens (2012; 2017; 2022), holds that the moral normativity of socially constructed norms stems from the way in which

70 GROUNDING THE MORAL FORCE OF SOCIALLY CONSTRUCTED NORMS

such norms further a special class of interests we possess, which Owens calls *normative interests*.[22]

We are familiar with interests that can be expressed in non-normative language. An interest is something that—if fulfilled—contributes to making our lives go well. So, for example, we have interests in access to food, shelter, sanitation, in having a certain degree of freedom, in having some control over our surrounding environment, and so forth.

But, Owens argues, in order to be able to explain a variety of normative phenomena, we also need to postulate the existence of *normative interests*. These are interests, namely things that make our lives go well, which must be expressed in normative language. Owens recognizes a variety of such interests. These include: (i) *deontic interests*—namely interests in binding ourselves to other people through, for instance, friendships and family relationships, (ii) *authority interests and permissive interests*—namely interests in determining, by declaration, when certain acts are permissible, obligatory, or forbidden, and (iii) *remissive interests*, namely interests in determining when a wrong qualifies as blameworthy (Owens 2012: 10–11). These interests, in turn, explain a variety of important normative phenomena. For instance, at least part of the reason why we are genuinely bound by family and friendship obligations is that those obligations further our deontic interests: they have deontic value for us. Similarly, the reason why we possess the normative power to release a promisor from his promise and to consent to medical treatment is that these powers further our authority and permissive interests. Finally, our moral power to forgive exists insofar as it serves our remissive interests: it gives us control over whether certain wrongs qualify as blameworthy.

So far, so good. But how does Owens' story about normative interests connect to the present focus of our analysis, namely, the moral normativity of socially constructed norms? The point of connection is to be found in Owens' claim that our normative interests ground moral powers and obligations *only when* corresponding socially constructed norms (which Owens calls "conventions"[23]) give such powers and obligations social existence. In Owens' words:

> Whether what is in question is the ability to make friends or forgive wrongdoers, or else a normative power like the power to promise or to consent, possession of this ability or power does us no good unless it is recognized in some form. It would make no sense for us to bother to exercise such abilities or powers unless their exercise had some social significance. So rights and powers grounded

---

[22] Since, at the time of writing, Owens' book on the moral normativity of social rules, *Bound by Convention*, was not yet published, in my discussion I mostly rely on his previous work. Having seen parts of the book's draft, my sense is that the way I characterize Owens' view here is consistent with how it is developed in the book. In fact, Owens himself notes that the view defended in *Bound by Convention* was already implicit in his earlier work.

[23] It is clear that what Owens has in mind is close to socially constructed norms in my sense.

in our normative interests exist only where the relevant social conventions [i.e., norms] are in force.   (Owens 2012: 10)

This means that Owens' thesis about normative interests, although not originally offered as an explanation for the moral normativity of socially constructed norms, does provide one. Indeed, Owens (2017; 2022) has recently explicitly extended his theory in this direction.

Let us consider some familiar socially constructed norms, such as the norm that it is wrong to use other people's property without consent, or the norm that one ought to keep one's promises and that the promisee may release the promisor from his/her obligations, or the norm that one ought to be loyal to one's friends, and so forth. Of course, there are often many good independent reasons why we should act in the way such norms prescribe. That is, often, acting in line with the relevant norms furthers some of our non-normative interests, such that violating the norms counts as wrongful for this reason. This line of reasoning is central to the deflationary view.

But, as we have seen, there are cases in which norm-violations appear to set back no interests. This was the case in *Barbeque*, which described harmless violations of property rights. Similarly, we can easily imagine cases in which violations of promises or instances of disloyalty to one's friends—e.g., those which are never discovered—result in no setback of anyone's interests. Yet, we often have the intuition that such violations are wrongful and morally problematic all the same. Owens' normative-interests view explains why: the reason why property norms, friendship norms, and promissory norms retain moral normativity even when breaches do not result in any harm is that *the very existence of* those norms furthers our *normative interests.*

The reason why it is wrong for others to take our property harmlessly without consent is that *it being wrong is good for us*: it furthers our (normative) interests in being the ones who determine whether an action is permitted or not. Similarly, the reason why it is wrong to breach promises even when such breaches are harmless is that *it being wrong* to breach promises—hence people being bound by promissory obligations—is good for us: it furthers our interests in having the authority to determine whether the promisor ought to perform or not (Owens 2006).

The normative-interests view, Owens argues, also helps us explain the moral normativity of norms that would otherwise strike us as somewhat arbitrarily context-dependent. Consider, for example, socially constructed norms concerning parents' duties of care towards their children (Owens 2017). Owens notes that different societies are characterized by different such norms. Southern European societies (or, as Owens puts it, "the Italians") have cultures governed by norms that require parents to let children live in their family homes as dependents until they get married. Pushing a child out of one's home as soon as she turns 18 or 21 would be perceived as a violation of one's parental duties. Northern European societies (or, as Owens puts it, "the English") are characterized by different norms. There, it is perfectly permissible to ask of one's children to become independent at around age 20.

It is clear that the different shapes of these obligations are a matter of pure social construction. Both systems of norms seem morally permissible. Yet, in Southern Europe, where the demanding care norms are in operation, their violation gives rise precisely to the reactive attitudes associated with violations of moral duties. The same goes for the somewhat lighter-touch care norms of Northern Europe. Owens again argues that these norms are binding because their very existence furthers our normative interests: specifically, our deontic interests in being bound in particular ways to members of our families. Moreover, even though "there is likely more than one set of familial rights and obligations that would be good for us and so would bind us were they recognized...social convention gets to determine which of these normative structures is actually in force" (Owens 2017: 570).[24] Differently put, once a social convention (i.e., a set of norms) is in force, if it can be shown that its existence furthers our normative interests, then that convention is morally binding.

In sum, for Owens the moral force of socially constructed norms stems from the way in which they further our normative interests. Violations of those norms "qua norms" are wrong, and rightly elicit the reactive attitudes associated with wrongdoing, because and insofar as their doing so is good for us.

Owens' view is appealing, and the thought that our normative relationships to others contribute to enriching our lives—i.e., the thought that we have an interest in them—is highly plausible. But does the view succeed in grounding the moral normativity of socially constructed norms? To address this question, let us begin by mapping the view onto our reference grounding sequence. This time, I take *Barbeque* as our relevant scenario, since Owens himself mentions that normative interests can help us account for the wrongings involved in cases of harmless trespass (Owens 2012: 64).[25]

Normative-interests grounding sequence
- Action required: You ought to φ (φ = refrain from taking other people's pots and pans without their consent).
- By virtue of what ought I to φ?
- Empirical fact: Because there is a socially constructed norm that requires you to φ.

---

[24] Compare here Scanlon's principle of established practices, discussed in Section 4.
[25] Owens (2022: Ch. 7) includes a broader discussion of property rights, which he regards as conventional and partly grounded in our authority interests over certain objects.

- By virtue of what does the fact that there is a socially constructed norm that requires me to φ ground my obligation to φ?
- <u>Target general moral principle</u>: Because people, including you, have a *normative interest* in determining whether others' actions wrong them, and the norm in question furthers that interest.

There are a few things to note about the normative-interests grounding sequence. The first and most important one is that the target moral principle is, actually, not a normative principle at all. Instead, it is an evaluative statement, coupled with a descriptive one. It says that we possess a particular interest: that it is good for us if such and such is the case. It also asserts that the existence of a given socially constructed norm—namely a property norm—as a matter of fact, furthers that interest.

It is unclear, however, how a fact about what is good for us, coupled with an empirical observation about what furthers our good, can itself give rise to an "ought", how it can ground a duty. This line of thought clearly violates the general, Cohen-inspired rule I said I would subscribe to at the start. Consider a simple example. It is good for me to have a new, well-functioning smartphone. This is an evaluative statement, a statement of fact about the good. It is, however, unclear how this fact alone could give rise to any duties or normative phenomena more generally. If something is good, we have reason to value it; but it is not clear how the fact of goodness, per se, generates obligations.[26]

This gap in the sequence, one might think, is just a matter of appearance. A tacit principle lies at the bottom of it: "One ought to act in ways that are consistent with, or promote, people's interests". A principle of this kind would inject the required normativity into the sequence: it would tell us that we ought to respect socially constructed norms—i.e., that these norms are morally binding—because, and to the extent that, doing so furthers people's normative interests.

While this is a plausible explanation of how interests ground duties—something I do not dispute—I am not convinced that it can be used to supplement the normative-interests view. This is because, on that view, it is not acting in conformity with certain norms that furthers our normative interests. It is *the very existence* of those norms qua norms that does. When someone takes my pots and pans without my consent, "society" reacts by condemning their conduct as wrongful. And *this*—the broad acceptance and recognition of the wrong—furthers my normative interests. Unauthorized harmless use of my pots and pans is wrongful

---

[26] Owens (2006: 52, n. 3) mentions that, for some theorists, obligations make sense as phenomena, or give reasons for action, only if they can be linked to human interests, to what is good for us. Even so, there seems to be a difference between arguing that obligations must be somehow connected to the human good and arguing that obligations exist *by virtue of the fact that* their existence is good for us. Owens' normative-interests view appears close to the latter, controversial statement. Cf. Owens (2012: 9).

because its socially counting as wrongful is good for me: it furthers my normative interests. Normative interests are not set back by norm-violations, they are furthered by the existence of norms. And, typically, unless violations occur "en masse", any specific norm-violation does not threaten the existence of a norm.

This reveals that what, for Owens, genuinely matters is people's displaying the attitudes that constitute socially constructed norms. It is the existence of particular webs of beliefs, emotions, and intentions, among a large enough number of people, and as a matter of common awareness, that furthers our normative interests. This is what is good for us. In turn, the evaluative fact that the relevant social fact—i.e., the existence of certain norms—is good for us is meant to explain why those norms are morally binding.

Once its structure is uncovered in this way, the normative-interests view seems to suffer from an *explanatory gap*. It suggests that people's normative attitudes, when their possessing them is in some ways good for us—i.e., it furthers our interests—can bootstrap various moral powers and obligations into existence. If (i) people believe that X is wrong and have corresponding action-guiding attitudes, and (ii) it is good for people to believe that X is wrong, and to develop corresponding action-guiding attitudes, then X really is genuinely morally wrong. It is, however, unclear how alleged facts about goodness (i.e., normative interests) coupled with beliefs and attitudes about wrongness can bring moral obligations and powers into existence.

To put the point more concretely, consider Owens' own example, concerning context-specific familial obligations binding parents and children. Suppose that, in Italy, there is a socially constructed norm that requires parents to "help pay for the children's tertiary education" (Owens 2017: 570). The content of this norm, it is assumed, is not independently morally mandated. The reason why parents are bound by this obligation, on the normative-interests view, is that it is good for them and their children to be so bound, independently of whether parents actually abide by the obligation. In Owens' words: "[t]he normative interest here is an interest in the *recognition of the obligation*, and the obligation in which we have an interest does not exist until that obligation is recognized" (Owens 2017: 570, added emphases).

But how can recognition of an obligation bring that obligation into existence? In fact, talk of "recognition" is somewhat misleading. It is not that there is an obligation, and *then* that obligation is recognized. The obligation is *created* by people's believing in its existence and acting accordingly. What, in turn, makes that obligation binding is that its "recognition"—as opposed to its performance—is good for us. But there is something explanatorily unsatisfactory in the suggestion that treating a piece of conduct *as if* it were morally obligatory makes it actually morally obligatory, so long as our treating it as morally obligatory is good for us.

Consider the implications of this view for the following type of scenario (cf. Owens 2017: 567). An Italian mother tells her son that, contrary to Italian norms, he will be expected to move out of the family home by the time he is 20. As she explains to him, her aim is to help him become independent and develop a sense of responsibility. In so doing, on the normative-interests view, the mother breaches a moral obligation whose existence depends on the presence of a generous family-care norm in Italy. Consequently, the son would be right to resent and blame the mother, and the mother should feel guilty. But why is this so, on the normative-interests view? Because it is good for the mother-son duo to relate to each other in this way, and to experience the relevant reactive attitudes.

Now suppose the son blames his mother for her decision, and suppose the mother asks why what she is doing is wrong. Intuitively plausible answers include: the fact that the son feels very close to his parents and thus has an interest in sharing a home with them, the fact that it would be hard for him to both finish his studies and hold down a job, and thus it is unduly harsh of his mother to force him out so soon, etc. Crucially, these are *not* the reasons the son would have to invoke, if the normative-interests view is correct. What makes the mother's decision wrongful, on that view, is that *it being treated as wrongful is good for both mother and son*. But this seems like a rather contrived explanation for its wrongfulness, and in all likelihood not one the son would invoke when blaming his mother. This casts doubt on the explanatory adequacy of the normative-interests view.

In sum, while having some appeal, upon scrutiny the normative-interests view reveals itself unable to provide a satisfactory explanation of the moral normativity of socially constructed norms. It might fit the phenomena, but the reasons it offers for treating such norms as binding do not convince.

7. The Joint-Commitments View

A final attempt to ground the moral normativity of socially constructed norms has been put forward by Margaret Gilbert. On her view, our obligations to obey such norms—especially the norms governing our common life in society—are grounded in *joint commitments*. For Gilbert, socially constructed norms themselves are constituted by joint commitments.[27] Such norm-constituting joint commitments exist when (i) the parties express their readiness to commit to a requirement together and (ii) their readiness is common knowledge among them (Gilbert 2006: 138–40). Joint commitments—paradigmatic examples of which include contracts and agreements—are binding: they give rise to rights-correlative obligations among the parties involved (Gilbert 2006: 156–61). As Gilbert puts it:

---

[27] In her words: "*There is a social rule in a population P* if and only if the members of P are jointly committed to accepting as a body a requirement...of the following form: members of P are to perform action A in circumstances C" (Gilbert 2006: 197, emphasis original). Gilbert further argues that those who are jointly committed form a "plural subject". I set aside this ontologically demanding aspect of Gilbert's view here.

"by virtue of the joint commitment present when there is a social rule, each member of the population in question has a right against every other member for conformity to the rule" (Gilbert 2006: 200).

As this short sketch shows, for Gilbert the normativity of socially constructed norms stems from the bindingness of *joint commitments* themselves. In the same way in which, by agreeing to sign a contract, the parties bind themselves to comply with the relevant terms and conditions, by jointly committing to acting in a certain way, the parties bind themselves to so act. The *source* of the normativity of socially constructed norms, on this view, is the obligation to respect the commitments one makes *to others* (Gilbert 2006: 201).

Let us once again systematize this view by reference to our model grounding sequence, this time taking our third example—namely *Non-proceduralist President*—as our starting point.

Joint commitments grounding sequence
- <u>Action required</u>: You ought to φ (φ = not unilaterally authorize the tracking of calls/e-communications of people inside the US without a court warrant).
- By virtue of what ought I to φ?
- <u>Empirical fact</u>: Because there is a socially constructed norm that requires you to φ, and socially constructed norms are constituted by joint commitments.
- By virtue of what does the fact that there is a socially constructed norm that requires me to φ ground an obligation to φ?
- <u>Target general moral principle</u>: Because one ought to honour one's commitments to other people (i.e., one's joint commitments).

The target general principle that appears at the bottom of the joint-commitments grounding sequence is both familiar and plausible. The idea that promises, agreements, contracts, and so forth should be honoured is a "fixed point" in our moral reasoning. Furthermore, the principle would allow us to defend content-independent obligations to obey socially constructed norms. According to this principle, it is the fact that such norms are the objects of joint commitments that grounds those obligations, not the substantive merits of the content of those norms.

For these reasons, Gilbert's view is certainly appealing. What is doubtful, however, is that the attitudes underpinning most socially constructed norms correspond to the commitments figuring in Gilbert's target general principle. While it is apparent how contracts, agreements, and perhaps norms that exist in small-scale contexts are constituted by obligation-generating joint commitments, it is much less obvious that the same can be said of society-wide norms.

For instance, I am personally committed to the queuing norm, and I know that many others around me are as well (and vice versa). I find it odd, however, to suggest that we have *jointly committed* to upholding the queuing norm. Violating that norm may be wrong, but not in the way breaching a contract is. If I skipped the queue and someone ahead of me protested by saying "You are violating *our* joint commitment, a commitment we all made to each other", I would respond that I do not know what commitment this person is referring to (cf. Gilbert 2006: 153). I certainly never agreed, whether tacitly or explicitly, to respecting the rules of queuing. I robustly intend for the queuing rule to function as a general standard of behaviour and, in this sense, I am *committed* to it. Furthermore, this commitment happens to be one that several others in my society share, and this is a matter of common awareness. Still, this is not a commitment we have made *to each other*. But it is precisely these interpersonal commitments that generate moral obligations.[28]

It might be thought that, while this objection works for a norm like queuing, it does not succeed in the case of our current lead-example: *Non-proceduralist President*. Upon taking office, the President does indeed make a commitment, and a public one: a commitment to protecting and respecting the Constitution (and the law more generally). That commitment, one might say, is akin to a promise made *to the people*, and by acting illegally the President violates that commitment. This, in turn, explains what is wrong with the case at hand, and does so in line with the joint-commitments view.

First, it is not clear that our intuitions about the wrong of *Non-proceduralist President* rest on the assumption that the President has taken an oath of office. For even if we supposed that no such oath had taken place, the President's actions would continue to appear wrongful. Second, even granting that the breach of an oath could contribute to explaining what is wrong with *Non-proceduralist President*, it would not help alleviate our original concern about the joint-commitments view. This is because the fact that the President publicly pledged to behave in a particular way does not lend support to the claim that socially constructed norms—e.g., the FISA—are constituted by obligation-generating joint commitments. The difficulty with the joint-commitments view does not rest with the principle that our interpersonal commitments give rise to obligations. Instead, it lies with the claim that this principle can ground the moral normativity of socially constructed norms *in general*. Plausibly, only very few such norms are the product of obligation-generating joint commitments.

It might be suggested that while joint commitments only underpin a small number of socially constructed norms (e.g., those existing in small-scale contexts), attitudes not too far from joint commitments sustain many more such norms. These are what Michael Bratman calls shared intentions. Recall that, as explained in the previous chapter, for Bratman (1999), those intentions obtain within a

---

[28] Gilbert is not unaware of this problem, and she explicitly considers the question of whether joint commitments can also exist within large populations, with a high degree of anonymity (Gilbert 2006: Ch. 8). She answers in the affirmative. Her argument is interesting and subtle, but my concern is that any affirmative answer to the relevant question must necessarily rely on too weak a notion of joint commitments for joint commitments so understood to generate obligations.

group when (i) the members of that group each hold intentions of the form "I intend that *we j*" (where "j" is a joint action), (ii) each is prepared to adjust their conduct so as to *j*, and (iii) this is common knowledge among group members. It may well be that, in the case of some socially constructed norms, each norm supporter (i) robustly "intends that *we* (i.e., everyone in context C) *j* (i.e., act so that certain requirements function as general standards of behaviour)", (ii) is prepared to adjust their conduct so as to *j*, and (iii) this is a matter of common awareness among those in C.

Let us assume, for argument's sake, that shared intentions lie behind many socially constructed norms. Might this fact help us ground their moral normativity? That is, are such shared intentions obligation-generating? To answer this question, consider, for instance, a norm shared by a family, according to which everyone has dinner together at 8 p.m. Each member, let us suppose, robustly intends that the family dines together at 8 p.m., as a matter of common awareness. Intuitively, we might think, family members seem obligated to show up for dinner at 8 p.m. in this case. But does this obligation come from shared intentions alone? It does not. As Bratman explains, per se, shared intentions do not generate obligations *in the way* promises or contracts do (Bratman 1999: 132–5).[29]

Our intuitions about the "dinner at 8 p.m." scenario can nonetheless be accounted for. In fact, even if shared intentions themselves are not obligation-generating—in the way promises or agreements are—they can be accompanied by obligations. As Bratman (1999: 138) puts it, independent moral principles are "quite typically, engaged in cases of shared intention". For instance, Bratman briefly conjectures that Scanlon's principle of fidelity might often ground mutual obligations in cases involving shared intentions with permissible content.[30] The principle's core idea is that those who share intentions are obligated to each other whenever shared intentions are accompanied by "purposive expectation creation" (Bratman 1999: 138). In our "dinner at 8 p.m." example, such purposive expectation creation may be implicitly present and explain our intuition that family members ought to show up for dinner at that particular time, since doing otherwise would frustrate the relevant expectations. The mere fact that family members share a particular intention—unlike the fact of joint commitment—does not generate obligations.

In sum, not very many socially constructed norms seem underpinned by obligation-generating joint commitments. Perhaps more such norms are underpinned by shared intentions, but shared intentions are not obligation-generating in the way promises and agreements (arguably) are. In light of this, we can

[29] Of course, one could imagine an alternative situation where the "8 p.m. norm" has been formed through a binding agreement or promise, but this is not the case we are considering.

[30] Scanlon (1990) himself appeals to that principle in order to ground promissory obligations, which he does not understand as involving the exercise of distinctive normative powers.

conclude that Gilbert's joint-commitments view, while appealing to a plausible moral principle, cannot offer a *general* vindication of the moral normativity of socially constructed norms.

A further aspect of the joint-commitments view merits attention. Obligations of joint commitment, says Gilbert, are always correlative to rights (Gilbert 2006: 200). The parties to a joint commitment owe it to one another to act in line with the content of the relevant commitment (Gilbert 2006: 153–56). From this, it follows that any breach of a socially constructed norm violates the rights of *everyone* who sustains it.

For example, if I skip the queue—granting, for argument's sake, Gilbert's view that a social norm like queuing is the product of binding joint commitments—I do not just violate the rights of those standing in line, but of everyone in society who upholds the queuing norm. My adhering to the queuing norm is owed to all of them, such that they should feel betrayed by my non-compliance (Gilbert 2006: 150–1). While I believe that there is some truth to this diagnosis of the situation, I do not think it is fully accurate. There is some truth to it because all supporters of the queuing norm have been, in some sense, disrespected by my breach. For an analogy, by shouting profanities in a place of religious worship, I disrespect not merely those believers who are physically present there, but all adherents to that religion.

At the same time, the joint-commitments view seems unable to capture the thought that the people whose spots in the queue I have taken are *distinctively wronged* by my actions. The view is thus affected by a partial version of the "wrong reasons" problem discussed earlier in the context of Nieswandt's conventionalism. While I agree with Gilbert that by violating the socially constructed norms of a given community we commit a "diffuse" wrong against its members, in the case of many such norms, particular individuals stand in a distinctive normative position in relation to the breach. A fully convincing explanation of the moral normativity of socially constructed norms should be able to capture this fact. As it stands, the joint-commitments view does not.

8. Conclusion

I have considered different accounts of the moral normativity of socially constructed norms. After raising doubts about the deflationary view and Scanlon's principle of established practices, I have discussed the conventionalist view, the normative-interests view, and the joint-commitments view. I have concluded that none of them offers a satisfactory explanation of where the moral normativity of socially constructed norms comes from. The conventionalist view, I have suggested, is poorly motivated. The normative-interests view, in turn, is problematic insofar as it exhibits an explanatory gap. Finally, the joint-commitments view has limited scope and is susceptible to a partial version of the "wrong reasons" problem.

While, as just outlined, the conclusions of this chapter are mostly negative, there are several positive lessons we can learn from it. In particular, the difficulties with the views explored here alert us to the pitfalls that a successful account of the moral normativity of socially constructed norms must avoid. In the next chapter, my aim is to present an account that avoids those pitfalls.

Morality and Socially Constructed Norms. Laura Valentini, Oxford University Press. © Laura Valentini 2023.
DOI: 10.1093/9780191938115.003.0003

3
The Agency-Respect View

In this chapter, I present the core of my account of the moral normativity of socially constructed norms.[1] This account begins with our common-sense moral reasons for obeying those norms and shows how they can fit into a robust philosophical framework. To detect those reasons, we can start by asking ourselves why, in many cases, disobeying socially constructed norms appears wrongful. For example: Why is it wrong to show up at church wearing a revealing top and hot pants? Why is it wrong to fail to take one's shoes off when entering a Hindu temple? Why is it wrong to skip the queue, in a context characterized by the queuing norm? Why is it wrong to harmlessly trespass onto others' property?

There are two perspectives from which these questions can be addressed. One is that of norm-supporters, namely those who subscribe to the relevant norms. This is the perspective of, say, the Hindu believer who takes her shoes off because this is what her religion requires and of the elderly British lady who patiently waits in line because she believes that queue-jumping is wrong. From this perspective, which we may call *internal*, our reasons for following existing norms often relate to the merits of the *content* of those norms: "taking one's shoes off is respectful towards gods and goddesses"; "not skipping the queue is the fair thing to do"; and so forth. Plausibly, the Hindu believer and the elderly lady abide by the norms because these norms mandate actions that, in their eyes, have independent merit. While those independent merits might give us good reasons to act in line with what socially constructed norms require, they do not explain why *the fact that* something is mandated by a socially constructed norm makes "that something" morally binding.

To explain the latter phenomenon, we need to take an *external* perspective.[2] We need to ask: why ought one morally to obey norm N, even if one does not think that N is morally binding by virtue of its content? Once we take such an external perspective, we are better able to isolate moral considerations that attach to the fact that there is a norm, as opposed to the specific merits of the actions mandated by the norm.

From this external perspective, disobeying socially constructed norms seems wrongful because it is *disrespectful* towards those who accept the requirements set

---

[1] The chapter draws heavily on Valentini (2021).
[2] Compare Hart's (1961: 56) distinction between internal and external "aspects" of rules.

82 THE AGENCY-RESPECT VIEW

by them. It is, in other words, disrespectful towards norm-supporters. Even if I am not a Hindu believer and, as an Italian, I am not too convinced by the queuing norm, I still think I ought to remove my shoes upon entering a Hindu temple and I still think I ought to queue at the bus stop in the UK.[3] Why? Because doing otherwise would be disrespectful towards the locals, who subscribe to the relevant norms.

I believe that there is much truth to this disrespect intuition. My defence of the moral normativity of socially constructed norms builds on and systematizes it. I call it the *agency-respect view*. In a nutshell, I argue that the moral normativity of socially constructed norms stems from our duty to give people agency respect: to respect their authentic commitments as agents, provided those commitments are morally permissible and respecting them isn't too costly for us.[4] I show that this duty accounts for when and why the fact that a socially constructed norm requires something of us places us under an obligation to comply.

I proceed as follows. In Section 1, drawing on the lessons learnt in the previous chapter, and in line with the book's Introduction, I set out two desiderata that a plausible account of the moral normativity of socially constructed norms should satisfy: explanatory power and fit with evidence. In Section 2, I informally introduce the agency-respect view, by way of an analogy. In Sections 3 to 5, I offer a systematic defence of that view. First, I outline the agency-respect principle. This principle requires respecting the *concrete ways* in which people exercise their agency: their commitments (cf. Noggle 1999). I then argue that, since socially constructed norms exist by virtue of people's commitments, the duty to treat others with agency respect grounds the moral normativity of those norms. In Sections 6 and 7, I show that the agency-respect view meets the desiderata of explanatory power and fit. In Section 8, I consider objections. Section 9 concludes.

Before I begin, let me make one important clarification. The obligations to obey socially constructed norms I will be discussing are not all-things-considered obligations, but pro tanto obligations, namely obligations that can be overridden by other, weightier considerations. This is a familiar phenomenon. Importantly, when a pro tanto obligation is overridden, a moral remainder is left, which may call for some form of redress. Redress, in turn, may be minimal or rather demanding, depending on the case at hand. Unless otherwise stated, whenever I speak of an obligation to obey socially constructed norms, I mean a pro tanto obligation.[5]

---

[3] Having lived many years in the UK before moving to Germany, I am actually no longer that sceptical about the queuing norm.

[4] Note that I am not referring to *joint* commitments like those discussed by Gilbert and examined in the previous chapter, but to personal commitments. This will become clear as I proceed.

[5] Also, here and elsewhere in the book, I use the language of duty and obligation interchangeably.

1. Desiderata

In Chapter 2, I argued that vindicating the moral normativity of socially constructed norms requires identifying a moral principle P, capable of explaining why one ought to φ *because* there is a socially constructed norm that requires one to φ. I then looked at several candidates for P and concluded that none was up to this explanatory task.

There are, however, positive lessons we can draw from this negative conclusion. In particular, the difficulties highlighted with existing accounts of the moral normativity of socially constructed norms help us identify desiderata that a successful vindication of such normativity should satisfy. These desiderata can be grouped under two, familiar headings: explanatory power and fit. I begin by offering a broad formulation of the desiderata and then flesh them out in relation to our specific topic.

Explanatory power: the explanation is powerful, which means that it makes the phenomenon in question less surprising.[6]

When we try to explain a phenomenon, we seek to understand why it is the case. A good answer, in turn, renders the phenomenon no longer surprising. Suppose that you visit a friend and notice a small fluffy toy on her sofa. You do not think much of it and head out with her for a coffee. Upon your return, you notice that the fluffy toy is no longer on the sofa, but on the floor. "Why?" you might ask yourself. You left the house in your friend's company and, to the best of your knowledge, there was nobody else around. How could the fluffy toy have moved? This is your explanandum.

When you bring your friend's attention to the mysterious movement of the fluffy toy, she immediately responds: "Oh, it must have been the cat!". Unbeknownst to you, your friend has a cat, who typically hangs out upstairs in the bedroom, but apparently visited the sitting room downstairs during your absence. Now the otherwise mysterious movements of the fluffy toy have an explanation and are no longer surprising. It is only natural that fluffy toys would move around if there's a cat who habitually plays with them.

Note that the "cat explanation" is successful in part because it appeals to a familiar phenomenon—i.e., that cats move toys around. If your friend had instead responded—"Oh, there must have been an earthquake, weak enough for us not to feel it, but powerful enough to make the toy slip off the sofa"—you would probably not have found her explanation particularly convincing. It would have come

---

[6] Explanatory power is a topic much debated in the philosophy of science. I am here following Schupbach and Sprenger (2011: 108), who essentially understand explanatory power in terms of surprise-reduction.

84 THE AGENCY-RESPECT VIEW

across as rather ad hoc and *far-fetched*. In fact, the explanans, namely this peculiar earthquake, would be more surprising than the explanandum: that a fluffy toy fell off the sofa. Likewise, if your friend had tried to explain what happened by suggesting that "there must have been a power cut in the building", you would have found her explanation perplexing. It is just *mysterious* how a power cut would cause a toy to fall from a sofa, as opposed to, say, a burglar alarm to go off.

Let us bring these reflections to bear on our phenomenon of interest, namely the obligation-generating power of socially constructed norms. The phenomenon is somewhat puzzling because empirical facts by themselves cannot generate moral demands. As discussed in Chapter 2, an explanation of this phenomenon requires identifying a moral principle P that lends moral significance to the empirical fact that a given norm prescribes a certain conduct. The moral principles we have explored so far have proven unsatisfactory, in part due to failures of explanatory power. Some provided a *far-fetched* explanation for the wrong of norm-breaches, others were ad hoc and lacked independent plausibility, and others still made the move from socially constructed norms to moral obligations rather *mysterious*.

First, recall Gilbert's proposed principle, discussed in the previous chapter, namely that one ought to honour one's commitments to other people. While the principle is independently plausible, the explanation for the moral normativity of socially constructed norms that we obtain by appeal to it seems, at least partly, far-fetched. Consider, for instance, the wrong of violating someone's legitimate property rights. Gilbert's "joint-commitments" view holds that any such violation equally wrongs everyone in society—and not the individual owner *specifically*—insofar as they have (allegedly) jointly committed to abiding by property rules. While I agree that violations of a society's rules offend that society as a whole, a satisfactory explanation of the wrong of property violations must also account for the special moral position of the owner, who is the most immediate victim of the wrong.

Now take the conventionalist principle proposed by Nieswandt, according to which the rules of a justified practice are, ipso facto, morally binding on their own terms. As we saw in the previous chapter, the principle appears reverse-engineered to deliver a particular conclusion. Absent further argument, conventionalism comes across as ad hoc and thus falls short in terms of explanatory power.

Finally, let us go back to Owens' view, according to which socially constructed norms have moral normativity because they serve our normative interests. The problem, there, was a perceived gap in the argument. It is just not clear how the fact that being bound by certain obligations is good for us—since they serve our normative interests—can ground those obligations. The explanation proposed by Owens, then, seemed problematic due to its somewhat *mysterious* connection to the explanandum. This is analogous to the explanatory gap existing between the fact that a toy fell from the sofa and a power cut. It is puzzling how the former could result from the latter.

In sum, in order to meet the desideratum of explanatory power and make the phenomenon of socially constructed norms' moral normativity unsurprising, our target explanation must avoid the aforementioned vices. Let me now turn to our second desideratum.

Fit: the explanation fits the available evidence.

This is once again a familiar desideratum, which—in the empirical sciences—is known as "empirical adequacy" (van Fraassen 1980: Ch. 3). Scientific explanations, which deal with matters of empirical fact, must fit the relevant observations in order to be satisfactory. Similarly, normative explanations must fit the relevant "observations". Of course, it is not obvious what, exactly, qualifies as an observation in the normative domain. Current philosophical practice suggests that the best proxies for observations are our considered moral judgements or intuitions.[7] Fit with those judgements, then, would make our explanations "normatively" (as opposed to empirically) adequate.

This means that principle P we invoke to explain the moral normativity of socially constructed norms should account for cases in which we find violations of those norms intuitively wrongful, while avoiding declaring as wrongful violations that strike us as unproblematic. The principle should neither over-generate nor under-generate judgements of wrongdoing relative to our intuitions about the moral status of norm-violations. To be sure, given the somewhat uncertain status of considered judgements as evidence, in the process of reflective equilibrium some such judgements may be ultimately discounted (Rawls 1999a). But, in the main, the more such judgements we can account for, the more successful our explanation will be.

As we saw in the previous chapter, the deflationary view fails to satisfy this desideratum. It is unable to account for our intuitions in cases like *Traffic Light, Barbeque,* and *Non-proceduralist President.*[8] A successful defence of the moral

---

[7] Here I am using these terms interchangeably. For the broader methodological stance taken in this book, see the book's Introduction.

[8] I restate the cases for the reader's convenience.

Traffic Light: My German father-in-law, Jürgen, was driving late at night, through a village in his home region. He came to an intersection in the road. The traffic light went red. He looked in every direction: there was no car, person, or speed camera in sight. It would have been physically impossible for anyone to get hurt if he had continued straight, ignoring the red light. Moreover, nobody would have witnessed the breach. The only outcome would have been a happy one: an earlier arrival home. Yet my father-in-law stopped at the red light.

Barbeque: You are on a camping trip. You call some friends and make plans to spend the day with them, only to return in the late evening. Your barbeque set, pots, and pans are stored outside your tent. The Rossi family, whose tent is just a few metres from yours, notices your absence, and decides to

86 THE AGENCY-RESPECT VIEW

normativity of socially constructed norms, by contrast, should fit our intuitions in these and similar cases. It should explain why norms that strike us as intuitively binding are indeed binding. What is more, it should match the strength or weakness of our intuitions, and thereby explain why we feel more strongly about the wrongness of the actions involved in *Barbeque* and *Non-proceduralist President* than we typically do in a case like *Traffic Light* (where many may actually think no wrong occurs).

My aim is to defend an account of the moral normativity of socially constructed norms that satisfies these desiderata. In what follows, I turn to offering an intuitive illustration of the core idea behind this account, before providing a systematic defence of it.

2. Respecting Normative Worlds

Suppose you are committed to building a sandcastle on the beach. This is a project that matters to you, and one that you have taken up authentically: without fear, pressure, or brainwashing. There are other beach-goers around you, but your building the castle, as well as the castle's presence on the beach, does not particularly inconvenience them. As you are busy finishing up your creation, you ask one of them whether they could kindly pass a couple of beach pebbles to you, to decorate the castle's walls. Since passing the pebbles along is no great inconvenience, it seems your request should be accommodated. After a day's hard work, your castle is ready. To avoid destroying it, people must walk around it, rather than straight through it. But again, this is hardly a big inconvenience.

Your fellow beach-goers, however, do not have much patience for your building activities: they step over the castle, they refuse to pass along the pebbles, and so forth. Some particularly inconsiderate ones even destroy the castle as you walk away from the beach in the evening. This behaviour seems to me blameworthy, hence morally wrong. But why is that so? A sandcastle is just that, a sandcastle. And one may reasonably believe that, as far as projects and commitments go, it is not such an important one after all.

The wrongness of damaging the castle, then, cannot so much stem from the intrinsic worth of the castle. (To make the point even more straightforward, let us

---

make use of your grill and related accessories for an improvised barbeque feast. They celebrate during the day, but put everything back in order prior to your return. When you get back, you notice nothing.

Non-proceduralist President: In the wake of the 9/11 terror attacks, President George W. Bush authorized the National Security Agency to track international calls and e-communications of people inside the US, without a court warrant. Once this became known, the President was criticized for acting ultra vires, in violation of the 1978 Foreign Intelligence Surveillance Act (FISA), which prohibits warrantless domestic electronic surveillance. In an open letter to Congress, published in the *New York Review of Books*, a group of leading legal scholars and former government officials insisted that, to be lawful, such surveillance would need to be authorized by Congress, through legislative amendment.

assume that, despite your efforts, the final product does not exude architectural beauty.) The relevant behaviour is wrong, primarily, because it reveals a lack of respect for your commitments, hence for your agency. You committed to building a castle: a perfectly permissible pursuit, whether we think of it as valuable or not. Yet, others fail to accommodate or actively undermine this pursuit, even if not doing so would come at little cost to them.

Bearing the sandcastle story in mind, let me go back to our topic and introduce the notion of a "normative community". This is a community of individuals whose interactions are governed by a set of socially constructed norms. As we saw in Chapter 1, these norms are constituted by people's public beliefs and commitments to treating given requirements as general standards of behaviour. Members of this community hold each other accountable by reference to those norms and criticize and sanction those who fail to abide by them. Through their attitudes and behaviour, members are therefore responsible for the creation and continued existence of what we might call a "normative world". This normative world, in turn, matters to them. Furthermore, this normative world is a benign one. Of course, there can be sinister normative worlds, containing oppressive and discriminatory norms. This, however, is not our case.

Suppose some of those who find themselves in the context of this community started to interfere with the community's normative world, by violating its norms. As it happens, some such norm-violations do not even cause disruption. Take the norm, present in our imagined community, that one should not consume alcohol in public parks. This goes back to the community's strongly held belief that nature is sacred and alcohol consumption in public parks is therefore inappropriate. Some individuals within the community find the norm unwarranted, and secretly consume alcohol in public parks at night, when they could instead do so at home, or in restaurants and bars. Their misconduct goes unnoticed, however. Even so, I feel uneasy about their behaviour, in the same way I would feel uneasy if I were told that some people secretly entered a Hindu temple without taking their footwear off. Furthermore, it would seem appropriate for the members of our community to criticize and reprimand the norm-violators, if they became aware of the violators' behaviour.

The reason why it is wrong to violate permissible socially constructed norms, I want to suggest, is analogous to the reason why it is wrong to interfere with your sandcastle. The norms, just like the castle, are the product of people's commitments. To respect your agency, others must not undermine your commitment to building the castle. To respect the agency of the members of our community, those who find themselves in the context of that community must not undermine, or interfere with, the normative world they have created. Not undermining or not interfering with that world typically requires abiding by the norms that constitute it. This is *not* because those norms have great independent merit— though of course they must not be wicked or sinister. It is because, and to the

88 THE AGENCY-RESPECT VIEW

extent that, they stem from people's commitments: they are their creation and an expression of their agency.

This, in a nutshell, is the core idea behind my account of the moral normativity of socially constructed norms, which I call the "agency-respect view". On this view, the relevant principle P is the agency-respect principle. Coupled with the account of the existence conditions of socially constructed norms developed in Chapter 1, the principle allows us to pinpoint when and why we have an obligation to φ because a socially constructed norm requires us to φ. To anticipate, this is what the agency-respect grounding sequence looks like.[9]

Agency-respect grounding sequence
- <u>Action required</u>: One has an obligation to respect the socially constructed norms that exist in a given context, provided the commitments of norm-supporters are authentic, morally permissible, and respecting them is not too costly.
- Why does one have an obligation to respect the socially constructed norms that exist in a given context, provided the commitments of norm-supporters are authentic, morally permissible, and respecting them is not too costly?
- <u>Empirical fact F</u>: Because if one does not respect the socially constructed norms that exist in a given context, one fails to respect the commitments of norm-supporters.
- Why does fact F (i.e., if one does not respect the socially constructed norms that exist in a given context, one fails to respect the commitments of norm-supporters) ground an obligation to respect the socially constructed norms that exist in a given context, provided the commitments of norm-supporters are authentic, morally permissible, and respecting them is not too costly?
- <u>Target general moral principle P</u>: Because one has an obligation to respect people's commitments (i.e., "to give *agency respect* to people"), provided those commitments are authentic, morally permissible, and respecting them is not too costly.

---

[9] The concept of a grounding sequence was introduced in Chapter 2. To put the sequence into argument form, "principle P" is premise 1, "empirical fact" is premise 2, while "action required" is our conclusion.

- P1: One has an obligation to respect people's commitments (i.e., "to give *agency respect* to people"), provided those commitments are authentic, morally permissible, and respecting them is not too costly.
- P2: If one does not respect the socially constructed norms that exist in a given context, one fails to respect the commitments of norm-supporters.
- C: One has an obligation to respect the socially constructed norms that exist in a given context, provided the commitments of norm-supporters are authentic, morally permissible, and respecting them is not too costly.

In what follows, I elaborate on each component of the sequence, starting from principle *P*, then turning to empirical fact *F*, and concluding with the action required.

3. Principle *P*: The Agency-Respect Principle

Almost nobody would deny that human beings ought morally to be treated with respect; that we should acknowledge others' status as persons and be "willing to constrain [our] behaviour" accordingly (Darwall 1977: 45).[10] But what does this, exactly, involve? A helpful cue is provided by Robert Noggle's observation that persons' moral standing attaches not only to their nature as autonomous end-setters in general, "but also to their status as *particular* individuals" (Noggle 1999: 457, added emphasis).[11] Respecting persons as the specific individuals that they are, in turn, requires respecting the ways in which they exercise their agency. It is through our exercises of agency that we constitute our concrete, individual selves (Ismael 2016; Korsgaard 2009; Schapiro 2012).

To see this, suppose I suddenly feel like taking a nap, or experience the urge to yell at my daughters in frustration. These feelings simply arise in me, I do not "author" them. I may, however, be in a position to control them. For instance, I may resist the temptation to take a nap in order to finish proofreading a paper. Or I may suppress my urge to raise my voice, even when I am frustrated, because I have decided to set a good example for my daughters. In these cases, "my will governs my wants": I am committed to meeting professional deadlines and to raising my daughters without aggression, and I act accordingly (Schapiro 2012). When I do so, I am not just passively driven by urges, I am actively steering my life in a certain direction—some would say, I am exercising my autonomy—thereby constituting myself as the particular agent that I am. I call respect for persons so understood, i.e., respect for persons as particular, self-constituted individuals, "agency-respect".

Commitments figure centrally in this process of self-constitution (cf. Chang 2009: 259). A commitment, as we saw in Chapter 1, is an exercise of will—specifically, a *robust intention*—with which we direct our agency in a certain way: e.g., in pursuit of a goal, a practice, a course of action, a value, etc. (Calhoun 2009: 618).[12] While commitments are always our creation, they can be formed in a variety of

---

[10] This is what Darwall calls "recognition respect", as opposed to "appraisal respect", which involves positive appraisal of the qualities displayed by particular individuals.

[11] Noggle defends what he calls "Kantian particularism", namely, "a limited theory of the nature of moral respect which replaces Kant's focus on the ends set by a rational will with a focus on those core motives that constitute the person's identity" (1999: 471). My discussion of agency respect is inspired by Noggle's Kantian-particularist approach.

[12] I am referring not to interpersonal commitments, such as those we make through promises and contracts, but to what Ruth Chang (2013a: 76–7) calls "internal commitments".

90 THE AGENCY-RESPECT VIEW

ways. Some, for instance, originate in a precise decision moment: say, someone's commitment to go on a diet, made after an anxiety-inducing visit to the doctor. Others develop over time, like one's commitment to painting, which has gradually grown over the years, starting as a hobby and then becoming a serious pursuit. Equally, commitments may be more or less central to one's identity. I may be committed to doing regular physical exercise and to being involved in all aspects of my daughters' upbringing. The latter commitment, however, is a lot more central to my sense of self than the former. While being prevented from acting on either commitment would put some strain on my agency, interference with my commitment to being an "involved mother" would amount to a much more serious agency harm than interference with my commitment to being reasonably physically active.

In sum, put metaphorically, just as a sculptor's carving of a block of marble gives shape to her creation, our commitments give shape to our lives and to who we are.[13] While all of the sculptor's chisel strokes contribute to making the statue the particular statue it is, some strokes will have greater impact on the statue's identity than others. Similarly, while all of our commitments contribute to determining our particular selves, some are more central to our identity than others.

Given our commitments' role in constituting who we are, it should come as no surprise that agency respect demands respect for them. The thought should be intuitive enough. For instance, suppose I am committed to the environment: I lead a low-carbon lifestyle, only buy organic produce, and take great care in separating my trash. My friend, who knows me well, comes to visit me and absent-mindedly throws food leftovers into the wrong bin, and plastic into the trash rather than into the recycling. As it happens, I think that what my friend has done is independently problematic, given the current ecological and climate emergency. But, on top of that, her behaviour is also disrespectful towards me and my commitments. I could rightly confront her and complain: "Why are you doing this? You know *I care* about recycling!".

While treating others with agency respect demands respecting their commitments, not *all* commitments are worthy of respect. We have pro tanto obligations to respect other people's commitments only *provided* these are genuine (i.e., authentic), morally permissible, and respecting them is not too costly to us (cf. Hill 2000: 79). Let me briefly elaborate on these three qualifications.

First, people's commitments are sometimes the product of coercion and manipulation, rather than an expression of their agency. To offer an extreme example, a slave may well robustly intend to satisfy his master's every wish, but we have reason to be suspicious that this commitment is an authentic one, and not a consequence of the coercive nature of slavery norms. Only *authentic*

---

[13] I owe this metaphor to Eidelson (2013: 214).

commitments, which genuinely express our agency, call for agency respect. This immediately prompts the question of how we can tell apart genuine commitments from inauthentic ones. The philosophical literature on autonomy, where a number of "authenticity tests" have been developed, can come to our aid here. But since reviewing that literature would take us too far from our present concerns, for now I limit myself to flagging that, in order to be operationalized, the agency-respect principle presupposes authenticity criteria. Different readers may then fill out the authenticity parameter in subtly different ways. (I will say more about how to interpret this parameter in the book's Conclusion.)

Second, the moral status of commitments varies widely: some are permissible (e.g., excelling at music), others obligatory (e.g., not harming the innocent), some supererogatory (e.g., donating 95 per cent of one's income to charity), and others impermissible (e.g., supporting the Mafia). We are morally required to respect others' genuine commitments only when these are morally permissible (see Hill 2000: 79ff.). Impermissible commitments, including commitments that entail a failure to respect others' capacity for agency, activate no respect-based demands. Many contemporary theories of basic justice or human rights may be regarded as articulating competing accounts of the requirements of moral permissibility. When individuals are tortured, enslaved, deprived of freedom of speech and association, or (avoidably) lack access to the means of subsistence, basic moral demands are violated. Once again, the agency-respect principle is compatible with different specifications of moral-permissibility standards, and readers may wish to refer to their preferred one. In what follows, I will rely on (hopefully) uncontroversial examples of moral permissibility and lack thereof. I will offer more detailed remarks about how I think the moral permissibility parameter should be interpreted later in the chapter. The tenability of the agency-respect principle should not depend on the plausibility of that interpretation.

Third, and finally, agency respect does not demand that we altogether sacrifice our own agency for the sake of respecting the agency of others. For example, my good friend may be committed to building a new home for his family and may need my help to do so. This would require me to devote half of my day to assisting him in his building activities, for at least half a year. While doing so would clearly be very kind on my part, it is not morally required by agency respect, since it is excessively costly. Assisting my good friend in realizing his commitments would prevent me from pursuing my own: it would be too burdensome for my own agency.

To make the implications of the agency-respect principle more vivid, consider the following examples. According to this principle, it is true to say that, in normal circumstances, I have a duty to:

- schedule a meeting with you one hour later than usual, so that you can attend a church service and thereby honour your religious commitments;

92 THE AGENCY-RESPECT VIEW

- take my shoes off when I enter your home, since you are committed to keeping your apartment hygienic; and
- refrain from asking you to lie to my parents about my habits, given your commitment to not lying.[14]

In all three cases, I have a respect-based duty to acknowledge your commitments and to accommodate them. Agency respect demands that I make reasonable allowances for your religious practice, that I adjust my behaviour in line with how you want to run your home, and that I think about the kind of person you are when I ask you for a favour. There is something disrespectful in asking you to choose between your loyalty to me and your integrity. By contrast, I lack a duty to, for example:

- allow my racist apprentice baker to refuse to sell bread rolls to ethnic minority customers (assuming I am a master baker who runs a bakery shop);
- not come into contact with members of higher castes (if I belong to a lower caste in a hierarchically organized society); and
- practice religion R because several adherents of R are committed to universal conversion to R.

Although my apprentice is committed to racist views, and does not want to serve minority customers, I am *not* required to accommodate her commitments. Why? Because they are morally impermissible: they presuppose a denial of persons' equal moral status. Similarly, the commitment of a caste society to segregating members of lower castes does not generate a valid claim to respect, since it is premised on a hierarchical view of human relations that is contrary to a plausible account of basic moral constraints (cf. Buss 1999: 810). Finally, others' commitments to my conversion to religion R do not make any agency-respect claim on me. Assisting them in the realization of their commitments would place too great a burden on my agency. Religious commitments are key to who we are, and it would be unreasonable—too costly from the perspective of our own agency—to demand that we form or give up such commitments for the sake of others.

I have argued that only authentic and morally permissible commitments can in principle trigger demands of agency respect: respect for the particular individuals that we are. The *strength* of these demands, in turn, depends on the commitments' centrality to one's life plans and sense of self (Noggle 1999: 473–5). The more failing to honour a commitment puts a strain on one's integrity, identity, and ability to pursue projects that one cares about, the weightier the agency-respect-based demand that commitment places on others. Plausibly, for instance, our duties to

---

[14] For further examples, see Noggle (1999: 472–3).

respect others' religious commitments are, by and large, stronger than our duties to respect commitments to football teams. Why? Because (and to the extent that) the former tend to be more central to persons' life plans and sense of self than the latter.

Crucially, from the perspective of agency respect, what gives commitments their moral significance is not their value, looked at from an independent, "objectively valid" conception of the good. Take the following example. Suppose Edward is a barber, committed to offering the best haircuts to his customers. Now consider Adam, a medical researcher, equally committed to finding a cure for cancer. You might find Adam's commitment more valuable—in some objective sense—than Edward's, since a great deal of good would be done if an effective cure for cancer were available, certainly more than whatever good is done by giving people stylish haircuts. But from the standpoint of agency respect, Adam's and Edward's commitments are equally deserving of respect, provided they're equally authentic, morally permissible, and central to their life plans and sense of self.

At the same time, we might have agency-respect-independent reasons for supporting Adam's project that we do not have in Edward's case. For instance, we may think that the cause of curing cancer is so important that we should contribute to funding Adam's research, while we have no comparable reason to assist Edward in buying shiny new hairdryers. But whatever targeted assistance Adam would receive in this case would not be offered out of agency respect for him. It would be offered with a view to finding a cure for a lethal disease.

Likewise, we may have greater "appraisal respect"—to use Darwall's (1977) terminology—for Adam, to the extent that we find his commitment particularly praiseworthy, and admire his intellect, dedication, and the scientific advances he has contributed to. Appraisal respect, however, is orthogonal to agency respect. Adam's qualities don't give him superior moral status as an agent. When it comes to agency respect, he is Edward's equal. The worth of his commitments or the excellence of his achievements does not make a difference to the agency respect he commands. It is the centrality of those commitments to his sense of self and life plans as an agent that determines the strength of the corresponding agency-respect claims. Ex hypothesi, if we were to prevent Adam from doing his research we would cause him an agency harm no greater and no lesser than the agency harm we'd cause Edward if we prevented him from giving people haircuts. This is not to deny that, say, in the context of the recent Covid pandemic, it would have been justified for the government to force Edward to temporarily close his shop, while still allowing Adam to pursue his research. All I am suggesting is that such a decision could not be supported *by appeal to* agency respect. Instead, it would have to be based on an evaluation of the society-wide risks involved in letting both continuing to work compared to the expected society-wide losses caused by forcing them to stay at home.

94 THE AGENCY-RESPECT VIEW

Having elucidated the agency-respect principle, let me now turn to empirical fact *F*.

4. Empirical Fact *F*: Socially Constructed Norms and People's Commitments

The agency-respect principle can help us explain why the fact that an action is prescribed by a socially constructed norm matters morally. This is because failing to respect socially constructed norms involves a failure to respect the commitments of norm-supporters, or so I will argue. To defend this claim, we need to remind ourselves of the relationship between people's commitments on the one hand and socially constructed norms on the other. Back in Chapter 1, we saw that socially constructed norms exist by virtue of people's acceptance of corresponding requirements, where "accepting a requirement" means believing its content and, crucially for our purposes, being committed to it as a general standard of behaviour.

Consider, again, the norms that: one ought not to drink alcohol in public places, one should offer one's bus seat to the elderly, one ought not to skip the queue, one ought not to interrupt others when they are speaking, one ought to wear modest clothes in church, and so forth. Their existence in any given context—in fact, often in a given community—depends on there being a large enough number of people who are publicly committed to the relevant requirements ("oughts") in that context. These are the agents I called "norm-supporters". Failing to respect the relevant requirements—i.e., acting contrary to their demands—is therefore tantamount to failing to respect the commitments of norm-supporters. This is precisely my claim.

The claim that respecting norm-supporters' commitments—in line with agency respect—requires respecting the corresponding norms may prompt three forms of scepticism. First, a critic might worry that, often, socially constructed norms are not genuine expressions of the agency of norm-supporters. That is, they are not the product of authentic commitments, but of coercion or false consciousness. For example, some South Asian women support norms requiring them to prioritize the nutritional needs of their husbands and male children. Several commentators argue that such support counts as coerced because it is developed against the background of oppressive gender relations (see, e.g., Stoljar 2014).

This is a valid point, but it does not threaten my claim. One can accept that the commitments of the oppressed to oppressive norms never count as authentic. This, however, does not go against the claim that socially constructed norms—including oppressive ones—are underpinned by agents' commitments, and that respecting those commitments would require respecting the corresponding norms. It only points to the fact that, in some cases, those commitments are not genuine, hence they *lack the moral significance* that commitments otherwise have. When commitments are not authentic, the agency-respect principle places no duties on us. And, as long as at least a good number of norms are underpinned by authentic commitments, the "coercion worry" is not threatening to my view.

The objector may reply that the problem of coercion is not the exception, but the rule. This is because socially constructed norms are accompanied by sanctions: some formal, others informal. Since a coercive element is inherent in *all* socially constructed norms, one might be tempted to conclude that no norm can be underpinned by authentic commitments, namely the kinds of commitments that activate obligations.

This conclusion would be too strong. After all, the fact that murder is punished severely does not undermine the claim that I am genuinely committed to not murdering people. As already mentioned, to determine whether commitments to the requirements of existing norms are authentic, we can rely on the authenticity tests developed in the philosophical literature on autonomy. For example, a possible test involves asking whether, upon reflection and independently of the sanctions associated with norm-breaches, norm-supporters would continue to endorse the norms in question or at least would not feel alienated from them (cf. Christman 2004: 154). If the answer is affirmative, then norm-supporters' commitments count as authentic. My impression is that, with many norms—from queuing, to standing up at high-table dinners and not swearing in sacred places— affirmative answers are to be expected. Of course, authenticity tests can take different forms, and different specifications of these tests will lead to slightly different verdicts. I will revisit this issue in the book's Conclusion. What matters, for the time being, is that the broad strategy offered by such tests can be employed to supplement the agency-respect framework.

A second worry may be that, instead of being underpinned by commitments, socially constructed norms are often just a matter of habit. To determine how damaging to my argument this worry is, we need to clarify what "following a norm out of habit" means. Habitual norm-following is consistent with at least two attitudes. The first is one of *indifference* towards the norm. This is the attitude of someone who, say, stands in line at the bus stop out of inertia and conformism, but who does not believe that one ought to queue and does not disapprove of queue-jumpers.

If this is what "following a norm out of habit" means, then the agent in question does not even *accept* the corresponding requirement. And if the majority of agents in the context under consideration have an equally indifferent attitude towards queuing, then that practice is not governed by a socially constructed norm in that context. It is a mere habit (Hart 1961: 54). The present argument is silent on habits.

A second possibility is that following a norm out of habit simply means following it without having explicitly reflected long and hard about its merits.

96 THE AGENCY-RESPECT VIEW

This understanding of habitual norm-following, unlike the previous one, is consistent with agents' robustly intending to be guided by the relevant oughts, and being prepared to sanction, or at least disapprove of, others' non-compliance. In this case, it remains true that these individuals are committed to the underlying oughts; it is just that they have developed this commitment without extensive prior deliberation.[15] As I have noted earlier, a commitment that does not stem from a precise decision moment preceded by deliberation is a commitment all the same. If, abstracting away from sanctions, norm-supporters are prepared to stick to that commitment, the commitment counts as authentic. Respecting that commitment, in turn, will require respect for the relevant norm.

Finally, a sceptic might insist that norms—in fact, their prescriptions and prohibitions—are rarely the objects of commitments. Instead, our commitments are often directed at the broader practices governed by those norms and the values those norms express. For example, my commitment to my university explains why I stably intend to be guided by its norms. Similarly, a believer in Hinduism is committed to the rule that shoes should be taken off when entering a Hindu temple, but this is because of her broader commitment to the Hindu religion.

The objection accurately characterizes the nature of many of our commitments, but it does not disprove the claim that we are committed to the requirements associated with socially constructed norms. Instead, it highlights the fact that our commitments to those requirements are often the product of broader commitments to certain practices or values: they are derivative. True, my commitment to, for example, the rule that students' papers should be marked within a certain timeframe stems from another commitment: that to my university. But this in no way invalidates the claim that I am committed to that rule. Similarly, our religious believer's commitment to the "no-shoes-in-the-temple" rule is not invalidated by the fact that it derives from her broader commitment to Hinduism.

If this is right, the claim that socially constructed norms exist by virtue of individuals' commitments to the corresponding requirements stands. There is one important qualification, however. A commitment to a norm's prescriptions and prohibitions—be it fundamental or derivative—must stem from reasons that relate to the value of the norm itself or of the practice of which the norm is a part. I do not count as committed *to certain requirements* if the only reason I comply with them is respect for those who embrace them: that is, for those who are genuinely committed to them. For example, I am not a supporter of the

---

[15] One might wonder how we should interpret the attitude of those who abide by socially constructed norms because "this is how things are done around here". Do they qualify as norm-supporters? I answer in the affirmative: if the people in question robustly intend for the relevant requirements to function as general standards of behaviour, and are prepared to sanction non-compliance and to stick to their commitments upon reflection, then their commitments place agency-respect demands on us. Of course, it may be that the commitments, in this case, are somewhat weak, depending on how attached to the value of "tradition"—if this is what the expression "this is how things are done around here" points to—norm-supporters are.

"no-shoes-in-the-temple" norm if I take my shoes off before entering a Hindu temple out of respect for the locals' religious beliefs. By contrast, those who take their shoes off for genuinely religious reasons, or reasons related to the merits of the practice, do count as norm-supporters.

5. Action Required: The Obligation to Obey Socially Constructed Norms

We can now combine the reflections advanced in the previous sections and conclude that the duty to give others agency respect—to respect their permissible and authentic commitments—lends moral normativity to socially constructed norms. This explains why the fact that φ-ing is required by a socially constructed norm makes a difference to the moral status of φ-ing.

To see the implications of this conclusion, consider some (by now familiar) socially constructed norms. Take the norm, prevalent in the UK, that people should queue up when waiting for the bus. Needless to say, we have prudential and fairness-based reasons to act in line with this norm, as proponents of the deflationary view also accept. But if we take agency respect seriously, those reasons are not the only ones that matter. The British are committed to the requirements associated with the queuing norm. Of course, this norm is probably not particularly central to their life plans and sense of self. Still, norm-supporters' adherence to the practice of queuing and willingness to sanction those who deviate from it show that it matters to them (Schmitt, Dubé, and Leclerc 1992: 807). This being so, we have an agency-respect pro tanto duty to queue up at the bus stop in contexts where the local norms prescribe it, just as we have a duty to take our shoes off when visiting people who support the "no-shoes indoors" norm. This is, of course, on the assumption that the British's commitment to queuing is genuine, morally permissible, and that respecting it doesn't place excessive burdens on our own agency.

For another example, in a country like Germany there is a norm that requires customers to tip approximately 5 to 10 per cent for service, except in cases where service is poor. This norm applies even in restaurants where—due to the reasonableness of the official wages—tips are not strictly necessary for waiters' subsistence, so that the action prescribed by the norm is not independently morally mandated. Even so, the demands of agency respect towards those who accept the norm give it some moral normativity—again, provided tipping is permissible, not too costly, and norm-supporters' commitment to it is authentic.

In so saying, I am implying neither that tipping is a core feature of German identity, nor that agency respect is the only or main reason why one should tip in Germany. My argument is consistent with tipping being a very weak commitment for many Germans, and with failures to tip being wrong primarily for other reasons: for example, the fact that they frustrate legitimate expectations. I am simply noting that, since (and to the extent that) the tipping norm exists by virtue of many Germans' permissibly exercising their agency in particular ways, the requirements of agency respect confer moral normativity—however weak—on that norm.

Finally, consider having to stand up when grace is said at Oxbridge high table. This norm is part of the broader practice of "Oxbridge college life". Many dons and students are committed to this practice and its associated prescriptions. Agency respect for them confers moral normativity on the corresponding norms. This, in turn, explains in what sense, at Oxbridge high table, one ought to stand up as grace is being said *because* there is a social norm requiring it (cf. Southwood 2011: 787–9).

More examples could be given, but the general spirit of the argument should be clear. If we take the demands of agency respect seriously, the fact that certain actions are mandated (or prohibited) by morally permissible socially constructed norms makes a difference to their moral status.[16] Just as we have duties to respect individuals' permissible and authentic commitments, so too we have duties to respect permissible socially constructed norms, when these are underpinned by authentic commitments, and doing so is not too costly to us. Furthermore, as explained earlier, the strength of these norm-related duties depends on how central the practices governed by the norms are to norm-supporters' plans of life and sense of self. This is why our duty not to swear in sacred places, for instance, is weightier than our duty to queue at the bus stop.

An objector may be concerned that my conclusion proves too much and is vulnerable to serious counterexamples. This is why. Respecting others' commitments places constraints on our agency. For instance, to respect the commitments of my Catholic friends, I must not interfere with their religious practice and, perhaps, even facilitate it. But it seems implausible to suggest that respect for their commitments requires that *I subject myself* to Catholic norms. Yet, the agency-respect view appears to prescribe precisely this. It says that we have obligations to respect—i.e., obey—socially constructed norms. Violating those norms would frustrate norm-supporters' commitments to the norms' requirements functioning as standards of behaviour.

The objector is right: the suggestion that I ought to abide by the rules of Catholicism is implausible. Luckily, the agency-respect view is not vulnerable to this, or similar, counterexamples. This is *either* because such counterexamples are based on a misinterpretation of the scope of the norms at issue *or* because those norms are morally impermissible, and therefore not binding. The "Catholicism" case illustrates both points well. First, the norms governing the practice of Catholicism do not typically count non-Catholics among their subjects. The

---

[16] Cf. Marmor's (2009) discussion of the morality of social conventions.

content of my Catholic friends' commitments is not, say, that "they *and I* should attend service on Sunday". Their commitments tend to be self-regarding. To that extent, respecting them does not require a non-Catholic to obey Catholic norms. What is more, if Catholics supported norms that required non-Catholics to practice Catholicism, their commitments would be impermissible: they would encroach on individual freedom of conscience. This is not to say that Catholics are not permitted to *believe* that Catholicism is the one, true religion. Nor is it to say that Catholics cannot be committed to trying to persuade others to convert to Catholicism. What is impermissible is supporting socially constructed norms that require everyone, no matter their convictions, to act in line with the demands of Catholicism, and thereby sanction them when they do not.

Still, very many socially constructed norms purport to bind classes of agents beyond those who are independently committed to their prescriptions and prohibitions. The queuing, tipping, and high-table norms are cases in point. They purport to apply to anyone who finds themselves in a given context: for example, a British supermarket, a German restaurant, or an Oxbridge college dining hall. I may be someone who is not particularly into queuing, tipping, or standing up when grace is said, yet, if I find myself in the aforementioned contexts, the corresponding norms apply to me too.

There is a crucial difference, however, between these other-regarding norms and a (hypothetical) norm requiring global conversion to Catholicism. The latter would be morally impermissible—it would ignore others' status as autonomous end-setters—while the former are arguably innocuous. There appears to be nothing particularly objectionable about the other-regarding nature of queuing, tipping, and "standing up at grace" norms. Therefore, if abiding by them is not excessively burdensome for our own agency, respect for the commitments of those who support them requires respect for the norms themselves.

At this point, the objector may retort that the constraints others' commitments impose on our agency should always be a matter of forbearance from interference, and never of obedience, even in cases where the relevant norms are morally permissible and obedience does not excessively burden our own agency. Anything else would be contrary precisely to respect for agency, which makes it impermissible for an individual to demand that others, who are her equals, become means to furthering her own conception of the good.[17]

There are two things to say in response. First, from an "agency-burdens" point of view, there is no clear distinction between the constraints involved in "refraining from interfering with" and "conforming to or facilitating" others' commitments. Suppose someone is very keen on attending a religious ceremony. Refraining from interfering with this commitment may mean not scheduling another important event that clashes with it, while conforming to or facilitating it may

---

[17] Thanks to Annie Stilz for raising this concern.

100 THE AGENCY-RESPECT VIEW

mean accompanying the person to the ceremony. Both types of conduct involve constraints on my actions, and it is not obvious that the former constraint is more acceptable or easier to defend than the latter. Plausibly, the defensibility of any given constraint will depend on the burdens it imposes on the agency of those whose conduct has to satisfy it. And while it may be the case that forbearance is often less costly than support, this needn't be so. After all, the magnitude of the burden imposed by any particular constraint is likely to depend on the specific nature of one's commitments, not on whether it can be most naturally described as a matter of non-interference vs conformity.

For instance, imagine three friends—Ada, Amy, and Annie—sharing the same room in a boarding school. Ada and Amy can't wait to read *Madame Bovary*: they're both fans of French literary realism and are committed to reading all of the relevant classics. Annie, by contrast, is not very much into literature, and is instead keener on visual arts. Unfortunately, the library only possesses one copy of Flaubert's classic, which Annie kindly checks out for her friends while picking up some books about cubism. Ada is the first to come home and get hold of the book. Unsurprisingly, she reads it avidly. Amy, who joins her roommates only a couple of hours later, needs to exercise a great deal of self-control in order not to snatch the book from Ada's hands (who, incidentally, has no greater claim to the book than Amy does). Now, Amy is forbearing from interfering with Ada's reading, while Annie facilitated her friends' pursuits. But it isn't at all clear that assisting her friends placed a greater burden on Annie's agency than forbearance places on Amy's. Given Annie's and Amy's different interests, it looks like forbearance is costlier for Amy than assistance is for Annie. And crucially, while the distinction between forbearance and assistance seems to have no independent moral weight—given that *both* involve constraints on agency—that between actions that place significant vs light burdens on our agency does.

Second, when it comes to socially constructed norms, the distinction between "not interfering" and "facilitating or conforming" becomes blurred. Consider, for instance, queuing or high-table norms. What does it mean to not interfere with the queuing norm if not obeying it? What does it mean to not interfere with high-table norms if not following them? After all, the moment I refuse to stand up when grace is being said, I automatically disrupt the functioning of the relevant norm. In sum, *if* we accept that others' commitments place constraints on our agency on respect grounds, the distinction between constraints involving forbearance and constraints involving positive actions or conformity appears of little significance, especially in the context of socially constructed norms.[18] What matters is how burdensome said constraints are for our own agency.

---

[18] One might wonder how the agency-respect view would respond to a "principled non-conformist": someone who is committed to not giving any normative significance to others' commitments. Since this would be someone committed to ignoring the demands of agency respect, from the perspective advanced here her commitment would be morally impermissible: contrary to respect for persons as particular agents.

In light of all this, the overall conclusion of my argument still stands: morally permissible socially constructed norms underpinned by authentic commitments place obligations on those who are subjected to them, provided fulfilling those obligations is not excessively burdensome.

6. The Explanatory Power of the Agency-Respect View

Having outlined the agency-respect view, I now turn to examining how it fares in relation to the desiderata proposed in Section 1. In this section, I consider the explanatory power of the view. In the next, I evaluate its ability to fit our considered judgements.

As I hope my discussion up to this point has shown, the agency-respect view renders the moral normativity of socially constructed norms *unsurprising*. The agency-respect principle is familiar from our day-to-day moral thinking and has much independent plausibility. Furthermore, the principle is arguably acceptable from within a variety of different moral theories: the kind of principle that could lie at the centre of a Rawlsian overlapping consensus (Rawls 1996). For example, a utilitarian could accept it on the ground that respecting persons' commitments maximizes aggregate welfare. A Kantian could regard the principle as mandated by the Categorical Imperative: as a maxim that one can will as a universal law. A Scanlonian contractualist may see the agency-respect principle as one that cannot be reasonably rejected, and so forth (Scanlon 1998). For present purposes, I need not subscribe to any further foundation for the principle in question. Different readers may choose their preferred one. All that I need to claim is that this is a familiar ethical principle, accepted across a variety of different traditions. And even if the latter claim is disputed, the principle is certainly central to contemporary deontological-liberal ethics. It is therefore not susceptible to the charge of being ad hoc: reverse-engineered to account for its explanandum.

The ground for the duty to obey socially constructed norms offered by the agency-respect principle is also *non-mysterious*. The principle sets out an abstract moral ought which, in conjunction with an empirical premise, gives rise to a more specific ought. The input to our reasoning is a deontic claim, not a piece of axiology as in the case of the normative-interests view. Consequently, while, as we saw in Chapter 2, it is arguably mysterious how we can have interests (axiological) as inputs, and oughts (deontic) as outputs, it is unsurprising that, with an ought as input to our reasoning, we obtain an ought as output.

But might the explanation offered by the agency-respect principle be *far-fetched* and, like the joint-commitments view, susceptible to a version of the "wrong reasons" problem? I believe not, but this requires some elaboration. After all, the duty to give others agency respect grounds the moral force of socially constructed norms, and the object of agency respect are norm-supporters, in the context under analysis. This may be taken to imply that those individuals *themselves* have their rights violated when the norms are breached. For instance, if I violate Bob's property rights, I do *not* wrong Bob specifically, but *all and only* those who support property norms in Bob's community. If this were the case, the agency-respect view would be vulnerable to the wrong reasons problem.

Luckily, it is not, or at least not to the same extent that some competitor views are. This is because whose rights, if anybody's, are violated depends on the *content* of the relevant norms (cf. Owens 2017: 558). In some—but not all—instances, the norms establish duties correlative to rights, by which I mean duties that the right-holder has the standing to waive or whose performance he may demand. Consider, for example, the norm that one ought not to jump the queue. If someone jumps the queue—e.g., arriving last, but putting himself at the top of the queue—he thereby breaches the entitlements of those who have been waiting in line until then. According to the queuing norm, each person has a right to a particular place in the queue (first, second, third, etc.), based on their time of arrival, and may either waive it by giving up their spot or demand that others not take it. The queue-jumper's actions violate those entitlements, thereby wronging *those standing in line.*[19]

Other socially constructed norms, such as the norm that one ought to stand up when grace is said at high table, establish oughts that are not correlative to rights. This means that failing to stand up at high table, in the context of an Oxbridge college, is wrong simpliciter, without involving any rights violation; no particular right-holders are wronged here.

On my account, then, the objects of agency respect (i.e., norm-supporters) and those whose rights may be breached by norm-violations need not coincide. Some may find this puzzling, insisting that my account avoids the wrong reasons problem by means of an ad hoc move. I do not think this is so. Respecting norm-supporters means taking seriously the *normative world* they have created. Since that world is partly crystallized in socially constructed norms, the demands of agency respect give those norms moral normativity. For example, those who support the British-style queuing norm see queue-jumping as a (mild) wrong primarily against people in the relevant queue, not themselves. Why should the demands of agency respect entail a structure of wrongdoing that deviates from the one they have created? Imagine I inadvertently jump the queue while waiting for the bus in a small English village. Upon realizing it, I proceed to apologize to everyone on the street, including random passers-by, on the assumption that they all support the queuing norm. This behaviour would be not just odd, but also not in line with the demands of agency respect. If the local norm implies that those standing in line are wronged when I skip the queue, then, in that context, I ought to apologize to them.

At the same time, there is a sense in which, by breaching a local norm, we also offend or disrespect the community whose norm that is. The agency-respect view

---

[19] For present purposes, I assume that rights violations wrong right-holders in particular.

is well placed to capture this idea, since it grounds the obligation to obey socially constructed norms precisely in respect for norm-supporters. The point is that its doing so does not prevent it from *also* identifying particular individuals as distinctively wronged by specific norm-breaches. In fact, it outsources the identification of these individuals to the norms themselves. (This aspect of the view will be further elaborated on in Chapter 4.)

An objector might protest that the way the agency-respect view identifies the specific individuals who are wronged by breaches of norms clashes with a widely shared assumption. This is that, when an action wrongs an agent A, the wrongness of that action must (at least in part) be explained by some morally significant feature of A.

Contrary to what the objector suggests, my view is *not* in tension with this assumption. On my view, when an action wrongs A, its wrongness *is* explained by a morally significant feature of A. The feature in question is that a binding socially constructed norm picks A out as the individual who is wronged by that action. If the objector were to insist that this feature is inadmissible as an explanation for why A is wronged, this would be tantamount to denying that socially constructed norms can have moral normativity. And in the present context, this denial would be question begging.

I thus conclude that the agency-respect view meets the desideratum of explanatory power and avoids the explanatory deficiencies detected in competing views.

7. How the Agency-Respect View Fits the Evidence

I now turn to whether the agency-respect view satisfies the desideratum of fit, by considering how it fares in relation to the three cases I introduced in Chapter 2: *Traffic Light*, *Barbeque*, and *Non-proceduralist President*. The agency-respect view will pass the "fit test" if it can be shown to align with our considered judgements in the aforementioned cases.[20] I argue that it can.

First, the view allows us to explain why a harmless failure to obey German traffic norms is wrong. To the extent that German traffic norms are morally permissible, and commitments to them are authentic, agency respect gives them moral normativity. We thus have a duty to obey them, and we commit a wrong, though not a rights violation, when we disregard them. This means that anyone driving on German roads would be doing something wrong by ignoring the red light in a situation like the one in which Jürgen found himself. Put in the form of the

---

[20] Of course, a complete "fit" test would require examining how the view fares in relation to *all* evidence. This, however, is clearly infeasible. Any argument to the effect that a view satisfies the criterion of fit must rely on core evidence, as opposed to all possible evidence.

104 THE AGENCY-RESPECT VIEW

grounding sequence we encountered in the previous chapter, the argument goes as follows:

- <u>Action required</u>: You ought to φ (φ = stop at the red light).
- By virtue of what ought I to φ?
- <u>Empirical fact</u>: Because a socially constructed norm—provided the norm is underpinned by people's authentic as well as permissible commitments, and respecting it is not too costly—requires that you φ.
- By virtue of what does the fact that φ-ing is required by a socially constructed norm—provided the norm is underpinned by people's authentic as well as permissible commitments, and respecting it is not too costly—ground my obligation to φ?
- <u>Target general moral principle</u>: Because you have an obligation to respect people's commitments (i.e., "to give *agency respect* to people"), provided those commitments are authentic, morally permissible, and respecting them is not too costly.

Note that my account can also explain why our hypothetical Southern Italian interviewees need not be *entirely* mistaken in denying that stopping at a red light would be wrongful. While they would be mistaken if the context of occurrence of the breach were Germany, they would not be if we shifted the context to, say, Naples. This is because, arguably, *in the specific context of Naples*, there is no socially constructed norm that requires obeying traffic signs. Furthermore, the agency-respect explanation allows us to make sense of why our duty to stop at a red light, in a context like Germany, is rather weak. No matter how law-abiding some Germans might be, it is hard to think that their commitments to traffic regulations are core aspects of their life-plans and self-understanding.[21] If Jürgen were to learn that, say, I have driven through a red light when absolutely nobody was around, he'd still think I ought not to have done it and tell me off for it, but I doubt he'd consider it a "big deal".

The agency-respect explanation, therefore, gives us exactly what we want: it accounts for why we may sometimes be bound to stop at a red light on an empty road, it allows us to make sense of many people's intuitions to the contrary, and it matches the judgement that the duty in question, when there is one, is rather weak.

The agency-respect view also explains the wrongdoing involved in *Barbeque*. (This time I omit to restate the grounding sequence, since its structure remains the same, no matter what action we substitute for "φ".) Here, the violated socially constructed obligation is correlative to rights. This means that *you*—namely, the

---

[21] A broader commitment to obeying legal norms might be, but presumably the strength of that commitment will also partly reflect the stakes involved in specific norms. On this view, while legal disobedience is always wrong, how wrong it is depends on the substance of the breach in question. More on this general line of thought will be said in Chapter 5.

owner of the barbeque set—are wronged by the Rossis' actions. The view also explains why this second case is more intuitively wrongful than the first. To begin with, private property requirements are ones most of us presuppose and are deeply committed to. Property norms shape and constrain the pursuit of our ends, projects, and goals in ways most of us have internalized.[22] Moreover, the violation of a right—hence of a duty owed to someone—is typically more intuitively problematic than the violation of a duty simpliciter. The fact that, in *Barbeque*, there is a clearly identifiable victim renders the wrongness of the breach all the more vivid.

Finally, the agency-respect view illuminates the nature of the wrong done in *Non-proceduralist President*. To the extent that the President violates the socially constructed norms that structure the US' collective decision-making—in fact, the norms via which laws are made—he acts wrongly. Officials, no matter how powerful, are supposed to be bound by the law. Legal violations on the part of officials undermine the ideal of the rule of law, to which citizens of democratic societies tend to be deeply committed. This is why, intuitively, the wrong involved in *Non-proceduralist President* is a serious one.

The agency-respect view, I hope to have shown, fulfils its promise: it fits our considered judgements and can match their varying strengths. Even so, readers may find some aspects of the view unsatisfactory. Before concluding, then, let me respond to possible objections to it.

8. Objections

In this section, I consider six worries about the agency-respect view. These are, respectively, that the view: (i) is implausibly demanding, (ii) is empty, (iii) cannot explain our obligations to obey "our own" norms, (iv) is ill-equipped to account for our intuitions in cases where different people's commitments clash, (v) has somewhat implausible, intrusive implications, and (vi) is biased in favour of the status quo. If these objections were successful, they would significantly undermine my claims about my view's ability to satisfy the "explanatory power" and "fit" desiderata.

8.1 Is the view implausibly demanding?

A critic might worry that the agency-respect principle is overdemanding.[23] After all, everything we do is an expression of our agency. And while it is true that some

---

[22] Of course, we are also externally constrained by such norms, since they are typically enforced by the state.

[23] The concerns discussed in this sub-section have been put to me by Daniel Statman and Arash Abizadeh, to whom I am grateful.

106 THE AGENCY-RESPECT VIEW

such expressions, namely those that are central to who we are and violations of which would undermine our integrity, call for respect, it is not true that every conceivable exercise of agency does. To better understand this concern, it is instructive to briefly look at the debate on religious rights, where a parallel concern emerges.

Some liberal theorists participating in that debate hold that religious rights stem from people's broader right to lead their lives in accordance with their conceptions of the good and commitments. Call this the "right to autonomy". But, as Cécile Laborde explains, pointing to a very general right to autonomy is not enough. One needs "to distinguish, among the vast range of commitments and conceptions of the good that people hold in pluralistic societies, those that deserve special protection" (Laborde 2015: 588). Here, liberal theorists typically point to the importance of freedom of conscience in particular. There is indeed something extremely valuable in leading one's life in accordance with one's own core ethical, moral, and religious commitments. The harm done to someone who is prevented from doing so is of the gravest kind, involving the erosion of their personal integrity (for discussion, see Laborde 2015: sec. 2).[24] These considerations, in turn, are meant to explain why religious agency deserves special protection from a liberal point of view.

Let us now return to our topic, namely the moral normativity of socially constructed norms and the agency-respect principle. It may be thought that the demands of this principle are plausible in relation to the kinds of commitments that fall under the purview of freedom of conscience. But the reach of the principle is in fact much broader than that, covering all sorts of commitments, not only those central to our personal integrity. This is why, a critic might say, it overgenerates moral demands. To echo Laborde's words, the principle fails to isolate the commitments "that deserve special protection".

For example, while respect for agency might satisfactorily explain why we ought to respect the commitments of religious believers, and even accommodate them, it is ill-suited to explaining why we should respect the commitments of those who subscribe to the queuing norm. This, the critic might continue, is not to say that we do not have a (moral) obligation to queue at the bus stop, just that respect for agency does not plausibly explain where it comes from. The commitments of those who support the queuing norm are far too weak to deserve moral protection qua commitments. No special agency-harm accrues to supporters of the norm when the norm is breached. They may perhaps be mildly annoyed but, the objector might observe, we are not ordinarily obligated to refrain from acting in ways that mildly annoy others. Contrary to these observations, the agency-respect principle implies that by skipping the queue one commits a wrong akin to the

---

[24] Note that Laborde herself does not find a conscience-based approach to religious rights convincing.

type of wrong involved in breaches of freedom of conscience. But, for the reasons just articulated, this seems implausible. The principle, therefore, over-reaches.

What is more, the objector might continue, if every exercise of agency underpinned by a robust enough intention generates pro tanto moral demands, there will remain very little scope for people to act at all. Every action one undertakes, every decision one makes is likely to have some impact on others' agency. In light of this, taking the demands of the agency-respect principle seriously would leave us in a world where everyone is "stuck in a cage", a cage whose bars are constituted by others' agency-respect claims.

Is the agency-respect view susceptible to these concerns? I believe not. Let me explain why. First, the agency-respect principle features important qualifications. Not every commitment calls for agency respect, only commitments that are authentic, morally permissible, and respect for which does not place excessive burdens on one's agency generate pro tanto obligations. Since being "stuck in a cage" clearly would involve excessive burdens on one's agency, it is not what the agency-respect principle requires.

Second, the agency-respect principle has indeed a rather wide scope: it demands respect for persons' commitments, but does not draw any categorical distinction between types of commitments based on their *content*. It is not that religious commitments are considered more respect-worthy than other such commitments, for instance. What matters, from an agency-respect perspective, is the centrality that such commitments have to one's life plans and sense of self. To the extent that religious commitments or commitments of conscience are particularly central to who we are, agency-respect obligations will be particularly weighty in relation to them. This, however, does not mean that more peripheral commitments generate *no* agency-respect demands. They do too, just much less weighty ones. And it is not clear to me why, if what we care about is respect for people's agency, we should switch to an on-off, categorical picture of when such respect is due, rather than accepting a graded picture like the one proposed here.

Third, and finally, let me emphasize that the demands of agency respect as I understand them are not meant to set out requirements that may be permissibly enforced by the law. While I think agency-respect considerations should inform law-making, not everything that is required by agency respect should become a matter of legislation. Plausibly, core legal freedoms should be determined based on the types of commitments that tend to be most central to individuals' lives: freedom of expression, conscience, movement, association, and so forth. But there may well be cases in which the overall best system of legal constraints, from an agency-respect point of view, gives individuals "rights to do wrong", including to fail to respect one another's agency (Waldron 1981).

For example, let us suppose that property rights are valuable legal mechanisms to protect people's agency, by giving them a secure space within which they may pursue their ends and goals. Consider a case involving someone whose religion

108 THE AGENCY-RESPECT VIEW

forbids him from taking his shoes off in front of others, but who is invited into a household where a "no-shoes" norm applies. The hosts have a right to force their guest to take his shoes off or leave. But, in the circumstances, I think that they would be wrong to do so: their commitment to the no-shoes policy is likely much less central to their life plans than the guest's commitment to not showing his feet in public. Morally speaking, the hosts should allow the guest to keep his footwear on. The agency-respect principle can thus help us explain both why, all-things-considered, property laws that give owners the right to force guests to take their shoes off are justified, and why it would in fact be wrong for these particular hosts to force this particular guest to do so. The macro-level enforceable rules that are, on the whole, most protective of everyone's agency may well leave scope for specific individuals to violate the demands of agency respect in particular circumstances. Not all that agency respect requires is thus something that should be made into law.

To sum up, once the qualifications inherent in the agency-respect principle and its status—i.e., as setting out moral demands not to be straightforwardly mirrored in the law—are appreciated, the worry about over-demandingness should dissipate.

8.2 Is the view empty?

These considerations are likely to generate a further concern: the qualifications that make the agency-respect view capable of addressing the over-demandingness worry also render it virtually empty, and therefore explanatorily inert.[25] To put the point rather uncharitably, but effectively: "according to my view, one has a pro tanto obligation to respect other people's exercises of agency in those cases where doing so seems plausible". The parameters of tolerable costliness and moral permissibility thus have to be adjusted accordingly. This, however, does not tell us *why* we should respect people's agency, and does not help us discriminate between difficult cases where different agency-respect demands conflict with one another.

Much of what the previous paragraph states, I think, is correct, but it does not show the agency-respect principle to be explanatorily inert. What it does show is that, as currently stated, the principle is not fully specified, and different readers may give it somewhat different interpretations, depending on how the parameters of "moral permissibility" and "tolerable costliness" are filled. While paradigmatic cases—e.g., not swearing in sacred places—are such that any specification of the parameters should be able to account for them, in other cases we will obtain different verdicts depending on our views on moral permissibility and costs. This, however, strikes me as a feature, not a bug of the view. It allows the view to retain

---

[25] Thanks to Daniel Statman for raising this worry.

the core insight that respect for agency is what lends moral normativity to socially constructed norms, while being compatible with different substantive views about which norms do, in fact, have moral normativity.

One might worry that leaving a parameter like moral permissibility under-specified opens the way to interpretations of it that are so demanding as to virtually render any socially constructed norm that isn't morally perfect morally inert. For example, the queueing norm might be criticized as "ableist". The grace norm at Oxbridge high table may be questioned for privileging a majority religion. And so forth.[26]

In response to this worry, I am happy to concede that if most socially constructed norms failed to reach the moral-permissibility threshold, then indeed they would lack moral normativity. Having said that, I am not too concerned about this possibility, for two reasons. First, it seems plausible that morality is somewhat coarse-grained and does not specifically mandate how exactly we are to organize our lives together. It rules out arrangements that are manifestly contrary to our moral equality, but it doesn't provide us with a blueprint detailing what norms, conventions, and habits we should live by. Of course, if the balance of reasons clearly showed that the queueing norm unfairly discriminates against those with physical disabilities, or that the grace norm still retains strong religious connotations that are problematically exclusionary vis-à-vis certain individuals, we would be in the presence of objectionable norms whose moral normativity would have to be put into question. I am sceptical that this is the case, but I might be wrong.

Second, morality isn't only coarse-grained, but when it comes to important questions that arise in our shared social and political lives, we *reasonably disagree* about its demands. This means that people who are sincerely committed to values such as equality and respect for others' agency may end up having different views about what honouring such values more specifically requires. This is not due to manifest errors in reasoning, but to the complexity of the matter at hand coupled with the fact that people assess it from their different, situated perspectives.[27] And if individuals who reasonably disagree about what morality requires are to peace-fully live together, they need to accept even norms they do not find morally optimal, but which nonetheless fall within the realm of the reasonable. Since, for any given norm that doesn't simply state the morally obvious—e.g., the injustice of slavery, or the wrongness of murder, or the unacceptability of discrimination based on race and gender—there will be some who disagree with it, acceptance of

---

[26] I am grateful to Annie Stilz for raising this concern.

[27] This may be traced to the phenomenon which Rawls (1996: 55–8) famously calls the "burdens of judgement", according to which our different perspectives and experiences may lead us to develop different but competing accounts of justice and the good. As he puts it, "many of our most important judgments are made under conditions where it is not to be expected that conscientious persons with full powers of reason, even after free discussion, will arrive at the same conclusion" (Rawls 1996: 58).

norms falling within the domain of reasonable disagreement is necessary for us to build a rich enough social life. This means that norms which fall within the realm of the reasonable—and I suspect the queuing norm and grace norm are among them—are not ruled out by the moral permissibility qualification built into the agency-respect principle.

In sum, while it is possible that, under a very demanding and fine-grained account of the demands of morality, most socially constructed norms would lack moral normativity (according to the agency-respect view), on what strikes me as a more plausible picture of morality—i.e., one that is coarse-grained and leaves room for reasonable disagreement—this concern isn't as worrisome.

An objector might insist that, setting aside worries about how the various parameters in the agency-respect principle should be interpreted, my view does not explain *why* we should respect people's agency in the first place. What is so valuable about respect for agency? Here, it seems to me, two responses are available. The first involves pointing to those freedoms and rights that are widely considered valuable within liberal democratic societies, and asking the objector whether he agrees that they are, in fact, valuable. I am assuming that it will be hard for the objector to say "no". Presumably, both the objector and I care about freedom of movement, association, speech, religion, conscience, and so forth. We care about these freedoms because, among other things, they allow individuals to express their agency, to shape their lives in line with their ends, goals, and commitments, which is, in turn, essential to their nature as deliberative, reflective agents. The agency-respect principle articulates this widely shared agreement (see also Eidelson 2013). I am thus treating this principle as a starting point that I assume my reader and I both already accept.

The second response to the objector would be to suggest, as I did earlier, that the agency-respect principle need not be fundamental, but may itself be grounded in more basic moral principles, be they contractualist, teleological, and so forth. While I am not committed to this view, it seems quite plausible. And, if the principle could indeed lie at the heart of a Rawlsian-style overlapping consensus, this would make it all the more powerful, since it could be accepted from a variety of competing overall ethical perspectives (Rawls 1996: lecture IV).

In sum, the agency-respect principle is not explanatorily empty. What some might mistake for emptiness is in fact a virtue of the principle: namely its being susceptible to a variety of interpretations (depending on how its parameters are filled), and thus its core insights being compatible with different underlying substantive views. And while it is true that I do not offer any "deeper" justification for the agency-respect principle (without ruling out its possibility), it is not obvious to me that doing so is needed. Moral argument needs to start from somewhere, and the agency-respect principle, given its wide appeal to those with broadly liberal-deontological dispositions, seems like a good place to start.

8.3 What about the moral normativity of "one's own" norms?

A reasonably sympathetic reader may find that the agency-respect view success-fully explains when and why the fact that "foreign norms" demand that we φ places us under a duty to φ. That is, she may be convinced that the view accounts for our obligation to obey the (formal and informal) norms of communities *other than our own*. But she may also be sceptical about its ability to vindicate our obligation to obey the norms structuring our own community. What to say in response to this concern?

First, the question of why we should obey the norms of societies other than our own is independently important and seldom discussed. To that extent, my argument would still have merit, even if it only explained the obligation to obey the norms of societies we are visiting. But I think the potential of my argument is greater than the objector believes. To see this, we should keep membership-based or associative obligations—i.e., the obligations one putatively has as a member of a community—and our obligation to obey socially constructed norms separate (for discussion of the former, see van der Vossen 2011). As Joseph Raz points out, the obligations that, in his view, arise out of membership in a given society are not limited to—and sometimes do not even include—the obligation to obey various socially constructed norms. In fact, our membership-based responsibilities may require us to disobey existing norms (when they are unjust), as well as to do things on which existing norms are silent (e.g., show solidarity towards our fellow members in circumstances that are not the object of formal or informal regula-tion) (Raz 2006: 1004–5). So, the relationship between putative associative obliga-tions and the moral bindingness of socially constructed norms is not one of identity. Here, I have remained silent about associative obligations, and have only focused on the moral normativity of socially constructed norms.[28]

Furthermore, the presupposition that the moral normativity of a society's norms is tied to membership appears unsupported by day-to-day experience. Most of us do not think that, while we ought to obey legal and informal norms in our country of citizenship (and/or residence), we have no such obligation when we visit a different country. My sense of obligation tracks the set of norms I am actually subjected to, in the jurisdiction in which I find myself. If I move to Australia for a short academic visit, I consider myself under an obligation to do what Australian law requires, because it so requires. In fact, I consider that

---

[28] I will briefly talk about associative obligations in Chapter 5, mostly expressing scepticism about them in the context of political communities. This, however, isn't to deny that citizens have obligations towards their polity and each other that go beyond obeying the law. All I will be suggesting is that those further obligations are not best understood as being of an associative kind.

obligation no different from the obligation to obey the law and informal norms of the country where I normally reside or of which I am a citizen.

To be sure, I do not think that my obligations with respect to the Australian polity extend as far as my obligations to "my own" society. For example, as a citizen, I have greater responsibility for the justice of the society of which I am a member. I may have duties to engage in political activity, I may have more stringent obligations to assist the poor in my own society than abroad, and so forth. But the moral grip that socially constructed norms have on me seems independent of my political membership.

Second, I grant that one may have *additional reasons*, beyond agency respect, to act as the norms of one's own community prescribe. This is so *when and because* one is committed to the oughts making up the norms of that community. Under appropriate conditions, commitments may well generate reasons for those who make them (Chang 2013a). Moreover, if one strongly identifies with and values certain norms, acting as they require may carry expressive significance (on valuing, see Scheffler 2011). In the same way in which, say, members of Oxbridge colleges engage in a number of rituals to express their commitment to, and identification with, college life, so too members of political communities might follow the formal and informal norms of their polities to express their commitment to a political project they find valuable and with which they identify (see Stilz 2016).

But although commitments to certain oughts and identification with the associated practices may generate additional reasons to act on their demands, it is not clear that they give rise to any additional *moral obligation* to obey socially constructed norms (cf. Southwood 2011: 787–9). Affirming the norms' demands "from within" may be valuable for an agent, but it is not morally obligatory. This parallels the way in which appreciation of the arts is valuable, but not obligatory. The moral grip socially constructed norms have on us—whether at home or abroad—can be accounted for by the agency-respect principle. In fact, that principle allows us to explain why even a non-committed member of a community, who is not particularly invested in its norms, nonetheless has an obligation to obey them.

An objector might point out that there must be reasons—what I called *internal* reasons—why the members of a given community commit to particular requirements.[29] For example, they implement a given set of traffic rules because they find those rules efficient and effective; they adopt a specific political decision-making system because, in their view, "it delivers the best results overall", and so forth. While the grounds of visitors' obligations to obey those norms need not refer back to those reasons, any plausible account of members' own norm-generated obligations should. The agency-respect view, it might be thought, is problematic because it does not satisfy this desideratum.

---

[29] I thank Samuel Scheffler for pressing me on this.

This objection conflates the grounds of the moral normativity of socially constructed norms—which explain why the fact that a given norm requires one to φ generates an obligation to φ—and the considerations justifying norms-supporters' commitments. The moral normativity of socially constructed norms cannot rest on the substantive virtues of the actions they prescribe. A focus on those virtues leads us to what, in Chapter 2, I called the deflationary view. But a commitment to treating the demands of socially constructed norms as standards of behaviour often rests precisely on the substantive merits of those demands. Take, again, traffic norms established on grounds of safety and efficiency. Safety and efficiency are reasons for adopting traffic norms, but they cannot ground the moral normativity of those norms. Once again, when a socially constructed norm has moral normativity, it is true to say that one ought to φ *because* the norm prescribes that one should φ, not in light of the virtues of the prescription's content (e.g., "φ-ing is safe").[30] This is why the grounds for accepting (committing to) the demands of socially constructed norms and the grounds of the norms' moral normativity cannot be the same.

8.4 What about people whose commitments clash with the commitments underpinning existing norms?

We know that, in any given context, and all the more so in a multicultural world, there are bound to be minorities whose commitments are at odds with majority-supported socially constructed norms. What does agency respect recommend in relation to them? Consider this low-stakes scenario; the lessons drawn from it carry over to high-stakes ones.

Japanese Tourist: A Japanese tourist at a traditional German restaurant, in Germany, wishes to express his satisfaction with the meal and service. In Japan, there is a socially constructed norm that one ought *not* to tip, but instead verbally thank service providers. In Germany, there is a reasonably entrenched tipping norm. The Japanese tourist feels uncomfortable at the prospect of tipping someone.

Here, we are confronted with agency respect pulling in different directions: the tourist should tip (in line with the commitments of local norm-supporters); the restaurant should not expect a tip from him (in line with his own commitments). Most people's intuitions would probably suggest that, all things considered, the tourist should tip, and this would continue to be the case even if the tourist's

---

[30] Though, as discussed, the obligation to obey is *conditional* on socially constructed norms having morally acceptable content.

114 THE AGENCY-RESPECT VIEW

commitment to the no-tip norm were more central to his sense of self than locals' attachment to the tipping norm. Can the agency-respect view help us make sense of cases like this?

I think it can. Except in private and personal contexts, where others' commitments are well known to us, satisfying the demands of agency respect presents considerable epistemic obstacles. Other people's commitments are not public; they are not transparent to us. And it would be practically impossible—as well as undesirable—for us to get to know all of them, one person at a time. This is why, outside private and personal contexts, we tend to assume that one should simply obey local norms, as concisely expressed in the old saying "When in Rome, do as the Romans do". After all, more often than not, the content of those norms is easily accessible to us—by definition, such norms are public—and tracks the commitments of those with whom we interact. Provided local norms are morally permissible, underpinned by genuine commitments, and obeying them is not too costly, obeying them "by default" is a perfectly reasonable—in fact, a justified—rule of conduct in light of agency respect combined with efficiency and publicity concerns (cf. Scanlon 1998: 339).[31]

This explains the underlying intuition in *Japanese Tourist*—i.e., that the customer ought to obey local norms and tip—while at the same time allowing us to acknowledge that asking the tourist to obey local rules involves a mild, though inevitable, agency-harm. This acknowledgement is important. Consider higher-stakes cases, such as those involving refugees being accepted into a new country and culture. In such cases, we typically regard it as morally appropriate that, within the limits imposed by moral permissibility, refugees be asked to integrate and obey local norms. Yet it is crucial to acknowledge that this rule is one the justification of which also depends on considerations of publicity, coordination, and practicality. While the demands of agency respect per se certainly push in the direction of refugee integration, they also push in the direction of accommodating the valued practices of refugees. When refugees make considerable sacrifices in terms of integration and adaptation, we should recognize that their agency is burdened. And if the burdens in question are too great, demands for integration cannot be defended on agency-respect grounds, but must appeal to other values, such as social stability. Furthermore, if there exist reasonable strategies for minimizing the agency burdens faced by refugees, they should be pursued.

The examples offered up to this point involve "outsiders" (refugees, tourists) entering a particular community. This, it might be thought, makes matters easier, insofar as we already intuitively expect newcomers to conform with established local customs. Moreover, so long as "outsiders" only temporarily visit or reside in a new society, whatever burdens conformity with local norms places on them

---

[31] See also G. A. Cohen's (2003) notion of a "rule of regulation".

won't have to be endured for too long. But in contemporary, pluralistic societies, it is often the case that members themselves reasonably disagree about the norms governing their communities. What such reasonable disagreement implies for minorities who dissent with majority-endorsed *formal legal norms* will be discussed in Chapters 5 and 6. Here, I limit myself to saying a few words about majority-minority dynamics when *informal norms* are concerned.[32]

For example, in Europe there are dominant norms of etiquette and self-presentation in public, professional contexts: people are supposed to be bare-headed and clean-shaven; they are supposed to greet through handshakes, etc. Some such norms, however, are at odds with the religious commitments of citizens belonging to minority groups. What is more, for members of religious minorities, adhering to these norms often involves violating demands that are quite central to their sense of self and integrity, while deviating from them doesn't have the same significance for secular citizens. What would the agency-respect view say in cases of this sort? I'll answer by focusing on the handshake norm. First, to the extent that it is possible to accommodate the commitments of minority citizens through exemptions, without thereby undermining the valued practices of the majority, this should clearly be done. If one's religion forbids certain types of bodily contact, it would be wrong to insist on handshakes with members of that religion. This exemption, however, would in no significant way undermine the relevant practice among members of the majority, nor would make civilized greetings in general impossible: minority members could still greet through other bodily gestures.

Second, in cases where such "targeted" exemptions are not feasible, we will have to consider (i) the independent merits of the majority norm in question— namely what values, if any, it serves, (ii) the centrality of the norm to the agency of the majority, and (iii) the burden placed by the majority norm on the agency of the minority, given their commitments. For example, suppose that, for whatever reason, exemptions from handshaking were not feasible. The values served by the handshake norm are civility and mutual recognition. The norm, though, is not particularly central—at least so far as I can tell—to the self-understanding of members of the majority. What does matter to them is the existence of a shared norm for mutual greeting. Ex hypothesi, the handshake norm places significant agency-burdens on members of the religious minority. In a case of this sort, the agency-respect view would speak in favour of modifying the relevant norm, finding an alternative way of greeting in professional contexts which does not involve bodily contact. Such an alternative norm would come at very little cost to the majority (if any), and no longer burden the minority.

---

[32] I am grateful to Cécile Laborde for pressing me on this. For the distinction between formal and informal norms, see Chapter 1.

116 THE AGENCY-RESPECT VIEW

This is admittedly an easy case. Trickier cases involve, for example, norms concerning identifiability in public, such as a norm banning a full-face veil. Such a norm arguably serves an important public interest in safety and recognizability.[33] Yet, violating that norm—on the assumption that the competing norm requiring a full-face veil is genuinely endorsed by the religious women to whom it applies—constitutes a significant agency-harm for those adhering to it. Furthermore, there does not appear to exist an alternative norm capable of serving the underlying values without imposing agency burdens on women belonging to the relevant minority religion. This is a hard case, and I will return to it in Chapter 5. To briefly anticipate, my sense is that expecting minority religious citizens to conform to the relevant norm may be all-things-considered justified, given the importance of the values independently served by the norm. At the same time, in light of the agency burdens it places on them, the norm lacks moral normativity vis-à-vis minority citizens on *agency-respect grounds*. Muslim women committed to wearing a full-face veil have no agency-respect-based reasons for refraining from doing so in public spaces. They may, however, have other reasons to forego the veil in public: for example, the morally mandatory contribution each citizen must make to ensuring safety and transparency in public spaces.

In sum, whether permissible dominant norms place moral demands on dissenting minorities on agency-respect grounds depends on the burdens such norms impose on the agency of said minorities. When those burdens are trivial— i.e., the norms are not at odds with commitments central to a minority's sense of self and life plans—then the norms are still binding on agency-respect grounds. When those burdens are significant, the relevant norms do not trigger moral demands based on agency respect. Of course, if those norms independently further some important public values, they may still place demands for compliance on minority members. But those demands will directly stem from the merits of the actions prescribed (or prohibited) by the norms, not from the fact that those actions are norm-prescribed.

8.5 Counterexamples?

An objector might suggest that my view is susceptible to counterexamples. Here is one.[34] Imagine two friends visiting a country where there exists the following socially constructed norm: one ought not to drink alcohol, whether in public or in private. Assume, further, that the two friends know fully well that neither of them is committed to the relevant prohibition, and find themselves in a private hotel room with a bottle of wine. Do they have any agency-respect obligation not

---

[33] The European debate on the matter in the early 2000s referred to a variety of different considerations, including, but not limited to, public safety. For an overview, see Grillo and Shah (2012).

[34] Thanks to Richard Fallon for proposing it. Gabriel Wollner independently suggested a similar example to me.

to drink? Most readers, the objector would continue, would say: "They do not". Yet it is not clear what my view implies for a case like this.

I agree that my view does not deliver a straightforward verdict in this case, but this need not count against it. The agency-respect view is meant to offer a framework for analysing complex cases, not a recipe for answering all difficult questions. That said, the view has the resources to vindicate a negative answer to the question posed. There are two avenues for doing so. The first consists in adopting a particular substantive account of what is morally permissible, and concluding that the socially constructed norm under discussion is inconsistent with it. On this account, prohibitions on what an individual should do in private—provided that the actions in question are not harmful to others—are morally impermissible because problematically intrusive.

A second line of argument could instead focus on the relevant context of analysis. Throughout, I have spoken about socially constructed norms that "exist in a given context". I have then treated the context as exogenously given: I assumed various contexts and drew conclusions about them. I have said nothing about what the right context of analysis for each given question is. Now, one possibility may be that, when it comes to our two friends, the relevant context of analysis is precisely "the two of them in a private hotel room". Since, in *that* context, no socially constructed norm against drinking exists, there is no agency-respect obligation not to drink.

What I have said in relation to the example just described also applies to structurally similar cases. One's views about what agency respect demands depend on (i) what is morally permissible and (ii) what the relevant context of analysis is. Here, I have not offered a substantive account of either (i) or (ii), and different ways of filling these parameters will satisfy different objectors. As I announced in the book's Introduction, the agency-respect framework is meant to be modular.

8.6 Status quo bias?

Finally, an objector might be concerned that my view is inherently conservative, since it vindicates moral obligations to obey existing norms. This problematically implies that informal-norm change will always involve wrongdoing. Why? Because informal norms lack established procedures for changing them and can most readily be changed by consistently breaking them. But if consistently breaking them is wrong, then there is no "morally clean way" of changing informal socially constructed norms.

This is not quite right, though my view is admittedly not too far from supporting this conclusion. Breaching socially constructed norms is wrong to the extent that agency respect gives them moral normativity, but *only provided* that those norms (hence the commitments generating them) are morally permissible. This means that the conservative pull of my view can be felt only when norms are permissible. And once this qualification is appreciated, it is no longer mysterious, or problematic, why we might have pro tanto obligations to obey them, provided doing so isn't too costly to us.

This does not rule out the possibility of justified informal-norm change. A socially constructed norm may be morally permissible, not particularly burdensome, but quite inefficient, and some might reasonably wish to change it for this reason. Friends have told me, for instance, that in Japan one is not supposed to eat while walking on the street. There is a socially constructed norm that forbids it. I would not find it unreasonable for someone to think that this norm is worth changing: people are busy, and it's often quite convenient to eat a sandwich on the go. To change the norm, though, many would have to start breaking it, by eating on the street. On my view, doing so would be wrong (even if mildly so), and would require the "norm-entrepreneurs" in question to both apologize to the wider community and justify their actions.[35] For instance, they could create a website explaining their motives. Still, I am happy to bite the bullet (in fact, I am not even sure it is a bullet) and conclude that breaching morally admissible and not-too-burdensome socially constructed norms is always wrong (remember, by this I mean pro tanto wrong), even when the breach is done with a view to justifiably changing the norms in question.

9. Conclusion

In this chapter, I have developed my answer to the "moral normativity" question: the agency-respect view. The view offers a normative-individualist defence of the moral normativity of socially constructed norms: it rests on the importance of respect for persons qua autonomous, self-constituting, commitment-making agents. It relies on the familiar thought that respecting individuals requires respecting their commitments—provided those commitments are authentic, morally permissible, and respecting them isn't too costly to us.

If I am correct, the agency-respect view can be used to derive and explain a number of important moral phenomena: in fact, as many as there are socially constructed norms underpinned by authentic and morally permissible commitments. Surveying all of the phenomena in question would obviously go well beyond what is feasible within a single book. In Part 2 of the book, therefore, I limit myself to considering how the agency-respect view can help us answer three important questions, which have been at the heart of lively debates in moral, legal, and political philosophy. Showing that the view enables some progress in these different areas will hopefully provide further support for it.

---

[35] The term "norm entrepreneur" was coined by Cass R. Sunstein (1996).

Morality and Socially Constructed Norms. Laura Valentini, Oxford University Press. © Laura Valentini 2023.
DOI: 10.1093/9780191938115.003.0004

4

Grounding Moral Rights

This chapter is devoted to examining the grounds of moral rights. By "the grounds of moral rights", I mean those facts or preconditions by virtue of which moral rights exist. In particular, I am interested in asking whether moral rights can exist independently of socially constructed norms (i.e., whether they can be natural), or whether all moral rights include such norms among their existence conditions.

This question has been the object of much debate in the history of modern moral and political philosophy, with figures like Grotius, Locke, Hume, and Bentham among its protagonists (for an overview, see Tuck 1979). Locke, for example, defended natural rights, while Bentham famously thought they were "nonsense upon stilts". The debate is still very much ongoing, attracting renewed interest in recent years thanks to the rise of human rights discourse. Just like their historical counterparts, some contemporary theorists find the existence of pre-institutional rights an almost obvious moral truth (e.g., Kamm 2007: 271; Nagel 1995; Quinn 1989), while others find conventionalism about rights the only plausible position to take (e.g., Darby 2009; Nieswandt 2016; Sumner 1987).

In this chapter, I bring the framework developed in Part 1 of this book to bear on this long-standing debate and, in so doing, I apply it to a class of socially constructed norms to which I have devoted relatively little attention so far: power-conferring ones. The chapter proceeds as follows. In Section 1, I distinguish between two understandings of the notion of a right: "rights as inviolability" and "rights as control". After briefly explaining why I accept that rights as inviolability exist independently of socially constructed norms, I turn to rights as control. In Section 2, I characterize rights as control as involving two familiar normative powers: the power to demand the performance of others' actions and the power to waive obligations to perform them. I then show, in Section 3, that possession of these powers is dependent on the existence of socially constructed norms. This is because, for anyone to be able to possess the power of demand or waiver, there must be "something"—a communicative act—that *publicly counts* as the exercise of that power in the relevant context. Power-conferring socially constructed norms are indispensable to determine what that "something" is. In Sections 4, 5, and 6, I consider some objections to, and implications of, the view that rights as control are parasitic on power-conferring norms. In Section 7, I explore the relationship between de facto powers of demand and waiver, namely those conferred upon us by socially constructed norms, and corresponding moral powers. I outline two mechanisms through which de facto powers acquire moral significance.

120 GROUNDING MORAL RIGHTS

First, de facto powers become moral powers when their creation is independently morally mandated. Second, in line with the view advanced in Chapter 3, I argue that, so long as socially constructed norms confer powers on us that are morally permissible (even if not morally mandated), those powers acquire moral significance on agency-respect grounds. In Section 8, I discuss the implications of my account of the grounds of rights—both rights as inviolability and rights as control—for the associated notion of wronging another person. Section 9 concludes.

Overall, by distinguishing between rights as inviolability and rights as control, the view advanced in the chapter shows that both advocates and critics of natural rights have a point. Ultimately, whether moral rights can be natural or not depends on what particular understanding of moral rights we have in mind.

1. Two Types of Rights: Rights as Inviolability and Rights as Control

The notion of rights is widely discussed in moral, legal, and political philosophy. Many scholars in these fields have attempted to offer a unified, compelling account of this notion: one that both vindicates the intuitive importance of rights as a moral category and accords with our ordinary-language rights talk. The debate is still alive, though perhaps not so well, since scepticism is mounting about whether this conceptual enterprise can ultimately be successful (see, e.g., Van Duffel 2012; Hayward 2013). My aim, here, is not to engage in conceptual disputes about the nature of rights. I therefore set aside the question of what exactly we should call "a right". Instead, I start by distinguishing between two understandings of the notion of a right, which are prominent in the literature and each of which aligns with some aspects of ordinary-language talk of rights. I call these understandings "rights as inviolability" and "rights as control", and characterize them as follows. (Readers will notice similarities between these notions and the concept of a right as understood, respectively, by the so-called "interest" and "will" theories. I explain why I do not directly refer to those theories in this footnote.[1])

---

[1] Rights as inviolability are closely associated with the interest theory, according to which rights exist whenever the interests of creatures with ultimate moral status are weighty enough to ground duties in others (see, famously, Raz 1986: Ch. 7). Rights as control instead echo the will theory, according to which rights give their holders the power to claim and waive others' duties (see, e.g., Hart 1955). Relevant to rights as control is also the so-called demand theory of rights, see Feinberg (1970), Skorupski (2010: 12.6), and Gilbert (2018). Incidentally, the fact that no fully satisfactory way out of the impasse between these competing views has been found to date, despite several attempts (e.g., Sreenivasan 2005; Wenar 2013), seems to give us preliminary support for the view that rights in these two senses are conceptually separate, with no satisfactory "compromise concept" available (see, e.g., Van Duffel 2012; Hayward 2013). In the main text, I avoid the labels "will" and "interest" theory for three reasons. First, given how fraught the debate on the concept of rights is, and given the existence of several versions of will and interest theories, referring directly to those theories is likely to generate

Rights as inviolability:
- designate creatures' status as fundamental units of moral concern;
- imply that others are under certain duties towards these creatures, typically aimed at protecting their interests.

Rights as control:
- designate special normative powers that give one normative control over a range of others' actions;
- these are the powers to demand the performance of given actions, thereby making them obligatory, and to waive obligations to perform such actions.

Consider, for example, someone's (e.g., Bob's) right to physical integrity. From an inviolability perspective, Bob's having this right is a marker of his status as an ultimate unit of moral concern and implies that others have duties not to physically interfere with him in certain ways. From a control perspective, Bob's right to physical integrity consists in Bob's "sovereignty" over the ways in which others physically interact with him. For example, Bob may waive another person's duty not to physically interfere with him by agreeing to having his hair cut. In doing so, he makes it permissible for his chosen barber—Nic—to touch his hair. Now suppose that, as Nic picks up a hair clipper, with the intention of shaving some of the hair at the back of Bob's head, Bob says: "Stop! Not with the hair clipper. Please, do it the traditional way, with scissors". By saying so, Bob places Nic under an obligation to use scissors instead of a hair clipper; that is, he has (politely) exercised his demand-power.

As the example of physical integrity shows, rights as inviolability and rights as control can be, and often are, coinstantiated in practice. Conceptually, however, they are separate, and there are concrete cases in which they come apart. For instance, suppose you encounter a stranger in need—an elderly lady carrying some heavy shopping who is struggling to cross the street—and you are uniquely positioned to help her. Assisting her would come at little cost to you, so you ought to offer assistance. Your duty is grounded in the elderly lady's status as an ultimate unit of moral concern with an interest in being helped. In that sense, she has a right to your assistance. Yet, she seems to lack the power to demand that you assist her. Suppose she were to start issuing commands such as "Give me some help!", "Take my shopping bag!", and "Let me hold on to your arm!". It would seem appropriate for you to wonder "Who does this lady think she is?". Instead of obligating you to help in the way she seeks to prescribe, her demands would seem

---

confusion. Second, those theories are typically treated as competitors, rather than as parallel understandings of rights, such that referring to them directly would probably generate in readers the expectation that I should take sides. Third, and finally, I find the labels "inviolability" and "control" more informative: they better convey the phenomena I am interested in. I am grateful to Pablo Gilabert for inviting me to clarify this.

122 GROUNDING MORAL RIGHTS

to give you reason not to offer assistance in the first place. By issuing those demands, the lady is "acting entitled". While you ought to offer help—hence she possesses a "right as inviolability" to your help—she has no "right as control" to it.[2]

This is just one instance of a more general phenomenon, whereby one is under an obligation to do (or not do) something for other people, on account of these people's status as ultimate units of moral concern, without these people having a right—in the control sense—to the performance of those obligations. To see this, consider the rights of non-human animals. While non-human animals (arguably) enjoy moral protections on account of their ultimate moral status, hence they possess rights as inviolability, they lack the powers to issue obligation-generating demands and to waive existing obligations. They therefore lack rights as control.

Alternatively, take the case of children's rights. Consider, for instance, a child's right to bodily integrity. This right is clearly grounded in the importance of bodily integrity for the child herself. The right-holder, from an inviolability perspective, is the child. But from a control perspective, those in a position to allow or forbid certain forms of interference with children are their parents or legal guardians. A child cannot consent to medical treatment; only a parent or guardian can do so on her behalf, and thereby turn what would otherwise be a violation of bodily integrity into a permissible medical intervention. For another example, a parent may demand that a nanny showers their child before taking him to bed, despite the child's protestations to the contrary. In a control sense, the parent possesses the power to waive the nanny's obligation of non-interference with the child and to demand the performance of particular actions from her. These examples hopefully show that the distinction I have drawn is a meaningful one. From now on, I shall take that distinction for granted.

Recall that the purpose of this chapter is to determine whether moral rights can exist in the absence of socially constructed norms, or whether their existence presupposes such norms. Since, I have argued, there are (at least) two concepts of rights, the question needs to be asked twice.

In the case of rights as inviolability, my answer is straightforwardly affirmative. I have no inclination to challenge the widely held view that our moral inviolability is independent of any socially constructed norms. Why? Because rights as inviolability are a sine qua non of any moral outlook that minimally accords with our considered judgements. Denying the existence of rights as inviolability is like denying the existence of fundamental constraints on action—i.e., duties—imposed upon us by virtue of the intrinsic worth of others. Such constraints have figured prominently in my argument up to now. The very pro tanto obligation to give others agency respect is a case in point. It is others' nature as creatures of a certain sort—commitment-making, with lives of their own to lead—that explains

---

[2] She does have the power to *refuse* your help. This, however, doesn't show that she possesses a right as control to your help, only that she possesses a right as control against interference.

why we ought to give them this kind of respect. Furthermore, rights as inviolability play a key part in determining what is and what is not morally permissible, hence what commitments call for agency respect in the first place. For instance, norms that support slavery or discrimination based on race and gender and norms the operation of which is likely to cause severe bodily harm are impermissible precisely because they are at odds with individuals' rights as inviolability. In light of this, questioning the social-norm-independent reality of this class of rights would be tantamount to questioning one of the moral presuppositions on which my argument is based. I see little reason to do so. This is not to say that grounding rights as inviolability is a philosophically trivial matter; far from it. However, it is not my task here. My focus, instead, will be on rights as control.

2. Rights as Control

Rights language is routinely associated with possession of particular *normative powers* in relation to others' actions: the powers to demand their performance and to waive obligations to perform them. But what, exactly, is a normative power? A normative power is the ability to alter others' or one's own normative situation by performing a communicative act.[3] Put informally, a normative power changes someone's normative situation through one's say so. Altering someone's normative situation means altering the permissions, prohibitions, powers, or immunities she has.[4] There are many familiar examples of exercises of normative powers. By *promising*, for instance, I alter my own and the promisee's normative situation: I place myself under a duty to abide by the promise and confer on the promisee the power to release me from my duty. Similarly, by *consenting* to intimate physical contact, I give the recipient permission to do something to me that he or she would otherwise be forbidden from doing. Or else, by *commanding* a soldier to move closer to the enemy, a general places the soldier under an obligation to proceed that the soldier would not otherwise have, and so forth (Watson 2009: 160).

---

[3] Compare Hohfeld's notion of a legal power (Hohfeld 1913: 44). Some characterize normative powers as the ability to alter others' or one's own normative situation *by communicating one's intention to do so* (Owens 2012: 4). This definition, however, doesn't quite correctly capture the idea, since it is possible to exercise a normative power without intending to—e.g., making "a binding contract without realizing that one did" (Raz 1975: 104). In Raz's view, what marks out normative powers, at a fundamental level, is the reason why they bring about normative changes: namely, that it is typically desirable for people to have the ability to change the normative situation in certain ways, if they wish to do so (Raz 1975: 102). This may lead normative powers to sometimes misfire, namely when they are being exercised without the powerholder realizing that they are doing just that.

[4] See Raz (1975: 3.2). To have an immunity, following Hohfeld (1913), is to not be susceptible to the exercise of normative powers. E.g., one may have an immunity against one's marriage being annulled arbitrarily: this means that it is impossible for the marriage to be so annulled (hence that nobody has the power to annul it arbitrarily). The notion of an immunity will not figure in my discussion.

124 GROUNDING MORAL RIGHTS

These are just some familiar examples of normative powers. There are, of course, many more, including the power to marry, to enter into contracts, to pronounce the defendant guilty, etc.

Rights as control, I have mentioned, involve two normative powers in particular: the power to *demand* the performance of particular actions and the power to *waive* obligations to perform those actions.[5] More precisely, I characterize them as follows.

The normative power to demand (or "demand-power"): the power to give someone a pro tanto obligation to perform a given action by one's say so.[6]

An exercise of the normative power to demand something results in the addressee's acquiring a pro tanto obligation to perform the action that is the object of one's demand. One's demanding—one's say so—is enough for the addressee to be bound to act in the required way, assuming there are no relevant countervailing considerations.

To see this, suppose we are having tea in my apartment. At one point, the conversation gets uncomfortable and I demand that you leave. In these circumstances, it seems that the fact that I demand that you leave gives you a pro tanto obligation to leave. If you were to ask me "why should I leave?", I could rightly answer "because I said so". Similarly, when my Head of Department (or line manager, more generally) says "please mark these essays", the very fact that he demands this of me, however politely, gives me a corresponding pro tanto obligation to act.

Of course, it may be that I had independent reason—or indeed an independent obligation—to mark those essays: say, I had promised students I would return the grades by a certain deadline. Be that as it may, if my Head of Department has the power to demand prompt marking of the essays from me, his issuing a demand places me under an overridable obligation to do so.[7] The obligation is overridable (i.e., pro tanto) because there may be important, competing considerations that outweigh it. If, while I am in your apartment, you show signs of mental instability and the potential of harming yourself, your demand—however legitimate—does

---

[5] For the importance of the power to demand in connection with rights, see Feinberg (1970), Gilbert (2018), and Skorupski (2010: 12.6). For the importance of the power to waive, see Hart (1955) and proponents of the will theory more generally, e.g., Steiner (2013).

[6] Cf. the analysis offered in Gilbert (2018: 60), who argues that "a demand implies that its addressee should comply irrespective of what pleases him".

[7] As Margaret Gilbert (2018: 2.2) points out, demands have something in common with requests, but should not be conflated with them. Requests do not give an agent a pro tanto obligation to act: when you issue a request to me, it's up to me to deliberate over whether to fulfil it. By contrast, demands are somewhat more peremptory. As Gilbert again suggests, echoing the Razian framework of exclusionary reasons, when I issue a demand your inclinations seem ruled out as relevant reasons for action: you should act "because I demanded", independently of your preferences. See also Raz (1975: 100).

not give me an all-things-considered duty to leave. Still, the duty is at least pro tanto: were it not the case that you are a danger to yourself, your say so would all-things-considered require me to leave. Furthermore, your say so generates a moral remainder, such that I at least owe you an explanation, if not an apology, for ignoring your request that I leave.

Before turning to the power of waiver, let me make one point of clarification.[8] The notion of "demanding" is ambiguous between (at least) two meanings. Demanding, as we have seen, may designate the exercise of a normative power by which one gives another pro tanto obligations through one's say so. However, "demanding" may also designate the act of "pressing" existing obligations on someone (Abizadeh 2018: 190). For example, suppose you owe me one hundred dollars, and I demand that you pay your debt. Demanding, in this sense, does not seem to designate a normative power to generate *new* obligations. Instead, the demand here "presses" an existing obligation upon someone. When I demand that you pay me, I insist on the payment, I verbally push you to pay and thereby confirm that I have not waived your duty to pay.[9]

It should be clear from my discussion that the demanding I have in mind is of the first kind: a source of obligations. While what we may call "demanding as pressing" is often something right-holders have the standing to do, it does not appear to be particularly distinctive of right-holders. It seems, for example, that a third party could also have the standing to demand payment of your debt in the pressing sense: she may put pressure on you with a view to getting you to discharge your obligation. While we may all sometimes be justified in speaking in a demanding tone, trying thereby to push others to act, it is the power to obligate and release from obligation through one's say so that is distinctive of right-holders (in the control sense).

Let me now examine the power of waiver in greater detail.

The normative power to waive others' duties (or "waiver-power"): the power to release others from duties—i.e., to give them permissions—through one's say so.

Waiver-powers are very familiar from day-to-day life. The much-discussed power of consent is itself a form of waiver-power. When I consent to something, I remove someone else's duty (i.e., I give them a permission). For instance, when I consent to intimate contact with someone, I waive their duty not to physically interfere with me in certain ways. When I consent to your coming to visit me at home this afternoon, I waive your duty not to get into my apartment. When I release you from the promise you made to me to meet me for lunch, I waive your promissory obligation to meet me for lunch. And so forth.

---

[8] I thank Arash Abizadeh for prompting me to clarify this point.
[9] Thanks to Matt Kramer and Hillel Steiner for discussion of this point.

126   GROUNDING MORAL RIGHTS

As it is easy to see, demanding and waiving are two sides of the same coin. Together, they give the power-holder normative control over someone else's action, by making that action either *pro tanto obligatory* or *permissible through one's say so*. Rights, in the control sense, then, give their holders a special kind of authority over duty-bearers. To echo H. L. A. Hart (1982: 183), the individual is a "small-scale sovereign" within his or her space of rights as control.

Having clarified what rights as control are, let me turn to our main question, namely whether the type of control they confer on their holders can exist in the absence of socially constructed norms. May an agent have normative control over the duties of another by nature alone, independently of complex social constructions? An affirmative answer to this question seems implicitly presupposed by much contemporary work on moral rights. The reasoning behind the answer—which I informally report here—goes as follows.

It seems obvious that morality requires us to be able to, for example, consent to or demand the performance of others' actions in certain circumstances. For instance, we should have the moral power to demand that others not interfere with us in a variety of ways. Equally, we should have the moral power to waive others' duties of non-interference, so as to enter into meaningful relationships with them (Shiffrin 2008; cf. Owens 2012). If we are prepared to accept that we have certain duties towards others just by virtue of their humanity, as presupposed by rights as inviolability, then we should be equally prepared to accept that we hold certain moral powers just by virtue of our humanity. Intuitively, *both* first-order permissions as well as prohibitions *and* the second-order powers to issue demands and waive duties are morally necessary. So, once we accept the former, we should also accept the latter.

While this line of reasoning appears attractive, I do not think it is correct. Positing natural rights in the control sense encounters more obstacles than positing natural rights in the inviolability sense does. I explain why in what follows.

3. Normative Powers, Publicity, and Socially Constructed Norms

Let us begin by focusing on the function of normative powers in general, and of the powers of demand and waiver specifically. By exercising these powers, we bring about changes in the ways in which we normatively relate to one another: in our duties and permissions. In so doing, we *modify the terms of our mutual accountability*.[10] We shape the circumstances in which it is appropriate for us to resent one another, blame one another, rebuke one another, feel remorse and

---

[10] If there are *purely* self-regarding normative powers, they are set aside for the purposes of the present discussion.

NORMATIVE POWERS, PUBLICITY, AND SOCIALLY CONSTRUCTED   127

guilt, and so forth. This is the core structural feature of normative powers (cf. Dougherty 2015,:245).[11]

For illustration, once I demand that you leave my apartment, I may resent and blame you if you fail to comply with my demand. Equally, it may be appropriate for you to apologize in case you overstay your welcome. By contrast, once I permit you to enter my apartment—thereby waiving your duty to stay out—I make it no longer appropriate for me to resent you for your presence there, nor should you feel guilty or embarrassed.

Appreciating the function of the powers of demand and waiver as shapers of our mutual accountability relations is key to determining whether we can possess them independently of socially constructed norms. This is because, for a normative power to perform the said function, its exercise must be *public*. In any given context, there must be something that publicly counts as the exercise of that power. Socially constructed norms, in turn, are necessary to determine what that "something" is. Let me elaborate on both the publicity requirement and the claim that socially constructed norms are indispensable to satisfying it.

The rationale behind publicity is well articulated by Stephen Darwall, who notes that "we cannot intelligibly hold someone accountable for complying with an inaccessible esoteric principle" (Darwall 2014: 98).[12] If right and wrong are entirely opaque, we cannot plausibly blame, criticize, or reproach one another for failing to comply with moral demands. This is why "[n]ormative powers can only be exercised second personally, through a reciprocally recognizing transaction with another person" (Darwall 2012: 345). For the transaction to be reciprocally recognizing, it is for it to be public: mutually accessible to the parties involved. This, in turn, presupposes a *shared standard* by which the parties can determine whether a given normative power has been exercised or not.

To see this, consider the following example. Jill asks Jack whether she can cross Jack's field. Jack reacts by vigorously waving his hand from left to right. What, exactly, is Jack doing there? Is he giving Jill permission to cross the field? Is he denying Jill permission to do so? Is he informing Jill of some danger? Is he greeting Jill? Suppose Jill sincerely interprets that signal as a permission, while in fact Jack intended to forbid Jill from crossing the field. How are we to determine whether a permission has in fact been granted (or not), in a way that would make it appropriate to hold Jill correspondingly accountable? For that, it seems, we need a public system of standards that specifies which communicative acts, performed by which agents and in what circumstances, constitute the exercise of which normative powers. If, according to those standards, waving one's hand

---

[11] Dougherty focuses on the accountability-shaping function of consent in particular. The present section extends that argument to normative powers more generally. (It is not clear whether Dougherty would agree with that extension.)

[12] My attention to Darwall's discussion of this matter was drawn by Dougherty's (2015: 245) work.

from left to right constitutes an act of giving permission, then Jill has done nothing wrong, independently of Jack's original intentions. If, however, it constitutes an act of refusal, then Jill has indeed done something wrong, and is the appropriate target of criticism and blame (or at least redress, in case she was excusably ignorant of the convention).

Morality alone cannot tell us what those standards are. Abstract morality does not come with instructions on how to differentiate an act of consenting from an act of demanding, an act of promising from one of marrying. It does not specify whether a nod of one's head, a handshake, or an utterance such as "yes" or "okay" count as instances of waiver. Nor can it help us ascertain whether expressions such as "I want that apple!" or "Go away!" qualify as demands. While morality may judge certain specifications of the relevant standards impermissible—e.g., because they make the exercise of normative powers too costly[13]—it cannot positively determine what those standards are. That, it seems to me, is a job that only socially constructed norms are fit to accomplish (see Searle 2006 for discussion). It is those norms that tell us, in any given context, which act corresponds to the exercise of which normative power.

This is my simple argument for the claim that the powers of demand and waiver presuppose socially constructed norms. As it stands, however, the argument is perhaps a little too simple, and thus open to a number of objections. I consider them in what follows. Doing so will also allow me to elaborate on several aspects of my argument, thereby corroborating the conclusion that rights as control presuppose socially constructed norms.

4. Linguistic Conventions, Speech Acts, and Normative Powers

I have stated that socially constructed norms are existence conditions of the normative powers of demand and waiver, hence of rights as control. An objector may challenge this claim by conceding that some form of social construction is required for the exercise of normative powers, but insisting that socially constructed *norms*, in particular, are not. She may instead believe that shared linguistic conventions suffice to bring those powers into existence. Once formulations such as "I consent" or "You may" or "I demand" are available, so are normative powers. The trouble for my view, the objector might continue, is that while linguistic conventions are socially constructed, they are not constituted by socially constructed *norms*. The rules of language, fixing grammar (syntax) and meaning

---

[13] For instance, if what publicly counts as consent, in the context of sexual relations, is the lack of resistance, the local norms that govern the exercise of this normative power are morally problematic, since they make refusing consent (i.e., via resistance) too costly for individuals. For discussion, see Bolinger (2019: 22–3).

(semantics) are not normative. At most, they set out what John Broome calls "property requirements" (Broome 2013: Ch. 7): requirements that must be met for a particular property to be satisfied—for instance, requirements that must be met for a sentence to be grammatical, where there is no "ought" requiring grammaticality in the first place.

This "property" sense of requirement is involved in claims such as "keeping physically fit requires determination" or "helping others requires generosity" or "being a good cook requires a lot of practice", and so forth. Determination, generosity, and practice are what it takes to realize the *properties* of physical fitness, helpfulness to others, and good cookery. Similarly, the rules of syntax and semantics take the form of property requirements. They tell us what it takes to construct a grammatical or meaningful sentence in a given language. Take the following sequence of words "I cuts bottle chair". Whatever this sequence is, it is not a grammatical sentence (in English), nor is it meaningful. It lacks the properties of grammaticality and meaningfulness. But it is not clear that, per se, grammar and meaning are sources of normative requirements. "I cuts bottle chair" does not violate any oughts; it just makes no sense (in English).

Of course, in our world, we do tend to superimpose a veneer of normativity on linguistic rules, by codifying language and reproaching each other for spelling and grammar mistakes. But, it could be argued, this is simply because there is a further, socially constructed "ought", which says that one ought to speak grammatically. Language itself, namely what is needed for successful communication, does not appear to be governed by normative requirements.[14]

Our objector may then conclude that, since all we need for exercising normative powers is successful communication, and all we need for that is language, contrary to what I have argued, normative powers—hence rights from a control perspective—do not presuppose socially constructed *norms*.

I am happy to concede to the objector that syntax and semantics set out property requirements, rather than normative requirements. But does this concession threaten my view? I believe not. This depends on the kind of communication required for exercising normative powers in general, and the powers of demand and waiver specifically. For that kind of communication, the availability of linguistic expressions such as "I consent" or "I pronounce you husband and wife" or "Stop!" or "You may now leave the table" is not sufficient. This is because the normative powers of demand and waiver are exercised through *speech acts* (Austin 1962; Searle 1969).

The core idea behind the notion of a speech act is that in speaking—i.e., in uttering given words—one also performs different kinds of actions. Utterances can, in this sense, have a specific "force" (Austin 1962). For instance, through

---

[14] I thank Christian List for discussion of this objection, which he sees as in line with Chomsky's (1975) understanding of language and grammaticality.

130 GROUNDING MORAL RIGHTS

one's utterances, one might be warning, informing, joking, ordering, permitting, promising, marrying, rebuking, and so forth. Crucially, what particular actions one is "doing with words" is not only a function of the words and grammatical forms one uses (Asudeh 2019: 539). Instead, it is a function of "a wide array of explicit and implicit conventions governing context, tone, gesture, [and] etiquette" (Kukla 2014: 440–41). The exact same words and grammatical forms can *count as different actions*, depending on context and conventions.

Consider the following proposition—"Martha has a cold"—uttered by Martha's mother. In so saying, Martha's mother could be either *informing* Martha's GP of Martha's condition, or *warning* another child approaching Martha that he risks catching a cold from her. Or take the sentence "I pronounce you husband and wife". If uttered by a couple's friend, at a friends' reunion, it would count as an act of *joking*. But if uttered by a public official in the right settings, it would be act of *marrying*.[15] Grammar and syntax alone, then, do not suffice to determine which speech act one is performing. Other socially constructed materials are required.

Having established this, let us now zoom in on those speech acts that involve changes in normative situations—i.e., speech acts that create permissions, prohibitions, obligations, rights, etc.—namely speech acts that consist in the exercise of (de facto) normative powers. Call these "normative-power speech acts". Familiar examples include marrying, promising, consenting, pronouncing the defendant guilty, ordering, and so forth. Whether a particular utterance counts as a speech act of the relevant kind depends, in particular, on whether *applicable norms* confer that power on the individual making the utterance.

Simplifying considerably, the norms in question take the following form: "When agent X, in context C, does Y, normative change Z occurs". To see this, take the speech act of marrying. For the proposition "I pronounce you husband and wife" to count as an instance of marrying—hence for it to effect a change in the normative situation of the parties involved—it has to be uttered by a particular agent X (a public official), in a given context C (in front of witnesses). A private person cannot perform a marriage, nor can a public official without witnesses. And what it takes to successfully perform an act of marriage—what J. L. Austin (1962) would call a "felicitous" act of marriage—is set out by formal laws.

Similar considerations apply to "demand speech acts" and "waiver speech acts". Whether a given utterance counts as a speech act of demand or waiver depends on whether socially constructed norms—sometimes formal legal norms, other

---

[15] To use J. L. Austin's (1962: 108) famous terminology, "Martha has a cold" is the *locutionary act* (the uttering of a sentence with a conventional meaning), while informing or warning are *illocutionary acts* (specific actions one performs in speaking, which have a certain "force" by convention). Austin also includes a third category, namely *perlocutionary acts*, which designate the effects achieved by one's illocutions. For example, Martha's mother may convince the doctor to listen to Martha's breathing.

LINGUISTIC CONVENTIONS, SPEECH ACTS, AND NORMATIVE POWERS   131

times informal social norms—confer that power on the individuals making the utterance in the context at hand.

Once again simplifying matters, we can think of the exercise of demand-power as governed by a norm taking the following form: "When agent X, in context C, does Y, the addressee acquires a pro tanto *obligation* to φ (Z)". For instance, when the general (X), on the battlefield (C), tells the soldiers "fire" (Y), the soldiers acquire a pro tanto obligation to fire (Z).[16] Similarly, the exercise of waiver-power is governed by a rule taking the following form: "When agent X, in context C, does Y, the addressee acquires a *permission* to φ (Z)". For instance, when Jane (X), facing Mark on her doorstep (C), says to him "you may come in", Mark acquires a permission to enter Jane's apartment (Z).

It should be clear that the rules just stated, namely the rules conferring on individuals the standing to perform normative-power speech acts of demand and waiver, are socially constructed *norms* (Raz 1975: 106). Their formulation involves deontic operators, such as "ought" (obligation) and "may" (permission).

One might object that the rules conferring normative powers on us are, contrary to what I have argued, not normative. They too set out property requirements. Consider the following normative powers: consenting and promising. Roughly put, the rules governing consenting and promising state that: "When agent X, in context C, does Y, X *consents*" or "When agent X, in context C, does Y, X *promises*". These rules tell us what it takes for something to bear the property of "being a promise" or the property of "being an instance of consent".

I agree with the objector's reflections, but I do not think they threaten my main line of reasoning. This is because the properties "being a promise" and "being an instance of consent" are inherently normative in a way that the property "being grammatical" is not. To genuinely make a promise is to *bind oneself to another*; to consent is to *give another a permission*.[17]

While the objector is mistaken in suggesting that we are in the presence of mere property requirements, it is important to emphasize that the norms we are now dealing with are of a distinctive kind. Instead of being directive norms—namely

---

[16] Recall the standard formulation of a socially constructed norm introduced in Chapter 1: "Every A, in C, ought (not) to/may φ". We can easily rephrase the norm under analysis in the main text using this canonical form: "Every soldier, on the battlefield, ought to fire whenever the general says 'fire' ".

[17] To put the point in the language made famous by John Searle, deontic powers are created via status functions, and such functions are, at least superficially, not normative. A status function is a proposition of the form "X counts as Y in C"—e.g., "saying 'I do' counts as marrying if performed in the presence of a public official". However, as Searle himself admits, whenever we accept a status function we thereby also "accept a series of obligations, rights, responsibilities, duties, entitlements, authorizations, permissions, requirements and so on" (Searle 2006: 18). For example, the status function "X counts as promising in C" is, structurally, not a norm in my sense: it contains no deontic operators. However, since acts of promising are inherently normative, accepting this status function automatically involves acceptance of the rights and obligations that follow from acts of promising. That is, the status function can be restated as follows: "Whenever A says 'I promise to φ' to B, in context C, A thereby acquires an obligation to φ, owed to B". I thank Arash Abizadeh for inviting me to relate my discussion to Searle's views.

132 GROUNDING MORAL RIGHTS

norms mandating, prohibiting, or permitting particular types of conduct—they are what, in Chapter 1, following H. L. A. Hart, I called "power-conferring norms". They set out "recipes" that need to be followed in order to generate certain normative changes (Hart 1961: 32–3).

Formally speaking, power-conferring norms and directive ones have the same structure. Both types of norms can be stated using this formula: "If X, then normative consequence Y"—where normative consequences include permissions, prohibitions, duties, etc. To see this, take the following directive norm: "If you drive a car, you ought not to exceed a speed limit of 120 km/h". Now consider the following power-conferring norms: "If you are having a haircut, and you tell your hairdresser not to use any hair gel, they ought not to use hair gel" or "If someone asks you 'may I borrow your laptop', and you answer 'yes', they acquire a permission to take the laptop". As anticipated, both types of norms exhibit a "If X, then normative consequence Y" structure.

Although *structurally* parallel, directive and power-conferring norms are *functionally* different. The former directly regulate our conduct, they tell us what we may and may not do. The latter enable us to change the normative situation by generating permissions, duties, prohibitions (etc.) through our say so.[18]

To see more concretely how such power-conferring norms operate, it may be helpful to look at a few examples. The first set focuses on waiver-powers, the second on demand-powers.

1. I ask my friend, whom I am visiting, whether I can use the landline. A plumber, who is there trying to unclog the toilet, says: "Yes, of course".
2. I ask my friend, whom I am visiting, whether I can use the landline. She says: "Yes, of course".
3. A couple of adults are sitting at a restaurant table, and one of them tells the other: "You may now use the washrooms".
4. A group of children is having lunch in the school cafeteria. One of the teachers tells a child: "You may now use the washrooms".

All four cases feature linguistic formulations that typically imply waiver (i.e., giving permission). Yet, only 2 and 4 involve waiver proper: speech acts of *giving permission*. Utterance 1, despite having all the superficial semantic features of waiver, does not count as an instance of waiver in the context in which it is uttered, because the person who utters it—the plumber—lacks the power to give permission. Existing norms do not confer that power on him, since he is not the owner of the apartment where the landline is located. In all likelihood, upon hearing "Yes, of course" I'd assume the plumber is talking to someone else or to himself. I would not register his utterance as an instance of giving permission.

---

[18] Compare Searle's (1969) distinction between regulative and constitutive rules.

LINGUISTIC CONVENTIONS, SPEECH ACTS, AND NORMATIVE POWERS   133

By contrast, my friend—i.e., the owner of the apartment—does have waiver-power. Socially constructed norms confer that power on her such that, in that context, his "Yes, of course" qualifies as an exercise of that power.

Utterance 3 involves *informing* the other person that the washrooms are no longer busy. It is not an instance of giving permission because, according to background social norms, an adult lacks the authority to determine when another adult is permitted to use the facilities. Things are different in the school context, where the teacher clearly does have that authority, and, by making that utterance (in 4), she thereby releases the children from the obligation to stay at the table. In so saying, she *gives permission* to the pupils.

Similar considerations about norms and context-dependence apply to the power to demand. Consider the following examples.

1. A four-year-old child says, in a grumpy tone: "Mommy, give me the lollypop!".
2. A boss tells his employee: "I want that report by tomorrow at noon".
3. Someone you don't know, on the street, yells: "Stop! Stop!" at you.
4. A policeman on the street yells: "Stop! Stop!" at you.

Utterances 1, 3, and 4 take the typical grammatical form of demands: they are imperatives. Utterance 2, by contrast, takes the typical form of expressing a desire: "I want". Moreover, utterances 3 and 4 are linguistically identical, they are just uttered by different people, in the same situation. If the speech-act status of an utterance—e.g., as a demand or something else—depended on linguistic formulation only, we should expect 1, 3, and 4 to qualify as demands, and 2 to qualify as the expression of a desire. Yet, intuitively, 2 and 4 count as demands, while 1 expresses a desire and 3 a warning. How do we explain this? With the simple observation, made earlier, that whether an utterance counts as a demand or not does not merely depend on its grammatical form (an imperative), but on whether socially constructed norms confer on the person making the utterance the normative power to make demands in the context at hand.

The utterance in 1 is not a demand, though possibly an attempted one, because the norms that typically govern parent-child relations do not confer on a four-year-old child the standing to give her mother pro tanto obligations with her say so. The four-year-old expresses a strong desire in a demanding tone.[19] She might as well have said: "Mommy, mommy, I want the lollypop!" or "Lollypop, Lollypop!".

It may be objected that the four-year-old does indeed issue a demand, but not a valid one. I find this way of putting things unhelpful. As a matter of social fact, the four-year-old lacks the power to make demands. Socially constructed norms do not confer on her the power to place others under pro tanto obligations

---

[19] As Margaret Gilbert (2018: 242) explains, making a demand is not the same as "speaking in a demanding manner".

134 GROUNDING MORAL RIGHTS

through her say so. Given this, it seems odd to suggest that she has, in fact, issued a demand. We cannot do what we lack the power to do. Perhaps she *intended* to issue a demand. But intending to do something is not the same as doing it. Furthermore, it is opaque what the little girl's intention was: she clearly wanted the lollypop, but it is guesswork whether by saying what she said she intended to place her mother under an obligation.

We could, of course, distinguish between the power to issue demands and the power to issue felicitous demands (i.e., demands that give rise to pro tanto obligations), and say that the four-year-old possesses the former but not the latter. The problem with this suggestion is that it presupposes a much weaker sense of demand than that at issue here. If we were to adopt this terminology, the power to issue demands would become the power to use particular grammatical forms (imperatives) or expressions ("I demand that"). But this would not be a normative power. It would, at most, be a linguistic power. So, it would still remain true that the four-year-old lacks the power to issue demands in the sense under scrutiny here.

The utterance in 2 takes the semantic form of a desire expression, but in the context of a boss-employee relation, it counts as a demand. The boss is telling the employee: "You ought to deliver the report by tomorrow at noon, and my saying so places you under a duty to do it". The employee will see himself as being under a professional obligation to comply. The utterance in 3, in turn, is a warning. Given existing socially constructed norms, strangers typically lack the authority to make demands on us. Even if, for whatever reason, the stranger intended to make a demand, in the context, it will likely count as a warning. By contrast, when the policeman, as in 4, utters the same words in the same form, we do seem quite uncontroversially in the presence of a demand: the utterance counts as an exercise of a normative power on the part of the police, which has the authority to give one a duty to stop because of its saying so.

With demands too, then, a particular linguistic form, taken in isolation, is not enough. The possession of normative powers rests on whether existing norms— and not merely linguistic rules of grammar and semantics—confer those powers on individuals, in the particular context at hand. Of course, determining whether they do is a complex, at times very subtle, matter, especially when the norms in question are not formally codified. But the epistemic difficulties involved in determining whether something does indeed count as a demand or as an instance of waiver do not undermine the conclusion that socially constructed norms are key to the existence of the powers of demand and waiver.

5. Intentions and Normative Powers

This conclusion might be challenged by drawing on an argument often made in the literature on consent. Since, as we have seen, consent is a familiar vehicle for expressing one's waiver-power, that literature is perspicuous for our purposes.

The argument I have in mind holds that a purely mental act—such as an intention to remove a prohibition—is *sufficient* for an individual to bring about a change in someone else's normative situation, namely to give them permissions they would not otherwise have (see, e.g., Alexander 1996; Hurd 1996). The communication of that intention, by contrast, has purely epistemic status: it does not affect whether a permission has in fact been granted. Central to this view is the importance of consent for the autonomy of the individual, coupled with the thought that an act of will must be sufficient for consent, if its purpose is precisely to serve autonomy (Renzo 2022).

The obvious objection to a mental-act account of the normative power of consent is that we cannot hold people accountable for not responding adequately to alleged changes in normative situations which they cannot detect. And, if all that is needed for consent is a mental act, then one would be able to give others permissions, thereby changing their normative situation, without others ever knowing this. But recall here Darwall's observation: how can we hold each other accountable relative to standards that we cannot access?

Larry Alexander responds that this worry stems from a conflation between *wrongdoing* and *culpability*. While consent as a pure mental act can affect the status of an action as right or wrong, whether someone is culpable is a different matter. He offers the following scenario in support of this claim:

> D asks V to borrow V's car, V says 'Sure,' and is quite happy to lend D her car. D thinks the 'Sure' was sarcastic and was meant, not to signify consent, but to signify non-consent. Nonetheless, when V's back is turned, D takes V's car keys and drives away in V's car. Now D is surely culpable. He took V's car believing he lacked her permission to do so. But although he is as culpable as a thief—even a joyrider is a thief, though of a lesser sort than one who intends to deprive the owner of the car permanently—he did not in fact commit theft and thereby act wrongly. He had V's consent to borrow her car. (Alexander 2014: 105)

Alexander is certainly right about culpability here, but it is not clear that his example offers much support for the view that consent—hence the normative power of waiver—is best understood as a mental act. First, note that in this case consent is indeed communicated, and in a way that conventionally signifies consent. It is thus no surprise that, intuitively, we think consent has occurred. The plausibility of the mental-act view of consent is better tested assuming scenarios in which no communication actually takes place.

Second, it is not clear what is gained by divorcing culpability and wrongdoing in the way that the mental-act view suggests. The mental-act view, in essence, allows for the possibility that we could alter one another's obligations and permissions in ways that make it *inappropriate* for us to hold each other accountable relative to those altered obligations and permissions. We could change the status of actions as right or wrong, but not hold one another accountable in relation to

136   GROUNDING MORAL RIGHTS

that changed status, since that status was not accessible to us. This would severely undermine the mutual accountability function that is key to normative powers, including the power of consent (Dougherty 2015).[20] The world could be full of "bad people" who always do what is right (like D in Alexander's example) and of "good people" who always act wrongly. While not incoherent, this way of setting up our moral categories has the unfortunate potential result of making fitting moral reactive attitudes systematically divorced from rightful and wrongful conduct.

Finally, the mental-act view has been proposed in relation to consent but, interestingly, it does not have much traction when it comes to other normative powers, such as powers that generate obligations, including the power to demand.[21] It would seem strange (to put it mildly) to consider someone under an obligation to φ just because their boss intended them to be under such an obligation. After all, how could they know? Responding that, in fact, the employee acts wrongly by not φ-ing and yet she is not culpable appears rather far-fetched. What should the boss do, then? May the boss reproach the employee for not acting as she was obligated to do? And should the employee feel guilty? It seems not. But then what do we gain by saying that the employee was nonetheless under an obligation? This is the same problem we encountered in the case of consent, which appears all the more vivid in the case of the power to demand.

Much simpler and more natural, it seems to me, is the view that the employee is not under an obligation to comply in the first place. Similarly, the person who takes your possessions when you have mentally "agreed" to their doing so, but who has no evidence of this whatsoever, is indeed a thief and acts wrongly, in a way that disrespects you and your autonomy.

Overall, the suggestion that intentions alone can suffice for the exercise of normative powers does not convince. Those intentions need to be communicated through the conventions structured by socially constructed norms.

6. Demanding and Waiving Unintentionally

My account of the existence conditions of the normative powers to demand and waive has what might look like a somewhat unsettling implication. This is that normative powers may be exercised *without their holders intending to do so*. This possibility is opened up by the fact that, on my account, normative powers are exercised the moment one's actions, gestures, or utterances are picked out by

---

[20] Bolinger (2019) makes a similar argument, holding that the mental-act view of consent suffers from the problem of "normative opacity", and thus prevents consent from performing its coordinating function.

[21] For discussion in relation to the power to promise, see Dougherty (2015), from whose work I have learnt.

existing norms as exercises of the relevant normative powers. If the norms in question do not *also* include particular intentions among what is needed for a given normative power to be exercised, then that power can be exercised unintentionally.

For example, if I ask my husband "may I borrow your laptop charger?" and he absent-mindedly says "yes", without really paying attention to what I am asking, he thereby gives me permission to borrow his laptop charger, even if in fact he had no intention to lend it to me.[22] Alternatively, Kukla describes a situation in which a female manager keeps politely issuing what she intends to be demands to her employees but, due to prevalent gender norms and the fact that women are rarely in positions of power, her would-be demands count as requests—a different type of speech act, which does not generate obligations—in the context in which she utters them (Kukla 2014: 445–8).

As these examples illustrate, intention is not only insufficient for the exercise of the normative powers of demand and waiver, but it may also not be necessary. Perhaps unsettling at first, this seems to me to be exactly the right result and, in fact, something already acknowledged in discussions of normative powers (Bolinger 2019; Raz 1972: 453).[23] While it would be worrisome if exercises of normative powers *always* mis-matched their holders' intentions, the fact that occasionally they might do is an unavoidable byproduct of the imperfection of human relations. Sometimes we are distracted, sometimes we may be (blamefully or blamelessly) ignorant about existing conventions, sometimes we just misunderstand, and so forth. What matters is that, for the most part, what counts as the expression of a demand, or of an act of waiver, does track the intentions of those who engage in the relevant acts.

When this condition is systematically not satisfied, we need to question the appropriateness of the norms that determine what counts as an exercise of this or that power. Take the example offered earlier, of the female manager who issued requests, while intending to issue orders. The gender norms structuring communication conventions within her society disable her in a way that is morally objectionable. In that case, the mismatch between her intentions and what she achieves is indeed of concern.

But in other scenarios, such as the scenario involving my husband's being distracted while engaging in typical consent-giving behaviour, the mismatch between intentions and power exercised should not worry us. Questions will, of course, arise as to how responsibility should precisely be apportioned in cases involving blameless ignorance of power-exercising conventions or simple

---

[22] Of course, if applicable existing norms regard the presence of intention as necessary for consent, on my view intention will also be necessary. The point is that intention is not always needed as a matter of principle. For discussion of an opposite view, see Alexander (2014: 104).

[23] Although, like me, Dougherty (2015: 229) places emphasis on the mutual-accountability function of consent, he denies that consent can be given unintentionally.

138 GROUNDING MORAL RIGHTS

misunderstandings. But this is bound to be so in moral life anyway. The fact that moral powers can be exercised unintentionally, but through acts that typically count as communicating an intention—whether the intention is there or not—is no reason to abandon my account of the existence conditions of the powers of consent and waiver.

7. De Facto Powers, Moral Powers, and Socially Constructed Norms

Let us suppose that readers have been convinced by my analysis of the normative powers of demand and waiver. Still, they may think that all that I have said only applies to *de facto* normative powers, rather than to *moral* normative powers. Here is what an objector could say:

> Sure, whether one has the de facto authority to issue demands or waive others' duties depends on socially constructed norms conferring that authority or power on her. But whether one has the *moral* power to issue demands or waive others' duties (and so forth), depends on whether *moral norms* confer that power on her.

The objector is correct in pointing out the existence of a difference between de facto and moral normative powers, of course. There may be all sorts of norms that confer normative powers on individuals that are morally abhorrent. Think about the norms of slavery, which confer almost limitless interpersonal authority on the master, and deprive the slave of any authority. Or think of the norms governing strongly patriarchal societies, in which women lack the power to sign work contracts and husbands have to consent to employment on their behalf. Obviously, these de facto powers are not moral powers, because they are unjustified: contrary to the moral equality of persons.

The question, however, is whether we can possess moral powers—powers that morality would regard as either mandatory or justified—without possessing corresponding de facto powers. The objector believes that we can. He thinks that, say, the slave in a slave society possesses the moral powers of waiver and demand, even if socially constructed norms do not confer them upon him, and even if, were he to "say the right words", he would not *count* as demanding or consenting but as begging or expressing a preference (cf. Langton 1993: 305, 316). The objector will insist that the slave possesses these moral powers and acts on them, and that his contemporaries do wrong because they fail to *recognize* them.

Contrary to the objector's, my view says that a slave society is morally problematic because slaves *lack powers* they morally ought to have. Key moral concerns, such as respect for human equality and autonomy, make possession of those powers morally mandatory. What reasons do we have to favour my account over the objector's?

First, as I have argued, normative powers—including moral powers—can only meaningfully perform their function if their exercise is marked by a certain *publicity*. Socially constructed norms, in turn, are required for that publicity. While there is a lot that the master does wrong in relation to the slave, the fact that the master does not take the slave's imperatives as giving him pro tanto obligations to act does not seem to be one of them, if those imperatives do in fact count as instances of "begging"—rather than as demands—in the context in which they are uttered. (Compare the earlier example of a female manager whose intended demands functioned as requests.) Of course, the fact that the slave does not count as making demands is *itself* highly problematic, but if he cannot make demands proper, then we cannot hold others accountable for not appropriately responding to the "would-be" demands. What we *can* hold them accountable for is their sustaining of norms and practices that disempower slaves in this way.[24]

Second, and relatedly, my reading is also preferable to the objector's because it allows for a deeper critique of those practices we find objectionable. On my account, the problem with slavery is not merely that the master fails to respond to a power the slave possesses, but that socially constructed norms are set up in such a way that the slave *lacks that power* in the first place.

For an analogy, consider Rae Langton's (1993) influential elaboration of Catherine MacKinnon's claim that "pornography silences women". Women often refuse consent to sex—i.e., they say "no"—and yet their male partners go ahead

---

[24] But what about a situation in which the slave speaks using the imperative form, intends to place obligations on the master through his say so, and the master correctly interprets the slave's intention? Should we not then say that the slave, in this case, has placed pro tanto moral obligations on the master (even if, de facto, he has not)? And if this is so, does this not mean that the slave has moral demand-power vis-à-vis the master? Ultimately, I believe not. This is because possession of a power must be somewhat robust. I do not have the power to φ—moral or otherwise—if my exercising it rests on someone else's ability to guess my intentions. In that sense, it is not "up to me" whether the master is obligated: it depends on his ability to correctly decode what I mean. A plausible notion of a power (moral or otherwise) cannot depend on others' insight into one's mental states.

For another example, consider a society where the concept of marital rape does not exist because husbands, qua husbands, are entitled to sex with their wives whenever they want. Suppose that, in that society, three wives one evening say to their husbands—"You may engage in intimate contact with me"—and they say so with the intention of giving permission. The husband of wife number one thinks his wife is just stating the obvious, and *reminding* him of how things are. The second husband understands his wife's intentions, and thinks to himself "How peculiar, she believes she has the power to give me permission, when of course she doesn't". It would be odd to say that wife number one lacks the power to consent, but wife number two possesses it, because her husband has understood her intentions. But what about the husband of wife number three, who understands the relevant intention and takes himself to have been given a permission, despite being in a society where norms do not confer the relevant power on his wife? In this case, one could argue that a norm, different from the society-wide norm, exists in the particular household under consideration, between husband and wife. According to that norm, the husband does not have an unqualified right to marital sex, and the wife thus must give consent for the permissibility of intercourse. Here too, then, the existence of her moral power rests on there being a (highly localized) socially constructed norm.

anyway. This occurs against a backdrop where pornographic materials routinely present women as ultimately consenting to sex, despite superficially refusing it, and where female submission is normalized in sexual encounters. Langton's conjecture is that the depiction of women's sexual behaviour in pornographic materials shapes sexual conventions among consumers of pornography, who see pornography as accurately depicting the "rules of the sexual game". This, in turn, undermines women's ability to refuse sexual intercourse. As Langton explains, pornography silences women not in the sense that although women are still able to refuse sex—such that their partners correctly interpret their "no" as a refusal—men flout the corresponding prohibition (though that might also happen). The problem runs even deeper: pornographic materials contribute to changing the de facto rules of the sexual game such that a "no" uttered by a woman in that context *no longer counts* as a refusal of consent (Langton 1993: 320ff.). It is not merely that women's refusal is locally disregarded; women are "silenced" in the sense that they lose the power to refuse in the first place. In Langton's words, "although the appropriate words can be uttered, those utterances fail to count as the actions they were intended to be" (Langton 1993: 299).

Of course, women ought to have the power to refuse, morally speaking. But, Langton says, in some circumstances they lack it altogether. And claiming that the power is missing allows for a deeper, more comprehensive critique of the status quo. It is not just that there are a few men who don't take women's authority in sexual matters seriously. Patriarchy and misogyny can be so entrenched as to deprive women of the authority that they ought to have in sexual matters. By analogy and contrary to first appearances, then, arguing that socially constructed norms are necessary conditions for possessing morally mandatory normative powers does not rob us of instruments for moral critique. In fact, it sharpens those instruments. It allows us to identify the full depth of the disempowerment suffered by those who are socially subordinate.

The third and final argument for preferring my diagnosis of the slavery scenario—and the underlying view about the existence conditions of rights as control—to the objector's is methodological, and traces back to Ockham's Razor principle. The principle famously states that we should not multiply entities unnecessarily. Necessity, here, is to be understood explanatorily: we should not postulate the existence of more entities or facts than strictly necessary to explain and account for the available evidence. In the present context, the assumption that there exist "natural moral powers" implies the existence of a class of entities—i.e., moral powers parallel to de facto ones—which my view does without. This greater parsimony would not be an advantage of my view if postulating the existence of moral powers independently of socially constructed norms were explanatorily necessary. However, as I have argued so far, doing away with natural moral powers does not prevent us from explaining the morally significant phenomena we're interested in. To the contrary, accepting that moral powers presuppose corresponding de facto ones seems explanatorily necessary, *given* the role of normative powers within our moral lives (the "publicity" argument). Moreover, as I have argued, the view that moral powers presuppose corresponding de facto powers allows us to mount penetrating critiques to morally objectionable practices and norms. Overall, then, Ockham's Razor is fully on the side of the view I have defended.

8. From De Facto to Moral Powers

So far, I have argued that there cannot be moral powers of consent and waiver in the absence of socially constructed norms that confer corresponding de facto powers on individuals. In the process of making this argument, I have also hinted at the fact that, when they are morally justified, de facto powers of waiver and demand acquire moral valence. Those hand-wavy remarks require a more systematic articulation. We need to examine what infuses de facto powers with moral normativity such that they also count as moral powers, giving rise to moral rights as control.

To conduct this examination, I will rely on the framework developed in Part 1 of the book and consider its implications relative to three classes of power-conferring norms: (a) morally mandatory norms; (b) morally prohibited norms; and (c) morally permissible but optional norms.

8.1 Morally mandatory power-conferring norms

Possession of some powers of waiver and, perhaps more controversially, of demand is necessary for persons to lead minimally decent lives qua equal, autonomous agents. To that extent, the creation of socially constructed norms conferring those powers on individuals is *morally mandatory*.

The logic here is similar to that encountered in arguments for the creation of the state inspired by Immanuel Kant. Kant famously held that, in order for us to honour one another's right to freedom, we must leave the state of nature and enter a civil condition: the state (Kant 1999/1797; for discussion, see Ebels-Duggan 2009; Ripstein 2009; Stilz 2009). Only within the state can our rights be given public, authoritative boundaries, such that enforcing those rights does not count as a unilateral imposition of a person's will, and hence a hindrance to others' freedom. From Kant's perspective, then, we have a duty to create a certain set of socially constructed norms, namely those making up a sovereign state. Similarly, I argue, some normative powers conferred upon us by socially constructed norms

142 GROUNDING MORAL RIGHTS

gain moral normativity by virtue of being independently morally mandated.[25] If those powers do not yet exist, we have a duty to create the norms that make them possible.

Which norms these are is not easy to determine. Apart from some obvious examples, there are bound to be grey areas. Furthermore, depending on the specific account of independent moral requirements one subscribes to, one's answers are likely to vary. Still, for illustrative purposes, we may point to a few instances in which normative powers are uncontroversially morally mandatory.

For example, we have natural duties—i.e., social-construction-independent duties—not to interfere with others in certain ways without their consent: not to touch their bodies, not to go on walks with them, not to occupy their personal space, and so forth. However, without norms of consent establishing waiver-powers, it would *always* be impermissible to touch other people or to take walks with them. This means that, inevitably, a whole host of valuable relationships—which involve contact, exchange, and interaction—would be morally tainted (Shiffrin 2008: 500–2). We may thus conclude that the creation of waiver norms, at least in the context of certain issue-domains, is morally required. When it is, the de facto waiver-powers created also become moral powers.

Similarly, some level of demand-power for individuals, relative to particular issue-areas, may also count as a fundamental moral requirement. *If* the conception of the person underpinning our moral outlook is a liberal one, involving individuals' standing as "self-authenticating sources of valid claims" (Rawls 1996), and demand-power is necessary for the realization of this standing, then at least *some* practices that confer such power on individuals—i.e., authority-conferring practices—will gain moral significance because they are independently morally mandated.

An argument to this effect is offered, for instance, in Joel Feinberg's (1970) famous account of the nature and value of rights. There, Feinberg notes how the standing to demand the performance of others' actions is tightly linked to our sense of self-worth, and our being able to "stand up like men" (or, indeed, women), looking others in the eye, and claim a certain kind of treatment from them. So, one could argue, demand-power within some issue-domains is morally mandated. For example, it may be morally mandatory that we have demand-power in relation to those issue-domains in which we ought to have waiver-power. Plausibly, if someone demands one's possessions back after having lent them, that should suffice to generate in others a pro tanto obligation to comply.

---

[25] Continuing with the Kantian analogy, one could say that normative powers are only "provisional" or "imperfect" in a state-of-nature situation (just like, for Kant, rights are only provisional there), since there is bound to be indeterminacy regarding whether any particular communicative act counts as the exercise of this or that power. For those powers to be definitively established, they must exhibit a certain "omnilateral quality", namely they must be publicly defined via socially constructed norms.

FROM DE FACTO TO MORAL POWERS   143

In sum, to put it in Hart's previously mentioned words, it is a moral imperative that individuals enjoy a domain in which they are "small scale sovereigns". Therefore, the socially constructed norms that confer that morally mandatory sovereignty on them—via de facto rights as control—automatically acquire moral valence. Those de facto rights—i.e., de facto powers of waiver and demand—are also moral rights: powers to change not only the de facto normative situation, but also the moral situation.

8.2 Morally forbidden power-conferring norms

At the opposite end of the spectrum, there are socially constructed norms that confer morally forbidden de facto powers on us. Take norms that are clearly contrary to equal respect for persons as autonomous agents, such as those of slavery, mentioned earlier in the discussion. The powers they confer on us as a de facto matter have no moral counterparts. The master's authority over the slave is morally inert. Similarly, norms that give men considerable demand-power over women, such that women count as subordinated to them, have no moral bite. More generally, socially constructed norms that distribute consent and demand-power unequally, in a morally objectionable manner[26]—e.g., along gender or ethnicity lines—lack moral significance.

8.3 Morally permissible power-conferring norms

We have briefly looked at power-conferring socially constructed norms that are either morally mandatory or morally forbidden. However, many of the powers of waiver and demand we actually possess are likely located in the area between these two extremes. That is, the powers are morally permissible, but not morally required. Some of the examples I have been discussing fall precisely within this middle category.

Take, for instance, the powers of demand and waiver conferred upon us by the queuing norm. Those in the queue have rights as control over their spots: it is up to them to decide whether to keep those spots or to give them to someone else. In other words, they determine whether others are obligated to stay away from those spots or whether they may take them. While the queuing norm, with its associated powers, is permissible, it is not morally mandated—or at least so it appears to

---

[26] The qualification "morally objectionable" is necessary insofar as unequal demand and consent power may be perfectly permissible, for example, when they go to the advantage of those in a position of local subordination. For instance, teachers have authority over their pupils. The demand-power of the former is greater than that of the latter: there's no equality here. Still, such inequality is not morally problematic, but in fact justified by the interests of children themselves.

144 GROUNDING MORAL RIGHTS

me. Alternatively, take the norm forbidding the harmless use of others' property without their consent. As already remarked in an earlier chapter, while some general norms regulating the possession and use of resources seem necessary for persons to lead decent lives, morality arguably does not require them to take this specific, rather individualistic form. More communal property norms, which do not contain such a prohibition, could also be perfectly permissible (Cohen 2009). Hence, an owner's power to demand that her property not be harmlessly used without her consent, even when she does not need it, is not independently morally mandated.

For another example, consider local norms setting out the obligations and rights, in the "control" sense, of parents and children. According to some such norms, parents are under an obligation to provide a roof for their children until they get married, unless the children willingly leave the parental home sooner, thereby releasing their parents from this obligation (for discussion, see Owens 2017). This norm does not appear morally mandatory. A different norm, requiring children to become independent sooner, would seem equally admissible. The list could go on.[27]

These power-conferring permissible norms vary widely from one society to the other. The ways in which (at least some) norms of friendship, parent-child relationships, boss-and-employee relationships, and so forth confer the relevant powers of waiver and demand on individuals exhibit considerable diachronic and geographical variation.

In accordance with the framework set out in Part 1 of the book, the powers conferred upon us by such morally permissible, but not mandatory, norms acquire moral normativity via *agency respect*.[28] It is respect for those who, through their agential commitments, sustain the relevant norms that make the powers they confer upon us morally significant.

Take queuing, for instance. As already mentioned, the norms of queuing confer on those standing in line the power to give their place away, thereby waiving others' duties not to take it. If I am right, the moral normativity of the norms sustaining this practice—including of the normative powers it confers on individuals—stems from the demands of agency respect, as these have been characterized in Chapter 3.

Similarly, recall our earlier example, *Barbeque*, involving someone secretly using your barbeque set for an improvised summer feast, without this causing you any harm. Property norms as we know them confer upon you the standing to

---

[27] An interesting question is where promissory norms fit in: are they morally mandatory or morally optional? I confess that I find answering this question rather difficult, though I lean towards Seana Shiffrin's (2008) view that the power to promise, or at any rate to enter into bonds that are much like those created by promising, is necessary for a full instantiation of our status as autonomous agents. Still, the validity of my view is independent of how we understand the power to make promises.

[28] I should also note that, consistently with my argument, agency respect will be a further ground conferring moral normativity on de facto normative powers that are independently morally mandated.

determine that others use your barbeque set only as you see fit, no matter whether their use of it harms you in any way. If you demand that they should only use it to grill vegetables, then they are under an obligation not to use it for any other purposes. But equally, if you tell them "you may do whatever you want with it", they are at liberty to use it in line with their own needs and preferences. If I am correct, these morally permissible—but not obligatory—powers of yours acquire moral valence by virtue of our broader obligation to give agency respect to those who support the underlying power-conferring norms.

The same can be said about norms that set out the rights that parents and children have vis-à-vis one another, but which go beyond whatever we may think abstract morality demands in terms of basic mutual care and non-harm. Agency-respect for the community supporting those local norms confers moral normativity on them, and therefore also on the powers of demand and waiver—if any—they establish.

The list could continue, but hopefully the general point I wish to make is clear, constituting an elaboration of what was argued in Chapter 3. The moral normativity of morally optional de facto powers is ultimately traceable to the demands of agency respect.

When I briefly discussed these examples in Chapter 3, and I addressed the question of whose rights are violated by breaches of morally permissible (or, indeed, mandatory) socially constructed norms, I anticipated that I would return to this matter. I have partly done so, but need to further elaborate on it. This is because, as some readers may have noticed, my account has a somewhat unusual implication. This is that some individuals' rights—in the control sense—can be violated, hence these individuals can be wronged (on the assumption that rights-violations always result in wrongings of specific individuals), even if what explains our obligation to respect those rights are not primarily the interests of those individuals. Instead, the ground of our obligation is agency respect *for norm-supporters* generally. More needs to be said to vindicate this upshot of my discussion. This is the topic of the next section.

9. Rights and Wrongings

I have assumed that there are two kinds of moral rights: rights as inviolability and rights as control. The former class of rights designates duties stemming from the inviolability of the person. The latter refers to moral powers over other people's duties. I have then argued that while rights in the inviolability sense can exist independently of socially constructed norms, rights in the control sense include socially constructed norms among their existence conditions.

We should explore the implications of this picture for a notion that is typically associated with the idea of rights, and rights-violations, namely that of *wronging*.

146   GROUNDING MORAL RIGHTS

Within moral philosophy specifically, discussions about rights tend to focus on what it is to be the victim of a wrong, to be *wronged* (Thompson 2004). Those who are wronged are in a special position vis-à-vis the relevant wrongdoer. For example, they may be in a position to seek compensation from him or to forgive him or to demand an apology, something that third parties may not do (Cornell 2015; Owens 2020). If my distinction between two senses of rights is plausible, then, we should also expect to identify two corresponding senses of wronging or being wronged. These can be characterized as follows.[29]

Wronging$_i$ of A (inviolability): the violation of a duty grounded in A's fundamental moral status.

Wronging$_c$ of A (control): the violation of a duty over which A has normative control.

Wrongings of the first kind, namely wrongings$_i$, include forbidden actions such as killing the innocent, depriving others of the means of subsistence, failing to perform easy rescues, and generally violating duties whose raison d'être lies in the interests of particular creatures, who are ultimate units of moral concern. Wrongings$_i$ are the most familiar variety, and intuitively easy to explain insofar as they are accompanied by harms that befall the right-holder. When we are operating in the realm of wrongings$_i$, the idea of a harmless wronging becomes puzzling: a wrong is always caused by someone not acting on duties whose aim is to further another person's interests. Consequently, wrongings$_i$ involve setbacks in interests, hence harms.

On my view, one can also be wronged in a very different sense—corresponding to the notion of rights as control—namely when a duty over which one has normative control is violated. Of course, if the duty in question is also a natural duty, that is, a duty that is independently morally necessary and would exist in the absence of socially constructed norms, a wronging$_i$ may also occur. But when it comes to wrongings in the second sense, namely wrongings$_c$, what we are witnessing is not primarily a forbidden harm, but an *authority-violation*, which may or may not be accompanied by wrongful harm.

This type of moral breach occurs when, say, subordinates fail to abide by the demands of those who have (legitimate) authority over them. Or it may occur when someone is guilty of a harmless trespass, or violates a promissory duty over the fulfilment of which the promisee has no interest. Wrongings$_c$ can account for the widely discussed, and often puzzling, phenomenon of "harmless wronging",

---

[29] Nicolas Cornell (2015) suggests that someone is wronged when the violation of a duty sets back her interests (even if the duty need not be *grounded* in her interests). This sense of wronging is distinct from the two I have set out here and may be somewhat over-expansive, for reasons outlined in Kramer (2010: 36).

precisely because authority violations need not always result in harms, let alone harms suffered by the authority-holders.[30]

Wrongings$_c$ can only occur against the backdrop of socially constructed norms, and they may gain moral significance in two different ways: either directly, when the relevant powers are mandated by fundamental moral demands, or indirectly, through agency respect. The second case, as I have mentioned in the previous section, may strike some as puzzling, insofar as it involves a separation between (a) what *grounds* someone's moral authority—i.e., agency respect for norm-supporters—and (b) *who* possesses the relevant authority. The latter individual, I suggest, counts as the wronged party—wronged$_c$—*even if* his or her possession of authority is ultimately justified by appeal to respect for norms supporters generally.

Let me begin by noting that this separation between the source of normativity and its "target" is not only coherent, but also familiar. Think, for example, of divine command theory, according to which God's law sets out what human beings owe to each other. Here, it seems perfectly plausible to say that by violating God's law, human beings wrong *each other*. Perhaps, they also disrespect God, and in some sense wrong him too. This, however, does not appear to invalidate the claim that violations of those laws result in wrongs human beings commit against one another.[31]

Still, an objector might worry that the introduction of two notions of wronging is unsatisfactory. Although there does not appear to be a clear consensus in the literature as to what it takes to wrong someone—other than the view that it is tantamount to violating their rights (but see Cornell 2015)—an objector may find the first understanding of wronging I have outlined (corresponding to rights as inviolability) to be primitive or, at any rate, more fundamental. The objector may thus feel that "multiplying wrongings" is a bit like cheating. What I am describing are different types of moral offences, and only one of them can be a "wronging proper".

To corroborate this point, the objector may offer the following—by now familiar—example. Consider again the practice of queuing. On my view, it is true to say that we have moral obligations not to skip the queue, and that people in the queue have "control-rights" against this. That is, it is up to them to decide how others should relate to the place they currently occupy in the queue—i.e., whether they may take it or whether they are obligated not to. Yet, the objector would continue, the reason why, on my view, the obligations and powers involved are also *moral* has to do with the principle of agency respect, which requires us to respect others' permissible and authentic commitments. What ultimately gives

---

[30] For discussions of harmless wronging which differ from mine, but from which I have learnt, see Ripstein (2006) and Owens (2012: Ch. 2).

[31] Thanks to Christian List for suggesting this example.

148 GROUNDING MORAL RIGHTS

moral force to the norm of queuing "qua norm"—with its associated deontic attributes—is a demand to respect *those who support* the norm in the context at hand, not the specific interests of the individuals in the queue under scrutiny. But this, the objector would continue, means that—highly counterintuitively—by skipping the queue, we wrong not so much those whose place we take, but everyone who is committed to the queuing norm in the context under analysis, including people outside the relevant queue. Given these implications, the notion of wronging$_c$, the objector concludes, appears bizarre, and so we would be better off dispensing with it.

Here, I want to partly bite the bullet, by showing that, in fact, it is not much of a bullet to bite anyway. On my view, there are two sets of individuals who may count as *wronged*, albeit in two different senses. On the one hand, it is indeed those who support the queuing norm whose commitments are being interfered with and who are *wronged$_i$* for this reason. They have an interest in their commitments not being disrupted or disrespected, and by flouting the queuing norm the queue-jumper does just that. After all, we have no difficulties in accepting the view that desecrating religious temples is disrespectful towards the adherents of the relevant religion and, therefore, wrongs them. The matter is very similar when it comes to our queuing example, though the stakes are much lower in the latter case.

What is more, in light of the moral powers that the queuing norm confers on specific individuals, we can say that queue-jumping wrongs$_c$ those standing in line *in particular*, whose authority—i.e., whose normative control over the specific spot they occupy in the queue—is being ignored. And, as argued in Chapter 3, singling them out as "distinctively wronged" is in line with the particular normative world created by norm-supporters. Taking that normative world seriously involves, among other things, acknowledging the special position of those in the queue vis-à-vis possible breaches of the queuing norm.

It seems to me that, far from implausible, the claim that two constituencies are being wronged—each in a different way—precisely accords with our judgements. I can imagine those in the queue feeling affronted but, similarly, I can imagine bystanders looking on disapprovingly, feeling that "these queue jumpers are not taking *our* norms seriously". Both groups have reason to be aggrieved, albeit in different ways. The two notions of wronging I have proposed account for this fact.

On the question of whether proposing two notions of wronging is cheating, let me say this. I use the "wronging" terminology because this has been traditionally associated with rights language, and it follows from my contention that there exist two notions of rights that there have to be two corresponding notions of wronging. Nothing would be lost, however, if we used "wronging" to designate only one of the phenomena under discussion and adopted a different label for the other. What matters—in fact, the point I have been trying to make here—is that there are indeed two types of moral affront: to one's status as an interest-bearer and to one's authority. Keeping them distinct gives us a more nuanced and accurate picture of the types of moral injury involved in rights violations.

10. Conclusion

Debates about rights are complex and intricate. Some such debates are conceptual, concerning the very notion of rights. Others are substantive, asking by virtue of what we possess the moral attributes the notion of rights is meant to capture. In this chapter, I have stipulatively taken a particular view about the conceptual question, distinguishing between rights as inviolability and rights as control, and asked the substantive question for each of them. I have granted that rights as inviolability can exist independently of socially constructed norms, but I have argued that rights as control include socially constructed norms among their existence conditions. This is because rights as control consist of the powers to demand and to waive others' duties, and these powers can only exist when socially constructed norms publicly determine what counts as their exercise. I have then explained how de facto rights as control gain moral normativity, by applying the agency-respect framework developed in the previous chapter.

Finally, I have shown how the familiar notion of wronging is itself twofold, and how appreciation of this can help us explain the phenomenon of harmless wronging. Such wronging occurs when rights as control are violated—i.e., someone's authority is being in some sense usurped—without this resulting in any particular harm.

Precisely the notion of authority and violations thereof, which we have started to explore in this chapter, will take centre stage in the following two.

Morality and Socially Constructed Norms. Laura Valentini, Oxford University Press. © Laura Valentini 2023.
DOI: 10.1093/9780191938115.003.0005

5
Grounding Political Obligation

Do we have a pro tanto—i.e., overridable—obligation to obey the law because it is the law?[1] Legal philosophers are divided on this matter. Advocates of the authority of law—let us call them "legal normativists"—answer in the affirmative.[2] Philosophical anarchists in the negative: they admit that we often ought to act *in conformity* with the law, because doing so brings all kinds of benefits, but they deny our obligation to *obey* it: to act as the law commands *because* the law commands it.[3]

To make the distinction more concrete, let us go back to *Traffic Light*, one of the scenarios originally introduced in Chapter 2. This involved my German father-in-law—Jürgen—stopping at a red light, in the middle of the night, on an empty street. Anarchists will be happy to agree that, very often, we have excellent reasons to stop at red lights: doing so is safe and efficient. However, they will deny that the fact that stopping is required by law places us under a pro tanto obligation to stop. When nobody is around, and driving through is safe, stopping is neither rationally nor morally required. Philosophical anarchists, in other words, adopt what I have called a "deflationary view" about the normativity of law in particular. Legal normativists disagree. For them, Jürgen did the right thing: he had an obligation to stop *because stopping was legally required*. So, which side of this dispute is correct? Is there an obligation to obey the law because it is the law?

In addressing this question, my aim is twofold: (a) raising concerns about existing accounts of political obligation and, most importantly, (b) showing that the agency-respect view developed in Part 1 of the book can help us tackle the problem of political obligation. To briefly anticipate, on this view, agency respect for those who are committed to the rule of law—i.e., for those who are committed to the bindingness of law—grounds an obligation to obey it. The resulting defence of political obligation steers a middle course between anarchists and legal normativists. Contrary to what the latter often imply, the obligation to obey the law is potentially rather weak: it all depends on the strength of the agential commitments sustaining the rule of law. Moreover, when formal legal norms clash with informal social norms, on the agency-respect view it does not automatically

---

[1] The pro tanto nature of the obligation to obey the law is generally accepted in the political-authority literature. See Edmundson (2004: 215–16) and Lefkowitz (2006: 573–4).

[2] I am using this label since the view in question holds that the law has normative (moral) power.

[3] For the distinction between conformity and obedience, see Raz (1985b: 141). For an analysis of different kinds of anarchism, see Simmons (2009).

follow that the former take priority over the latter. To that extent, the agency-respect view sides with anarchists in holding that the law is not morally special. If we have an obligation to obey the law, this is because we have obligations to obey the prescriptions of socially constructed norms more generally, legal norms being a particular class of such norms.

This is how I shall proceed. In Section 1, I define key terminology and set the stage for the discussion that follows. In Section 2, I cast doubt on prominent attempts to defend the obligation to obey the law: instrumentalist, fair-play, natural duty, and associative views. I suggest that most of them only succeed in grounding an obligation to act *in conformity with* the law by virtue of the merits of the law's content, rather than an obligation to *obey it* by virtue of its status as law (Klosko 2011; Valentini 2018). In Section 3, I turn to democratic approaches to political obligation. I show that, while promising, they exhibit a problematic explanatory gap. In Section 4, I explain how the agency-respect view can fill that gap. In Section 5, to showcase the virtues of this view, I illustrate how it helps us make sense of the practice of civil disobedience. Section 6 considers the broader implications of the view. Section 7 concludes.

Before beginning my discussion, I must make two caveats. First, readers familiar with the political-obligation literature are likely to have noticed a conspicuous absence from my outline: consent theory. On this theory, political obligation is grounded in the consent of the governed. The idea is simple: if I agree to being governed by law, then I am bound to perform given actions precisely because the law requires them. Consent theory offers an elegant but ultimately unsatisfactory solution to the problem of political obligation, and for reasons by now well known in the literature. As critics have convincingly pointed out, only very few people voluntarily consent to being governed: for example, those who take up a new citizenship (not under duress) and swear allegiance to a country's laws (e.g., Simmons 1976). A satisfactory account of political obligation should have wider reach than that, explaining how it is that most if not all citizens are bound by the law. This isn't something that consent theory is in a position to do. Since this weakness of consent theory is already well known, and not directly relevant to my discussion, I will not further discuss consent theory in what follows.

Second, my critiques of existing accounts of political obligation in Section 2 will be relatively brief. This brevity is motivated by two considerations. One is that I—and, in fact, many others—have developed similar critiques, at greater length, elsewhere (e.g., Klosko 2011; Simmons 1979; Valentini 2018).[4] While sketching those critiques here provides a useful background for my own positive argument, reproducing them in full seems unnecessary. The other is that I am eager to devote enough space to the more constructive part of the chapter, where I outline

---

[4] Section 2, in particular, offers shorter versions of arguments I have advanced in Valentini (2018).

152 GROUNDING POLITICAL OBLIGATION

my own view. Conveying what the agency-respect view implies for the obligation to obey the law matters more to me than highlighting the limitations of alternative views. I will be happy if, by the end of the chapter, I will have shown that the agency-respect view offers valuable insights on political obligation, even if readers find my doubts about existing approaches insufficient to invalidate them.

1. The Political-Obligation Debate: Terminology and Significance

Throughout the chapter, I shall be using terminology such as political authority, political obligation, content-independence, and content-sensitivity. Before embarking upon my substantive discussion, I should therefore clarify the meaning of these terms, starting with the notion of authority.

By *authority*, I mean one's power to place others under pro tanto obligations to act as one commands. Here, I am particularly interested in one's moral power to place others under such obligations, or what is sometimes called *legitimate authority*. A typical example of authority so conceived is that of parents over their children. A parent has legitimate authority over their child if their telling the child to do something places the child under a pro tanto obligation to do it. Consider a mother telling her daughter "Help me do the dishes!" and imagine the daughter asking "Why?". If the mother has legitimate authority over her daughter, she can correctly answer: "Because *I* said so". To put things in vocabulary familiar from the previous chapter, to have legitimate authority over a person is to have "demand-power" over her.

When speaking of *legitimate political authority*, I shall be referring to the authority of law in particular. Consider a traffic warden shouting "Stop!" as a driver is approaching a red light. Suppose the driver asks "Why should I stop?". If the law has legitimate authority, the traffic warden can correctly answer: "Because the law says so". The law has the power to place moral obligations on its addressees.

I call the obligations grounded in the law *political obligations*. These are pro tanto obligations of subjects of the law to do as the law requires *because the law so requires*: that is, they are obligations to *obey* the law. According to this terminology, political obligation is coextensive with legitimate political authority: when there is one, there is also the other.[5] While the notion of political obligation

---

[5] This is what Edmundson (2004: 218) calls "inseparability". Raz (2006: 1004–5) uses the term "political obligation" differently, to denote the obligation to support one's institutions, which is not coextensive with the obligation to obey the law. This is a purely terminological matter, and not much hinges on it. One subtlety worth noting, and helpfully pointed out by Ralf Bader (2021), is that citizens' obligation to do what the law requires "because the law so requires" may be generated through two different mechanisms. It may be that citizens have a standing duty to do what the law requires, a duty that is then activated whenever the law requires something of them. Alternatively, it may be that the law has the power to create new duties (not merely to activate them), and that citizens are morally

THE POLITICAL-OBLIGATION DEBATE   153

describes the normative position of those who are on the receiving end of authoritative commands, that of legitimate authority focuses on the normative privileges attached to their source.

Let me now clarify the meaning of the expression "doing as the law requires *because it so requires*", which I have been employing multiple times so far. That expression is open to two interpretations, and it is important to make clear which one I am using here (see, e.g., Hershovitz 2012: 69; Perry 2013: 14; Raz 1985a: 7; Valentini 2018). On the first interpretation, that expression specifies the *content* of the obligation to obey the law in a very particular way. On this interpretation, political obligations are obligations to *act as the law requires for the reason that the law requires it*. This implies that someone who acts in conformity with the law, but for reasons other than the fact that those actions are legally mandated, fails to *obey* the law. Suppose I pay taxes, refrain from stealing, follow traffic rules, and I am otherwise a very law-abiding citizen. Suppose, further, that I do all these things because I believe that this is what justice and respect for my fellow citizens require, not because these various acts are legally mandated. If the clause "doing as the law requires because it so requires" is meant to specify the content of the obligation to obey, then, in all such instances, I fail to obey the law. Manifestly, this interpretation of the clause leads to counter-intuitive implications. There is something rather odd in accusing impeccably law-abiding citizens of legal disobedience.

Fortunately, this is not the interpretation that matters for our purposes. The second interpretation, which I adopt here, takes the expression "doing as the law requires *because it so requires*" to refer to the *grounds* of the relevant obligation: what explains the fact that we are under that obligation. According to this alternative interpretation, if we abide by the law, we honour our political obligations independently of the reasons why we do so. Obedience to the law does not require the subject to correctly identify the law as the source of obligation, it just requires acting within the limits of the law.

Political obligation so conceived is also said to be *content-independent* (Hart 1982: Ch. 10; see also Raz 1986: Ch. 2). This means that, when the law requires us to φ, we have a pro tanto obligation to φ, not because of some substantive virtue of φ-ing (its content), but because φ-ing is required by law. What *grounds* our obligation is the fact that the law requires something of us (in conjunction with a suitable moral principle that lends normative significance to that fact). Our obligation thus persists across permissible variations in the content of the law,

---

liable to acquiring these new duties. In the former case, we might say that the law's authority amounts to a "weak power" (namely the power to *trigger/activate* duties), while in the latter it amounts to a "strong power" or "normative power proper" (namely the power to *create* duties). Cf. the discussion of normative powers in Chang (2020). Different accounts of political obligation implicitly presuppose one or the other of these mechanisms. Which one is presupposed, however, does not affect the present analysis.

154   GROUNDING POLITICAL OBLIGATION

because it is the status of given actions as legally mandated that confers obligatoriness on them (see also Adams 2017).

Of course, content-independence cannot be absolute. Nobody would argue that we have moral obligations to obey morally abhorrent laws. To account for this concern, legal normativists accept that the law has the power to generate obligations only provided that the content of the relevant obligations is morally acceptable. Imagine laws that condone slavery, arbitrary incarceration, apartheid, etc. In such cases, the otherwise obligation-generating power of law is blocked. Obligations to obey the law, we can say, are content-independent but *content-sensitive* (Valentini 2018: 139).

The combination of content-independence and content-sensitivity is far from unusual in moral reasoning. Consider, for instance, promise-based obligations. When you promise to φ, you ought to φ *because* you promised to φ, quite independently of the merits of φ-ing. However, if φ-ing turns out to be morally abhorrent—e.g., it involves committing a serious crime—the obligation-generating power of promising is thereby blocked. Promissory obligations too, then, are content-independent, but not content-insensitive. Our target explanandum, namely the obligation to obey the law, shares this structural feature with promissory obligation (Raz 2006: 1013).

The debate between anarchists and advocates of the authority of law concerns precisely whether the law can generate content-independent obligations—i.e., obligations to φ grounded in the fact that φ-ing is legally mandated, not in other merits of φ-ing—and if so, under what conditions. It is worth pointing out that the stakes involved in this debate are high, but perhaps less high than one might at first think. As anticipated, both parties to this debate agree that, very often, we ought to act as the law requires—i.e., act *in conformity with* the law—since doing so is necessary to achieve a variety of morally obligatory ends, including justice, safety, coordination, and so forth. A philosophical anarchist may thus accept that we ought to pay our taxes, follow traffic regulations, and refrain from harming innocent others. The question is whether we also have an obligation to *obey* the law: i.e., whether the fact that the law commands φ-ing places us under an obligation to φ. This means that, in a large set of cases, anarchists and their opponents will come to identical verdicts about what we ought to do. The *reasons* for their verdicts, however, will differ. Legal normativists will count the fact that certain independently desirable actions are legally mandated among the reasons for performing them; anarchists will not (Simmons 2009: 6).

Still, this does not make the question of political obligation insignificant. Being able to vindicate the obligation to obey the law is necessary if we are to make sense of our practices, and specifically of the idea of the rule of law. Even though the precise contours of this notion are contested, a commitment to the rule of law is typically taken to signify a commitment to the bindingness of law for both officials and ordinary citizens. To put it in Jeremy Waldron's words, according to the rule of law: "people in positions of authority should exercise their power within a constraining framework of well-established public norms" and "citizens should respect and comply with legal norms, even when they disagree with them" (Waldron 2020).

The practice of the rule of law, in turn, stands in need of justification since what morality independently demands and what justified law requires may come apart. Yet, we often think that violations of law—even when these are not independently immoral—are fitting objects of disapproval, sanctions, and punishment. That is, legal violations (within limits) invite the types of responses and reactive attitudes that are appropriate in cases of moral violations.

To see this, it suffices to recall the scenarios discussed in Chapter 2: *Traffic Light*, *Barbeque*, and *Non-proceduralist President*.[6] If violations of the law are wrongful only when they align with independent moral considerations, then it looks as if we would have to revise our considered judgements about right and wrong. Harmless trespass, harmless failures to abide by traffic rules, beneficial behaviour ultra vires, and other instances of innocuous legal violations would no longer count as wrongful and could not legitimately elicit the reactive attitudes we typically have towards wrongdoing.[7]

More generally, while moral demands constrain morally binding law, it would seem far-fetched to suggest that they entirely *determine* what the law ought to look like. In the words of Gerald Gaus (2013: 85), "there is a non-singleton set of morally eligible conventions or norms". Many laws may be consistent with morality—e.g., laws about building regulations, about public funding of the arts, about immigration, about school curricula, about appropriate clothing, and so

---

[6] To recall, these are the cases in questions.

Traffic Light: My German father-in-law, Jürgen, was driving late at night, through a village in his home region. He came to an intersection in the road. The traffic light went red. He looked in every direction: there was no car, person, or speed camera in sight. It would have been physically impossible for anyone to get hurt if he had continued straight, ignoring the red light. Moreover, nobody would have witnessed the breach. The only outcome would have been a happy one: an earlier arrival home. Yet my father-in-law stopped at the red light.

Barbeque: You are on a camping trip. You call some friends and make plans to spend the day with them, only to return in the late evening. Your barbeque set, pots, and pans are stored outside your tent. The Rossi family, whose tent is just a few metres from yours, notices your absence, and decides to make use of your grill and related accessories for an improvised barbeque feast. They celebrate during the day, but put everything back in order prior to your return. When you get back, you notice nothing.

Non-proceduralist President: In the wake of the 9/11 terror attacks, President George W. Bush authorized the National Security Agency to track international calls and e-communications of people inside the US, without a court warrant. Once this became known, the President was criticized for acting ultra vires, in violation of the 1978 Foreign Intelligence Surveillance Act (FISA), which prohibits warrantless domestic electronic surveillance. In an open letter to Congress, published in the *New York Review of Books*, a group of leading legal scholars and former government officials insisted that, to be lawful, such surveillance would need to be authorized by Congress, through legislative amendment.

[7] I grant, again, that only few will share the intuition that there is something ever so mildly wrong about failing to stop when the light is red and the street is empty.

156 GROUNDING POLITICAL OBLIGATION

on—without being morally mandated. Or else, there may be reasonable disagreement about the moral status of given laws. In either case, the violation of said laws is met with disapproval, sanctions, punishment, and blame—sometimes on the part of individual citizens themselves, but certainly by society as a whole via the official state apparatus. Vindicating the authority of law is necessary to justify these common responses to legal violations.

In sum, even if philosophical anarchists and advocates of the authority of law often converge in their judgements about particular cases—i.e., when the law reflects or implements independent moral demands—the search for a ground of the obligation to obey the law still matters. In order to determine what would count as a good ground, we need to find a plausible moral principle explaining why the fact that an action is required by law places us under a pro tanto obligation to perform it.

To see this, we can go back to the distinction, encountered in Chapter 2, between deflationary views and views that vindicate the moral normativity of socially constructed norms—here, of *legal norms* specifically. Philosophical anarchists are, essentially, deflationists about the moral normativity of law. They subscribe to the following grounding sequence (here reported in relation to the *Traffic Light* example).

Philosophical anarchist (deflationary) grounding sequence
- <u>Action required</u>: You ought to φ (φ = stop at the red light).
- By virtue of what ought I to φ?
- <u>Empirical fact</u>: Because stopping at the red light minimizes the risk of harming others.
- By virtue of what does the fact that stopping at the red light minimizes the risk of harming others ground my obligation to φ?
- <u>General moral principle</u>: Because one ought to minimize the risk of harming others.

No reference to the law is made in explaining where our obligation to stop at the red light comes from. If the explanation for our obligation to stop lies in the general principle figuring at the bottom of this sequence, then, in a situation like *Traffic Light*, we'd have *no* reason to stop. A successful defence of the obligation to obey the law, by contrast, needs to identify a principle that can play the right explanatory role in the target grounding sequence below.

Legal normativist (target) grounding sequence
- <u>Action required</u>: You ought to φ (φ = stop at the red light).
- By virtue of what ought I to φ?
- <u>Empirical fact</u>: Because the law requires you to φ.

THE DIFFICULTIES WITH EXISTING VIEWS   157

- By virtue of what does the fact that φ-ing is required by law ground my obligation to φ?
- <u>Target general moral principle</u>: Because P.

Different accounts of the authority of law propose competing candidates for P. In the next section, I offer brief critical discussions of four prominent such accounts.

2. The Difficulties with Existing Views

Among the most prominent theories of political obligation, we can find instrumentalist views, fair-play views, natural-duty views, and associative views. I raise concerns about all of them.[8] I argue that the first three views rest on independently appealing principles, but fail to vindicate a *content-independent* obligation to obey the law. Instead, they vindicate an obligation to act in conformity with the law when the law tracks independent moral demands sufficiently closely. In other words, their candidate principles P ground the obligatoriness of legally mandated actions on contingent features of their content, not on their status as legally mandated. I then turn to associative views and judge them problematic because the principle P to which they appeal lacks plausibility.

2.1 Instrumentalist views

A highly influential account of political obligation focuses on how obedience to the law enables us better to exercise our practical reason. The account is most tightly associated with the work of Joseph Raz and his "service conception of authority" (Raz 1985a; 2006). On the service conception, the obligation to obey the law is grounded in the following principle.

P: One ought to do what makes one better conform with the reasons that independently apply to one.

In Raz's (2006: 1013) own words, the law has authority over an agent whenever he "would better conform to reasons that apply to him anyway...if he intends to be guided by [legal] directives than if he does not".[9] Authority thereby provides a service: it is a means to better reason-compliance on whatever matter the authority is issuing directives.

---

[8] This section partly summarizes arguments offered in Valentini (2018).
[9] For an earlier statement of Raz's view, see Raz (1985a).

158 GROUNDING POLITICAL OBLIGATION

Principle *P* is highly plausible and correctly identifies a set of conditions under which we should follow the law: namely when doing so is instrumentally necessary to do what we independently have reason to do. It is unclear, however, how the principle can succeed in grounding a *content-independent* obligation to obey the law. Surely, whether acting as the law requires makes one better conform with one's reasons depends on the content of the law: on what the law demands in any given instance or domain. Whether you ought to act as the law requires, then, is ultimately a function of the law's content, of the actions it prescribes, not of its *status* as law.

For example, it seems certainly true that obeying traffic law generally better allows us to act on the reasons that independently apply to us, by enabling coordination and thereby increasing efficiency and safety. However, in the *Traffic Light* scenario, it is hard to see why this would be the case (Soper 1989: 227–8).[10] There, one better conforms with the reasons that apply to one by following one's own judgement and driving through despite the red light: one saves time at nobody's expense. The legally mandated action is stopping, but the action recommended by Raz's master-principle is driving through. The *status* of the action as legally required is therefore not obligation-generating.

Interestingly, Raz (1979: 25) denies that the law lacks authority in a scenario like *Traffic Light*. He observes that if we were to always act on our best judgement concerning traffic we'd often get it wrong, and this would cost us much effort. From this he concludes that, in the domain of traffic regulation, the law *always* has authority. This, however, is a non-sequitur. In cases like *Traffic Light*—where the superiority of our judgement is obvious—determining what to do costs us very little. It is mysterious how deferring to the law in *Traffic Light* better serves us than following our own judgement. Situations like *Traffic Light* should precisely fall outside the domain of the law's authority.

More generally, and to use a label introduced earlier in the book, Razian instrumentalism represents an instance of the *deflationary view* applied to a particular class of socially constructed norms, namely legal ones. It explains why we ought to perform the actions mandated by those norms *not* by appeal to the fact that those actions are norm-mandated, but by appeal to the good effects of doing so—namely reason-compliance—where those effects are typically a function of the content of the norms.[11]

---

[10] It is a well-known feature of Raz's account that different laws may or may not have authority with respect to different people at different times and in different contexts: it all depends on their being more or less conducive to any given person's correct exercise of practical reason. See Raz (1986: 74–5).

[11] It may be objected that reason-compliance may not depend on the content of the law, but on its procedural pedigree. Suppose we have reasons (e.g., grounded in equality) to obey democratically made law. In that case, the instrumentalist view will require us to do what democratically made law requires even if, at the level of substance, we'd be better off by following our own judgement. This response, though in principle open to the instrumentalist, robs the instrumentalist view of its

THE DIFFICULTIES WITH EXISTING VIEWS   159

In sum, since conduciveness to reason-compliance depends on the content of the law—i.e., on what the law mandates in a given domain—and not on its status as law, for structural reasons instrumentalists have difficulties vindicating a content-independent obligation to obey the law "because it is the law".[12]

2.2 Fair-play views

Fair-play views hold that political obligation stems from a broader obligation against free riding.[13] In particular, they ground political obligation in the following principle.

P: One ought to contribute one's fair share to a reasonably just cooperative practice, whenever that practice produces goods one benefits from (see, e.g., Arneson 1982; Hart 1955: 185; Klosko 1987).[14]

Benefitting from others' sacrifices without reciprocating by doing one's fair share, so the argument goes, is morally wrong. If everyone did it, the benefits in question would no longer be produced. Obedience to the law, the fair-play theorist claims, is precisely a benefit-generating practice. It delivers public services, security, clean air, traffic coordination, and much else. Those who enjoy these benefits should thus do their fair share and obey the law too. Failing to do so amounts to free riding.

It is unclear how the fair play principle succeeds in vindicating a content-independent obligation to obey the law. Consider again our paradigmatic case: *Traffic Light*. Failing to stop at a red light on an empty street could not plausibly count as an instance of free riding. Free riding involves the receipt of benefits without reciprocation and succeeds only thanks to others' continued compliance. Failing

---

distinctiveness. As Scott Hershovitz points out, it is a platitude that we conform to our reasons by obeying the directives of legitimate authorities since, by definition, we have obligations to obey those directives. But if this is all the instrumentalist is saying, then instrumentalism turns out to be compatible with any theory of political obligation/authority that happens to be true (Hershovitz 2011: 5). In order to count as a distinctive view, instrumentalism must make the obligation to obey the law dependent on better conformity with the reasons that apply to us *regarding the substantive matter at hand*.

[12] I realize that my treatment of Raz here is very brief, especially given how influential his view is. Still, my discussion highlights what I take to be the main difficulty with his view, and hopefully suffices for my limited aims in this chapter (i.e., highlighting some difficulties rather than offering a definitive refutation). For further replies, and counter-arguments, see Valentini (2018: 142–46).

[13] Here I only discuss versions of the fair-play approach that set aside whether benefits are accepted voluntarily. Such voluntarism would in fact bring us back to the well-known difficulties with consent theory. See Simmons (1979: Ch. 5) for discussion.

[14] For a critique, see Nozick (1974: 90–5). Interestingly, Klosko (2007: 3; 2011) himself now acknowledges that his fair-play approach does not deliver a content-independent obligation to obey the law, for reasons similar to those I offer here.

160 GROUNDING POLITICAL OBLIGATION

to pay one's taxes, for instance, counts as free riding. If everyone did it, the services provided via tax revenue would cease to exist. There is thus something exploitative, or at least unfair, in benefitting from those services without reciprocating. Things are different, though, in a case like *Traffic Light*. Ignoring red lights *when nobody is around* can be unproblematically universalized, without undermining the benefits of traffic regulation. In London, where I used to live, virtually everyone crosses the street when no cars are in sight, even if the light is red. In doing so, they violate the law, but they clearly do not free ride. Here we have a permissible legal demand, but the injunction against free riding cannot ground an obligation to adhere to it.

It might be replied that this objection misunderstands the fair-play view. For the benefits the view refers to are not piecemeal, that is, those generated by particular laws. Instead, they are comprehensive: the benefits delivered by general compliance with the law as a whole. The argument would then go as follows:

- Action required: One ought to do what the law requires (provided it is just enough[15]).
- By virtue of what ought one to do what the law requires?
- Empirical fact: Because doing what the law requires (a) is a reasonably just cooperative practice that produces goods from which one benefits, and (b) corresponds to one's fair share.
- Why does the fact that doing what the law requires (a) is a reasonably just cooperative practice that produces goods from which one benefits, and (b) corresponds to one's fair share ground an obligation to do what the law requires?
- Target general moral principle: Because one ought to contribute one's fair share to a reasonably just cooperative practice, whenever that practice produces goods one benefits from.

There are two difficulties with this line of reasoning, concerning (a) and (b), respectively. First, it is unclear why we should regard legal obedience as beneficial *in general*. Some laws may be silly or unhelpful. And citizens can fail to obey those laws without this bringing on any harms, and, indeed, without this undermining the rule of law (Smith 1973: 958). For example, in certain parts of Italy, where I am from, there exist some rather outdated but permissible laws, regulating the location and shape of bathrooms in private homes. Originally introduced for health-and-safety purposes, nowadays these regulations arguably serve no purpose other than complicating the lives of homeowners. As it happens, these

---

[15] I will take this qualification for granted in what follows and omit to restate it.

laws are often ignored, without this undermining the rule of law *in general* or having any other bad consequence.

Second, and related, it is not clear what ensures that doing what the law requires always corresponds to *one's fair share*. Imagine a society where taxes are not egregiously unjust, but only a little unfair: the rich are taxed too lightly, and the middle and lower-middle classes too heavily, though by a relatively small amount. In this case, it would simply not be true that, by paying all their taxes, members of the middle class would do their fair share of reciprocation: they would in fact do *more* than their fair share. Whether someone does their fair share or not, surely, depends on the *content* of the law.

In sum, on the fair-play view, whether we have an obligation to obey the law depends on the content of legal commands: on whether general obedience would in fact be beneficial (given that content), and on whether obeying would correspond to one's *fair share* of reciprocation. The fair-play view, then, succeeds in grounding a contingent obligation to act *in conformity with many laws*, but not an obligation to obey the law "because it is the law" (cf. Klosko 2007: 3).

2.3 Natural-duty-of-justice views

Another family of views claim that our obligation to obey the law stems from duties that we hold just by virtue of our humanity—independently of our benefitting from cooperative practices. On a particularly popular version of this type of view, the ground of political obligation is justice-based, and captured by the following principle.

P: One has a duty to do what is necessary to realize justice (i.e., to respect and protect people's rights).

Coupled with the empirical observation that obedience to the law of a reasonably just state is required for the realization of justice, proponents of the natural-duty view conclude that we ought to obey the law—of course, provided the law is reasonably just (Rawls 1999a: 99; Stilz 2009; Waldron 1993).[16]

There are again predictable difficulties with the natural-duty-of-justice view, not too dissimilar from those we encountered in the case of fair play. First, many laws seem to have very little to do with justice. For instance, in *Traffic Light*, no concerns of justice—on any plausible understanding of justice—are at stake.

---

[16] Other natural duties appealed to in the literature are Samaritan duties to help others (Wellman 2001), and the "duty not to pose unjust threats" (Renzo 2011). My argument applies, mutatis mutandis, to these other natural duties too. Note also that some natural-duty-of-justice views intersect with democratic ones, which I discuss later in the chapter. In this section, I treat natural-duty approaches as self-standing.

162 GROUNDING POLITICAL OBLIGATION

My father-in-law's obedience or disobedience would have no impact on anyone's interests other than his own (cf. Edmundson 2004, 235; Lefkowitz 2006, 590–2). Consequently, it is not clear what right could possibly be violated by his disobedience, other than a question-begging right—held by the state or perhaps by all citizens—that everyone always obeys the law.[17]

Second, not only are certain laws justice-irrelevant. Some laws can also be *justice-undermining*, even in a reasonably just state. Consider again the case of taxation, where a portion of the population is disproportionately burdened. It is not clear that, if this portion of the population were to pay a little less tax than what, in fact, it legally owes, justice would be undermined. If anything, it would be enhanced.

This is not to deny that doing as the law requires is often necessary for the pursuit of justice. A lawless world is not one in which justice would triumph: this much I can perfectly concede to the proponent of the natural-duty view. The issue is that whether doing as the law requires in any particular instance is most conducive to justice depends on *what* the law requires. On a natural-duty view, it is not the status of a particular action as legally mandated that triggers obligations, it is its conduciveness to justice. This, in turn, is a contingent and *content-dependent* matter.[18]

2.4 Associative views

Another well-known family of views hold that political obligation comes with our membership in political associations. These so-called "associative views" ground political obligation in the following principle.

P: One has a pro tanto obligation to adhere to the rules of a reasonably just association of which one is a member (see, e.g., Dworkin 1986; Horton 2010; Miller 1995; Stilz 2011: sec. 5; for discussion see van der Vossen 2011).

Much, of course, hinges on what makes someone a member of an association, where the association at stake here is a political community. Let us immediately clarify that membership is not based on consent. If it were, associative views would collapse into consent-based ones, and we already know that only very few people ever consent to being members of states. So, what does it take for one to be a member? Two options are available. On a subjectivist picture of membership,

---

[17] I am here assuming a typically tight connection between rights (as inviolability) and interests. For discussion, see the previous chapter.

[18] Structurally speaking, natural-duty approaches seem akin to instrumentalist ones; while instrumentalism focuses on reason-compliance generally, natural-duty approaches emphasize compliance with reasons of justice specifically.

members are those who identify with the aims and rules of the association. On an objectivist picture, members are those who are designated as members by the associations' rules. So, for instance, someone who is a citizen of Italy but does not identify with the Italian state would be a member on an objectivist account and not a member on a subjectivist one.

Associativism about political obligation is plagued by significant difficulties. Most importantly, it is unclear that principle *P* has much independent plausibility. I, for one, do not quite see why unchosen membership in a non-intimate association should give rise to an obligation to obey its rules. My perplexities are independent of whether we opt for an objectivist or a subjectivist account. My identification with a certain practice seems to make my participation in that practice *worthwhile* for me, but it is unclear why it should further bind me to obey its rules (see Chapter 3, Section 8.3). Similarly, it is unclear why the fact that some state regards me as a citizen automatically places an obligation on me to obey its commands. Of course, citizenship comes with benefits, and we may think that the benefits require some form of reciprocation. But this would bring us back to the fair-play approach (cf. Dagger 2000).

These difficulties are reflected in some implausible verdicts delivered by associative theories. Recall *Traffic Light*. On the subjectivist version of the associative view, someone's lack of identification with the German state would suffice to release him from the obligation to stop at the red light (Renzo 2012). On the objectivist version, someone's being a foreigner—i.e., not a member of the German state—would equally suffice to release him from the relevant obligation. Whatever we think about the obligatoriness of stopping at red lights on empty streets, it certainly seems that a mere lack of identification with the relevant state or a foreign citizenship should not automatically release one from legal obligations.

Overall, then, the associative view appears to stand on shaky grounds, insofar as its chosen principle *P* lacks plausibility, quite apart from whether that principle could give rise to obligations to obey the law that are structurally content-independent.

3. Democratic Theory

The most popular account of political obligation in contemporary times and in the Western world is democratic theory. There exist two main versions of democratic theory: instrumentalist and proceduralist (Christiano 2008a; Valentini 2013).[19] Instrumentalist accounts defend the authority of democracy based on the quality of the outcomes it produces (Arneson 2004). It should be clear, based

---

[19] Just to warn my reader: the literature on democracy is so vast that offering a comprehensive list of references on the topic would make this section extremely cumbersome. I here limit myself to citing the works I have personally found most relevant to the points I am discussing, including my previous work on the topic, of which the present section and chapter are a continuation.

164   GROUNDING POLITICAL OBLIGATION

on my critiques of instrumentalism, that this version of democratic theory is poorly placed to vindicate a content-independent obligation to obey the law. This is because whether following democratically approved law is best from the point of view of outcomes clearly depends on the content of the law. Perhaps, on the whole, democracies—at least under a certain class of conditions—produce better laws than alternative political systems. However, whether we are better off, from the perspective of the reasons that we have, by conforming with democratically made decisions depends on how good these decisions are. As we have seen, sometimes it may be better—more in line with reason—to ignore a red light, or to not pay all of one's taxes, or to engage in harmless trespass, even if the law of a democratic state forbids all of these actions.

Democratic theory is genuinely distinctive as an approach to political obligation when it takes a *proceduralist* form. Here, the democratic pedigree of the law matters *intrinsically*, not instrumentally (e.g., Christiano 2008b; Dahl 1989; Griffin 2003; Waldron 1999). Although there are several versions of the intrinsic argument, they share the claim that democratic decision procedures uniquely reflect *citizens' equal status*. By giving citizens an equal say in the making of collective decisions, on matters subject to reasonable disagreement—i.e., where intelligent people who care about justice and the common good might still be at odds with each other—the state treats them as equals. Since treating citizens as equals is a bedrock moral requirement of any plausible conception of socio-political justice, democracy itself is a requirement of justice, or so the argument goes (e.g., Valentini 2013). Principle *P*, in this case, can be stated as follows.

P: One has a pro tanto obligation to adhere to democratically made decisions to which one is subject.

Democratic theory can be seen as offering a proceduralist twist on natural-duty theory. What explains our obligation to obey democratic law is that doing so is necessary to realize justice. If we disobeyed democratically approved law, we'd fail to treat our fellow citizens as equals, and since we have obligations of justice to treat them as equals, we also have an obligation to obey democratic law.

Unlike its natural-duty cousin, democratic theory exhibits a structure that allows it to vindicate the content-independence of political obligation. After all, in a democratic state, by definition, genuine law is democratically arrived at. Provided the content of the law falls within the bounds of moral acceptability, the law will clearly be binding independently of its content. Its democratic pedigree explains its bindingness; and if rules and regulations are not democratically arrived at, they do not count as law.

Even if principle *P* underpinning democratic theory is both plausible and capable of delivering on content-independence, its justification exhibits some lacunae. It is, in fact, far from clear *both*:

- that democracy uniquely instantiates equal respect for persons, *and*
- that, even granting the "uniqueness" claim about democracy and equal respect, only the *particular instantiations* of democracy found in this or that context do.

Let me address each point in turn. First, as several democratic theorists have argued, it is not obvious that democracy—understood as involving a combination of free and fair elections, universal suffrage, and majoritarian voting procedures— is the only political decision-making system able to honour a commitment to citizens' equal status. In a democracy, citizens only nominally have equal decision-making power. Even in the best-organized democratic system, representatives have greater decision-making power than the rest of the citizenry, and people with considerable financial means have greater political influence than the less financially privileged. Moreover, it is not uncommon for democracies to include permanent minorities: groups of citizens who are routinely outvoted. In light of these facts, a "lottocratic system"—i.e., one in which at least some decisions are taken through randomized procedures, giving each outcome a chance— might be equally, if not more, responsive to the fundamental equality of persons (Guerrero 2014; Saunders 2010). While that system would also include winners and losers, unlike standard democratic majoritarianism it would give those whose voices tend to be silenced a chance of succeeding. In other words, democratic theorists seem unable to show that democracy is *uniquely* tied to equal respect.[20] This, in turn, casts doubt on the privileged status of P as a ground for political obligation.

What is more, even if democracy could be shown to be uniquely capable of honouring equal respect, this would still not suffice to explain why only law arrived at through a *particular* democratic procedure has binding force in a given context. Let me explain. There clearly exists a multiplicity of permissible instantiations of democracy, characterized by different electoral rules, principles for drawing constituencies, procedures for making and changing law, and so forth. Consider the political systems in the US, Australia, and Italy today. All three qualify as democratic, but function rather differently. Now, let us focus on how the legislature is elected. In the US, this is through the first-past-the-post system.[21] Australia, by contrast, adopts the Alternative Voting system (also known as the Preferential Voting system).[22] As of 2017, Italy elects its members of parliament

---

[20] In Valentini (2013), I briefly tried to show that it is. On reflection, however, I think there was something missing from that argument, which I try to make up for here.

[21] This is a familiar system whereby voters select their preferred candidate on the ballot papers, and the candidate with the most votes wins.

[22] According to this procedure, within each constituency each voter ranks all candidates, from first to last. If a candidate obtains an absolute majority of first preferences, he/she/they is/are elected. If no candidate obtains the absolute majority of first preferences, the candidate with the fewest total first preferences is eliminated from the ballot papers of those voters who had him/her/them at the top, and

166 GROUNDING POLITICAL OBLIGATION

via a mixed procedure, combining elements of first-past-the-post and proportional representation. In light of the multiplicity of institutional set-ups counting as bona fide democratic, the question is how can democratic theory explain the following type of case.

Election Official: An election takes place in Australia. The accepted electoral procedure is Alternative Voting (AV). The election official in charge of counting votes, however, performs the calculation using a different procedure: the Borda Count (BC).[23] Depending on the profile of votes, the Alternative Voting and Borda Count procedures may deliver the same verdict. In this case, they do. The official's use of the Borda Count therefore makes no difference to the final electoral outcome, though, of course, it could have.

Most readers, I assume, would want to say that what the election official did was wrong. If he were discovered, he would be charged with a criminal offence: he'd be guilty of election fraud. Yet, it is not clear that democratic proceduralism, at least as I have presented it, allows us to come to this conclusion. After all, the procedure followed by the official is a fully democratic one, and one that also makes an appearance in real-world political systems. It is used to elect members of Parliament in the Republic of Nauru (part of the Micronesian region) and also features, less prominently, in the electoral system of the Slovenian National Assembly ("IFES Election Guide" 2019). There is nothing in principle anti-democratic about the Borda Count. A society where election results depend on AV and one in which they depend on BC are both equally democratic, and egalitarian for that reason. So, why does the fact that, in Australia, the accepted procedure happens to be AV make it intuitively wrong for our election official to resort to his favoured procedure, namely BC, instead? Democratic theory, as currently stated, cannot answer this challenge.[24]

In sum, I have argued that, while superior to competing views, democratic theory is not fully convincing. It gives us reasons for believing that only a certain subset of political decision-making systems can have authority, but it fails to explain why only democratic ones do, and why the *particular instantiations* of democracy to be found in any given context have authority in *that* context.

---

the vote is reallocated to the next candidate in the ranking. The procedure continues until a candidate with an absolute majority of votes emerges.

[23] Assume that there are K candidates. According to the Borda Count, each voter assigns a score to each candidate: K to their top preference, K-1 to their second preference, and so on. The voters' scores are then added up for each candidate and the candidate with the highest total score wins the election.

[24] Note that the wrong involved in *Election Official* is not traceable to something akin to a breach of contract, of terms of interaction that have been mutually agreed upon. In fact, the overwhelming majority of those wronged by the official's actions—i.e., contemporary Australians—have not consented to being governed in accordance with this particular electoral procedure. The procedure was introduced in 1918 (Australian Electoral Commission 2019).

Our discussion of democratic theory thus leads us to a modified version of *P*, according to which "one has a pro tanto obligation to adhere to the decisions made via the particular egalitarian decision-making mechanism that are instantiated in one's social context". What we need is a convincing justification for that obligation. The agency-respect view, I believe, can provide such a justification.

4. The Agency-Respect View

In this section, I discuss the agency-respect view of political obligation. I do so by first laying out the view and then showing how it fills the lacunae of democratic theory.

4.1 Respect for persons' commitments to the rule of law

Recall that, on the agency-respect view, principle *P*, which grounds content-independent obligations to obey socially constructed norms in general, reads as follows.

P: One has a (pro tanto) obligation to respect people's commitments (i.e., "to give *agency respect* to people"), provided those commitments are authentic, morally permissible, and respecting them is not too costly.

As argued in Chapter 3, the principle grounds those obligations because socially constructed norms are constituted by people's commitments, specifically their commitments to the norms' demands functioning as general standards of behaviour. Breaches of norms, therefore, disrespect people's commitments. To the extent that legal norms belong to the broader category of socially constructed norms, the agency-respect view applies to those norms too, or so I argue in what follows.

To elucidate my argument, I must first clarify what I mean by *legal norms*. There is of course a long-standing controversy, between legal positivists and their opponents, about the ontology of law: about what makes it the case that something counts as a legal norm. This is not the place to delve into that controversy (for discussion, see Marmor and Sarch 2019). I will thus limit myself to adopting a simple, common-sense understanding of legal norms. These, I suggest, are a particularly salient type of what, in Chapter 1, I called "formal norms", characterized by Hart-style primary rules (prescribing and forbidding behaviour) and secondary rules (establishing how primary rules are to be created, interpreted, and modified). For present purposes, which combination of primary and secondary rules qualifies as law in any given context depends on what is conventionally considered law in that context. Legal requirements and prohibitions in society S are those requirements and prohibitions that satisfy the conditions for legality *as these are understood by officials and citizens in S*. I thus outsource the account of law to local conventional understandings of this notion (for discussion, see Marmor 2019: 161).

Having clarified what I mean by legal norms, I can now turn to explaining how the agency-respect view grounds an obligation to obey them, thereby vindicating our practice of sanctioning and disapproving of legal disobedience. Schematically put, the answer is captured by the following grounding sequence.

- <u>Action required</u>: You ought to do what the law requires.
- By virtue of what ought I to do what the law requires?
- <u>Empirical fact</u>: Because a socially constructed norm—provided the norm is underpinned by people's authentic as well as permissible commitments, and respecting it is not too costly—mandates that you do what the law requires (i.e., the *rule of law*).
- By virtue of what does the fact that doing what the law requires is mandated by a socially constructed norm—provided the norm is underpinned by people's authentic as well as permissible commitments, and respecting it is not too costly—ground my obligation to do as the law requires?
- <u>Target general moral principle</u>: Because you have an obligation to respect people's commitments (i.e., "to give *agency respect* to people"), provided those commitments are authentic, morally permissible, and respecting them is not too costly.

As the above-outlined grounding sequence shows, the agency-respect view can only ground an obligation to do what the law requires "because the law so requires" in the presence of a socially constructed norm demanding legal obedience. That norm amounts to a public belief in, and commitment to, the *rule of law*. The rule-of-law norm captures the idea that nobody should be above the law and that, therefore, all requirements counting as legal should be complied with by those subject to them. A society characterized by the rule of law is one in which a large enough number of citizens and officials think that the question "why ought I to φ?" may be suitably answered by pointing to the status of φ-ing as legally mandated. Legality, in other words, comes hand in hand with de facto or "social" normativity.

Importantly, if legality were not accompanied by de facto normativity—i.e., in the absence of a commitment to the rule of law—the very problem of political obligation as we know it would disappear. Legal disobedience qua legal disobedience would not be accompanied by sanctions and negative reactive attitudes, hence the question of whether those sanctions are justified would not arise. We would not need to ask whether there exists a moral obligation to obey the law violation of which justifies our practice of sanctioning legal disobedience, because that practice would not exist in the first place.

Having said that, according to the agency-respect principle, respect for people's commitment to the rule of law generates a moral obligation to obey the law only under specific conditions. First, such a commitment needs to be *morally permissible*, and whether it is or not depends on the law's consistency with fundamental moral demands. This condition allows the agency-respect view to incorporate the insights of natural-duty and democratic theories. To the extent that fundamental moral demands include honouring the moral equality of persons, and to the extent that basic requirements of justice and egalitarian political decision-making are a sine-qua-non of equal respect for persons, on the agency-respect view laws will only be binding if their content is consistent with these requirements. That is, the law needs to be suitably substantively and procedurally egalitarian.

Autocratic law, or law that cannot be reasonably seen as protecting people's fundamental interests as equals, will lack moral force. There are, of course, complex questions concerning what, concretely, equal respect demands. By way of first approximation, as I already noted in Chapter 3, we can be confident that a state that deprives its citizens of freedom of movement, association, speech, access to basic necessities, and equal entitlements to political participation fails to meet the relevant demands. Its laws lack moral force, no matter how strongly committed to the rule of law citizens and officials are.

Second, the agency-respect view only grounds an obligation to obey the law on condition that people's commitment to the rule of law is authentic, and not the product of coercion, oppression, or brainwashing. Manifestly, this "authenticity" requirement—which I briefly discussed in Chapter 3 and will be further discussed in the book's Conclusion—will be much easier to satisfy in circumstances where the law meets independent criteria of moral permissibility. Commitments to inegalitarian or oppressive law are in fact hard to regard as genuine, especially if exhibited by those who are disadvantaged by that law.

Third, and finally, the agency-respect principle gives rise to a demand to obey legal requirements only provided that complying with this demand does not excessively burden one's agency. As we shall see later in the chapter, if obedience to legal requirements were to undermine one's integrity, say because such requirements contradict one's deepest religious or ethical convictions, the agency-respect principle would not mandate obedience.

In sum, when (i) a state's law is reasonably just and procedurally egalitarian, (ii) people's commitment to the rule of law is authentic, and (iii) abiding by legal rules isn't too costly for one's own agency, agency respect for supporters of the rule of law generates an obligation to obey the law. The moral normativity of law stems from the duty to respect people's commitments to legal norms serving as standards of behaviour. The agency-respect view thus grounds an *obligation to obey the*

170 GROUNDING POLITICAL OBLIGATION

law because it is the law. Unlike instrumentalist, fair-play, and natural-duty-of-justice views, it doesn't vindicate conformity with particular (possibly many) laws by appeal to the good consequences of following them, or to the fact that failing to follow them would (sometimes) amount to free riding. Instead, it starts from an existing commitment to the rule of law, and derives the normativity of law "qua law" from a prior obligation to respect that already existing commitment under specified conditions. The obligation to obey the law, on this view, is clearly *content-sensitive*—since no obligation is generated in the case of morally abhorrent law—but also *content-independent*—since what explains the obligatoriness of law is not a feature of its content, but its status as the object of particular kinds of commitments. Furthermore, despite giving a prominent role to commitments in generating an obligation to obey the law, the agency-respect view does not exhibit some of the implausible implications of subjective associative views. On those views, one's subjective identification with or commitment to a given community grounds one's obligations to obey the norms governing that community. This means that one's obligation to obey the law kicks in or disappears purely based on one's conative attitudes. If I am not committed, I need not obey. This, however, is odd to say the least. On the agency-respect view, by contrast, it is respect for others' commitments to the rule of law that generates an obligation to obey it. The obligation is not a mere function of "how one feels about the law", but rests on a prior moral principle mandating respect for others.

4.2 Improving on democratic theory

The agency-respect view allows us to respond to the challenges encountered in the previous section, which democratic views had trouble tackling. Suppose someone asks: why are democratically made decisions binding in the UK, but decisions arrived at through lottocratic decision-procedures are not? The answer, from the perspective of the agency-respect view, is simple. In principle, both procedures might give rise to morally binding decisions, since they are both consistent with a commitment to equal respect. However, since what happens to count as the law in the UK is arrived at via democratic decision procedures, agency respect for those who support the rule of law in the UK grounds the authority of democracy. Switching to a lottocratic procedure—in a way that is unconstitutional or otherwise not in line with existing law—would violate their commitments.

Similar considerations allow us to respond to the challenge posed by *Election Official*. The reason why what the official did was wrong is that in Australia the Alternative Voting procedure counts as the law. Deviating from that procedure is tantamount to agency-disrespecting those who are committed to the rule of law. The agency-respect view, therefore, helps us explain how it is that existing, de facto democratic procedures are morally binding, even when we know that democracy can be instantiated in a multiplicity of different ways. In doing so, it explains why we have a pro tanto obligation to adhere to the decisions made via the particular egalitarian decision-making mechanisms that are instantiated in our social context. That obligation stems from agency respect towards those who are committed to said mechanisms—mechanisms that happen to be the law—provided their commitments are authentic and respecting them isn't too costly.[25]

These observations are likely to prompt a concern, which was briefly mentioned in Chapter 3, but resurfaces in the present context with full force. This is the worry that the agency-respect view exhibits unpalatable "majoritarian tendencies". On that view, a norm exists in context C whenever a large enough number of people in C (typically, a consistent majority) display certain beliefs and commitments. However, one might wonder, why should *a majority's* commitments take priority over the commitments of a minority? After all, even within the best egalitarian political systems, what counts as the law tends to reflect the commitments of existing majorities. Suppose—to go back to our earlier example—that, in Australia, the majority is committed to AV, but in fact there are a few, including our election official, who are convinced that the Borda Count would be a far superior method for aggregating votes. What about agency respect *for them*? Note that the same question could be raised in relation to a variety of different matters over which citizens are likely reasonably to disagree. These include, for example, vegetarianism, abortion, school curricula, the use of nuclear power, and much else. Doesn't respect for a commitment to the rule of (permissible) law imply "unqualified" respect for the commitments of the majority? And isn't this problematic?

To answer this question, we must first get clearer about some details of the envisaged situation. Disagreeing with the content of the law need not imply that one lacks a commitment to *legal* norms functioning as general standards of behaviour, that is, a commitment to the rule of law. I may be an Australian citizen, believe that the Borda Count would be a superior procedure for determining who wins an election, but be committed to the rule of law and thereby still condemn violations of the Alternative Voting system—such as the violation committed by our election official. In this case, I belong to the group of people whose commitments are violated by breaches of the AV rule, *even if* I do not particularly like that rule. It may be unfortunate that the content of the law does not match my preferences, but so long as I am committed to the rule of law, my agency-respect obligation to obey it does not clash with agency respect for my own commitments.

The tension we are exploring only arises when some individuals are not generally committed to legal requirements functioning as standards of behaviour, and the content of existing laws is at odds with their commitments. For example, consider an animal-rights activist with philosophical anarchist leanings. In his

---

[25] I do not mention permissibility because this condition is already implicitly satisfied by the mechanisms being appropriately egalitarian.

172 GROUNDING POLITICAL OBLIGATION

view, the legal permission to consume meat is morally abhorrent: it is inconsistent with a deep, principled commitment of his, namely, preventing meat consumption. Why does the fact that the majority is either happy with meat consumption, or indirectly accepts the permissibility of meat consumption because of its legal status, make it wrong for our animal-rights activist to illegally try to prevent others from eating meat? Doesn't existing law violate *his* reasonable commitments? After all, whether eating meat should be permissible or not is a complex matter on which there is reasonable disagreement.

The answer to the aforementioned questions is: yes. There is something morally unsatisfactory about a status quo where some people's commitments happen to be reflected in the law, and where those laws in fact themselves frustrate other people's—typically, a minority's—commitments, especially if said minority isn't itself committed to the rule of law. This, however, is an unavoidable fact of life, especially within pluralistic societies. A world in which everyone's reasonable and permissible commitments can equally coexist with each other is a regulative ideal we may aspire to but are unlikely ever to reach in full. There is no world, in other words, which doesn't involve frustrating valid agency-respect claims. The best we can do is build norms and broader decision-making systems that minimize such frustration and allow us to keep the limitations of the status quo—from the perspective of agency respect—firmly in sight. I therefore concede that the situation of our anarchist animal-rights activist involves an agency harm. While such harms are unavoidable, for the reasons just mentioned, we may still try to mitigate them, by giving minorities space for protesting and challenging the law.[26] Furthermore—as principle P states—when respecting others' commitments becomes too costly, in terms of one's own agency, others' commitments cease to place obligations on us. If this were the case for our animal-rights activist, a suggestion which I do not find implausible, then our activist would have no content-independent obligation to *obey* the law in the first place. Of course, whether he would be all-things-considered justified in violating it is a separate matter.

These considerations bring to mind the practices of civil disobedience and conscientious refusal. As I argue in the next section, the agency-respect view offers us a useful perspective on the value of these practices within a broadly democratic society.

5. The Agency-Respect View and Civil Disobedience

Civil disobedience can be defined as the conscientious, public violation of the law, with a distinctively communicative aim: alerting the rest of the citizenry to what

---

[26] Under appropriate circumstances, minorities may even have a right to political independence. See the discussion in Chapter 6, Section 8.1.

one perceives to be a serious injustice (Rawls 1999a: 320). Examples of civil disobedience abound: from Gandhi's historic non-violent resistance against British colonial rule to today's acts of disruption undertaken by environmental activist groups, such as Extinction Rebellion or Fridays for Future.

Conscientious refusal, by contrast, is a more private affair: it involves one's refusal to obey the law in cases where the law is felt to clash significantly with one's personal commitments. For instance, a pacifist may conscientiously refuse to go to war or serve in the military, despite being otherwise legally bound to do so (Dworkin 1985: Ch. 4; Rawls 1999a: 320).

Conscientious refusal and, even more so, civil disobedience have long puzzled advocates of political obligation. On the one hand, they appear to be admirable practices, and have in the past been used to combat egregiously unjust political arrangements, such as racial segregation in the US and colonial rule in India. On the other hand, if there is an obligation to obey the law, civil disobedience and conscientious refusal involve at least a pro tanto wrong. How to reconcile our admiration for these practices with their apparent wrongness?

The first thing to note, which David Lyons (1998) correctly alerts us to, is that in paradigmatic instances of civil disobedience—such as Gandhi's and that of the American Civil Rights movement—and conscientious refusal the conditions for political obligation are unambiguously absent. The regimes involved were too egregiously unjust for anyone to have an obligation to obey the law qua law. In relation to those regimes, by and large, disobedience to the law involved no pro tanto wrongs. The law, qua law, had no moral normativity.

That said, there exist (or at any rate there can be) reasonably just states in which citizens strongly oppose at least some democratically made laws. This may be for personal ethical or religious reasons, or because these laws are perceived to be seriously unjust—for instance, in the case of the animal-rights activist mentioned earlier. Note that these laws' opponents may be *either* (a) generally committed to the rule of law, and simply object to some particular laws, *or* (b) anarchists who have no commitment to the rule of law as such and also object to the content of some specific laws. Case (b) was briefly discussed earlier. For our purposes, cases of type (a) are particularly interesting, since they bring to light the tensions *internal* to civil disobedience and conscientious refusal. How does the agency-respect view help us make sense of, and navigate, such tensions?

Let us start with conscientious refusal. The agency-respect view allows for a rather seamless moral analysis of this practice. In situations where a person's deepest commitments clash with permissible legal demands, the view tells us that insisting on legal obedience would excessively burden the agency of that person. In such cases, a person may not only be all-things-considered justified in committing a pro tanto wrong and violating the law. If obeying the law would place unreasonable burdens on her agency, according to the agency-respect principle, the law will not be morally binding on her in the first place. Violations of the law "qua law" will thus not result in pro tanto wrongs. In this vein, the pacifist who is legally obliged to go to war may not be morally obligated to "do so because going to war is what the law requires". Agency respect for law-supporters would in fact come at too high a cost to the pacifist's own agency. Similarly, one might argue that a legal requirement to not wear headscarves in certain public spaces might place too heavy a burden on the conscience and integrity of Muslim women—on the assumption that they themselves genuinely endorse this clothing rule—such that the relevant requirement places no obligations on them *on agency-respect grounds*.

In recognition of the agency-burdens inflicted upon holders of minority views by the law, legal channels allowing individuals to conscientiously refuse without violating the law have been made available. Seeing the obligation to obey the law as itself grounded in respect for commitments, as the agency-respect view enables us to do, lends further legitimacy to the demands of those who conscientiously refuse. It shows that far from treating themselves as exceptions, their refusal to obey the law is consistent with a principle of *equal* respect for persons' commitments. In a pluralistic society, the majority's commitments—as expressed in the law—may at times clash with the deepest convictions of minorities. Making space for legal conscientious refusal, and exemptions more generally, is a way of acknowledging this fact and reducing the agency-burdens faced by those with unpopular commitments. Of course, in which cases conscientious refusal should be made available is itself a complex matter, where the strength of the agency-interests of individuals and the broader interests of society in the delivery of certain social goods (e.g., safety) have to be taken into account. For instance, while a special exemption might be granted for the wearing of a veil that only covers one's hair, arguably, such an exemption may not be equally all-things-considered justified in case of a full-face veil, out of safety concerns (i.e., since wearing such religious garments is tantamount to hiding one's identity). Enforcing the "burqa ban" could thus be justified even if, by evading the ban, women genuinely committed to wearing the burqa or niqab on religious grounds wouldn't be doing anything wrong *from the perspective of agency respect*, since the ban itself places too heavy a burden on their agency.

Let me now turn to civil disobedience. Suppose an environmentalist citizen chains herself to rail tracks to protest against the installation of a new nuclear power station. In her view, nuclear power should be outlawed (BBC News 2001). Chaining oneself to the rail tracks is illegal and our citizen is aware of this. In fact, she has a general commitment to obeying the law—she belongs to type (a) above—and feels like what she is doing is a pro tanto wrong. At the same time, she finds the state's acceptance of nuclear power deeply morally problematic and at odds with her commitments. By chaining herself to the rail tracks, she tries to alert the moral conscience of her fellow citizens to what strikes her as a big moral mistake.

THE AGENCY-RESPECT VIEW AND CIVIL DISOBEDIENCE   175

Looking at civil disobedience from the perspective of the agency-respect view allows us to see its raison d'être within a well-ordered democratic society. This practice allows citizens whose justice-commitments deeply clash with existing laws to express their frustration and dissatisfaction, and in a way that involves violations of agency respect, just as some existing law violates agency respect towards them. And once we realize that, even in well-ordered democratic systems, laws are bound to be contrary to at least some citizens' commitments, it should also become clear why a practice like civil disobedience should be responded to *with lenience*, rather than with harsh punishment (see, e.g., Brownlee 2012: Ch. 8). Put somewhat bluntly, what the genuine civilly disobedient agent does to the rest of the citizenry, in terms of agency-respect wrongs, the rest of the citizenry does to her on a regular basis, under the banner of legitimate law. While this unfortunate state of affairs is virtually unavoidable, it is also one we should acknowledge and remedy as much as possible.

Civil disobedience is a reminder of the fact that the socially constructed norms governing society—typically, laws—do not represent universal commitments, but partial ones, albeit widespread. While violating those laws may be pro tanto wrong, treating those who conscientiously break them as regular criminals would be even more problematic, since it would imply a failure to acknowledge the agency harms of which they are victims, by virtue of finding themselves in the minority.

This view tallies well with the defence of civil disobedience proposed by David Lefkowitz (2007), and which Emanuela Ceva draws upon in the following passage:

> That any single person finds herself in a majority or in a minority position within a certain social context is largely a matter of luck. But it should be a priority for a legitimate state to reduce as much as possible the impact of luck on the exercise of their autonomy, that is on the capacity citizens have to be the co-authors of the collective decisions binding on them. On this ground, those who were unfortunate enough to find themselves in a minority position should either endorse the majority's view or engage in public acts of disobedience to express their disagreement and try to modify the contested decision.   (Ceva 2015: 643)

The idea, put in the vocabulary of the agency-respect view, is that the practice of civil disobedience is required out of respect for the agency (i.e., autonomy) of individuals who find themselves within minorities. To the extent that the law does not reflect their commitments, strictly speaking, they are not "equal co-authors" of the law. To approximate this democratic regulative ideal, society should make mechanisms available for their expression of dissent and protest. Civil disobedience without (harsh) punishment is one of them. The agency-respect view thus helps us make moral sense of this practice.

176 GROUNDING POLITICAL OBLIGATION

6. Between Anarchism and Legal Normativism

I have argued that, to the extent that the rule of law is a norm within a given society S, the agency-respect view can explain our obligation to obey the law. In other words, it explains why it is pro tanto wrong to disobey the law qua law: it is agency-disrespectful to those whose attitudes sustain it. It should be emphasized that while this is good news for advocates of the authority of law, it is not such bad news for anarchists either. On the view that I have defended, the obligation to obey the law turns out to be potentially rather weak and is fundamentally no different from the obligation to queue up at bus stops, to wear modest clothes in church, to stand up at high table when grace is said, and so forth. My view thus has the virtue of doing justice to both anarchists and legal normativists.

On the one hand, it acknowledges that, under appropriate circumstances, there is something (pro tanto) wrong in disobeying the law. Action X being prohibited by a set of morally permissible laws gives us a pro tanto obligation not to do X— an obligation that would not exist were it not for the laws in question. However, and this is where my view leans in the direction of anarchism, the relevant obligation often only accounts for *a fraction* of the wrong involved in performing actions prohibited by morally permissible laws. Much—though not all—of what is wrong with performing those actions will likely be law-independent, as in the case of laws against murder and theft, as well as traffic and safety regulations. Several of those reasons are aptly captured by the views critically discussed in Section 2.

Furthermore, when those other considerations are absent, whether violations of legal norms are wrongful "because those are legal norms" will depend on the nature of people's commitments: i.e., whether those commitments concern the particular content of those norms or their legal status. Take again our familiar example, *Traffic Light*, and consider the following three scenarios (two of them are rather realistic, one isn't—you guess which one!). First, in Germany, there is a general commitment to the rule of law, which requires stopping at red lights even when doing so is not necessary for reasons of safety or coordination. Second, in Germany there is no general commitment to the rule of law, but people nonetheless are committed to the specific rule requiring obedience to traffic regulations. Third, in Naples, there is no general commitment to the rule of law, traffic signs are considered "legal", yet nobody, including officials, follows them. What does the agency-respect view imply in each of these cases?

The first case is rather simple: the agency-respect view requires people to obey traffic regulations because they are the law. The second case, by contrast, is one in which people have agency-respect obligations to stop at red lights because socially constructed norms require them to do so, independently of their status as legal norms. So, although there's a content-independent obligation to stop at red lights, the legally mandated nature of such behaviour doesn't contribute to grounding that obligation. Finally, the third case is one in which traffic regulations have no moral normativity per se, since they do not function as socially constructed norms proper. There's no general commitment to their demands, whether direct or whether mediated by a higher-order commitment to the rule of law.

On the agency-respect view, then, the law matters only as long as it features among people's commitments, and its status is no more special than that of other socially constructed norms. Furthermore, by not fetishizing the law, the agency-respect view reflects the common thought that, often, small legal infractions may strike us as wrongful, but not really "a big deal". At the same time, harmless breaches of laws which we regard as particularly important or fundamental—e.g., laws concerning the state's collective will formation, such as in *Election Official*—appear to us seriously wrong. Again, the agency-respect view is able to account for these judgements, by pointing to the greater weight of the agential commitments underpinning those laws.

The reason why advocates of the authority of law often defend a very weighty obligation to obey it, I suggest, is that they surreptitiously build into the force of that obligation independent moral reasons that have little to do with "something being required by law". Describing something as "a breach of law" may be a quick and parsimonious way of pointing to a variety of law-independent moral (and prudential) grounds for an action's wrongness. Since the empirical association between breaches of law and independent moral wrongs is rather regular—at least in decent legal systems—appeals to breaches of the law can function as "summaries" of these independent reasons. But note that, on this use, the obligation to obey the law, strictly understood, does not exist. The fact that a set of socially constructed norms prescribes a particular conduct, independently of its substantive merits, is not what explains the obligatoriness of that conduct.[27] As we have seen in the more critical portion of this chapter, this is arguably the route taken by instrumentalist, fair-play, and natural-duty approaches (cf. Klosko 2011). They do not establish an obligation to *obey* the law, but an obligation to do as the law requires contingent on the fact that doing so often (i) enables us to act on reasons that we independently have, (ii) is necessary to avoid free riding, and (iii) is conducive to justice.

But a second, more pertinent sense of the expression "X is wrong *because* it is a breach of (morally admissible) law" alludes to the law as explanatorily necessary to make sense of the relevant wrong. X is wrong—among other things—*because* it breaches the law. This is the sense I have been interested in throughout this chapter, and the only sense that vindicates a content-independent obligation to obey the law.

---

[27] I thank Kim Sterelny and Florian Ostmann for discussion.

7. Conclusion

In this chapter, I have brought the agency-respect view to bear on the question of the obligation to obey the law. I started by showing that prominent attempts to defend this obligation in fact only succeed in setting forth reasons for conformity with the law: the kinds of reasons a proponent of the deflationary view about the moral normativity of socially constructed norms would be ready to accept. I then argued that the agency-respect view provides a novel understanding of the moral normativity of law, and one that vindicates its content-independence.

Specifically, on the agency-respect view we have a content-independent obligation to obey the law to the extent that this is necessary to respect others' commitments to the rule of law. In doing so, the agency-respect view turns the question of political obligation on its head. While scholars have so far tried to vindicate political obligation by finding reasons that would justify a commitment to the rule of law—i.e., asking why we ought to be committed to the rule of law in the first place—the agency-respect view grounds the obligation to obey the law in respect for that commitment, assuming that commitment to be permissible. On the agency-respect view, without a widespread commitment to the rule of law, there is no obligation to obey it, though often plenty of duties to act in conformity with it.

The obligation to obey the law supported by the agency-respect view, however, is heavily qualified—it only applies to cases in which the law is morally permissible, commitments to the rule of law are authentic, and abiding by the law is not unduly costly. Furthermore, the agency-respect view does not give the law morally special status. Instead, it traces its moral normativity to the broader phenomenon of the moral normativity of socially constructed norms. In these respects, then, it sides with philosophical anarchists.

Finally, I have suggested that the agency-respect view can shed light on the practice of civil disobedience, as one of those cases in which the commitments crystallized in the law clash with those of some people subjected to it. This is just one specific instance of the broader phenomenon that, in a pluralistic world, people's commitments, and relatedly, their agency-respect claims, inevitably conflict with one another. Instead of pushing such clashes under the rug, the agency-respect view allows us to keep them in sight and take them into account in our moral reasoning.

Morality and Socially Constructed Norms. Laura Valentini, Oxford University Press. © Laura Valentini 2023.
DOI: 10.1093/9780191938115.003.0006

6

Explaining the Wrong of Sovereignty Violations

In recent years, political philosophers have become increasingly interested in the question of when and why violations of a political collective's sovereignty are wrongful. As these violations occur in multiple contexts, discussion of this matter can be found across several debates, ranging from just war theory and humanitarian intervention to territorial rights, from the ethics of secession to the nature of the wrong of colonialism.

Participants in these debates, by and large, agree that reasonably just political collectives have a justified claim to sovereignty, and that failing to honour this claim amounts to wrongdoing. A moment's reflection about paradigmatic examples of sovereignty violations—such as aggressive wars, colonialism, and annexations—lends plausibility to this consensus. Violations of a political collective's sovereignty are typically accompanied by severe bodily harm, exploitation, and oppression of individuals. Their wrongfulness thus comes as little surprise and creates no philosophical puzzle.

Philosophically more challenging is the question of whether violations of reasonably just collectives' sovereignty are wrongful *even when* they are not ostensibly accompanied by these other, familiar wrongs against individuals. Let us call these "pure sovereignty violations". For instance, consider an immigrant entering a territory illegally—hence disregarding the sovereign will of the host state—without thereby setting back the interests of local inhabitants. Or imagine a hypothetical peaceful unilateral annexation of a country by another: no individual is harmed in the process and the newly established political unit is governed justly. How can pure sovereignty violations such as these be wrongful if, on the face of it, they do not set back any obvious interests of individuals? The aim of this chapter is to bring the agency-respect view to bear on this question, a question that has recently been given significant attention by political philosophers, in an effort to better understand the relationship between the normative status of individuals and that of collectives (e.g., Altman and Wellman 2009: 13ff.; Miller 2016; Moore 2015: 89–110; Simmons 2013; Stilz 2019; Valentini 2015; Ypi 2013).

To anticipate, I will argue that pure sovereignty violations are wrongful to the extent that they are agency-disrespectful to the individuals whose commitments sustain the complex web of norms making up collectives' sovereignty. In this way, the agency-respect view allows us to explain the wrongfulness of the violation of

180   EXPLAINING THE WRONG OF SOVEREIGNTY VIOLATIONS

political collectives' sovereignty without having to give such collectives independent moral weight. Pure sovereignty violations are wrongful because they fail to give individuals the agency respect they are owed.

In developing this argument, the chapter proceeds as follows. In Section 1, I explicate the concept of sovereignty, drawing some parallels between the sovereignty of individuals and that of collectives. In Section 2, I provide some concrete examples of pure sovereignty violations and set out the puzzle animating this chapter, in the form of a trilemma. The puzzle stems from the impossibility of simultaneously holding the following three prima facie plausible claims:

  (i) there is no pro tanto wrong without setbacks in the legitimate interests of individuals;
 (ii) sovereignty violations of reasonably just political collectives are always pro tanto wrong;
(iii) violations of a reasonably just political collective's sovereignty need not set back individuals' legitimate interests.

In Sections 3 and 4, I consider views about the wrong of sovereignty violations that abandon, respectively, claim (i) and claim (ii). In Section 5, I focus on the most philosophically interesting set of views, namely those that abandon claim (iii). These views seek to show that sovereignty violations of reasonably just political collectives *always* involve setting back individuals' interests. According to these views, the category of "pure sovereignty violations" turns out to be an empty set. I consider two families of views: membership-based views and autonomy-based ones. I suggest that neither succeeds in accounting for all instances of sovereignty violations that strike us as wrongful. In Sections 6 and 7, I turn to the agency-respect view. Thanks to its focus on socially constructed norms, the view successfully relaxes claim (iii), and reveals how, even when seemingly harmless, collective sovereignty violations do in fact involve agency disrespect for individuals. In Section 8, I consider objections, and further elaborate on the agency-respect view, showing that it is also consistent with a mild relaxation of claim (ii). Specifically, on the agency-respect view, if respecting a just collective's sovereignty would place unreasonable burdens on the agency of a given set of individuals (for instance, a national minority wishing to secede), those individuals are not obligated to respect it. This means that certain sovereignty violations of reasonably just political collectives are not wrongful, contrary to claim (ii). Section 9 concludes.

Before I start, let me make two points of clarification. First, as this introduction reveals, the chapter is premised on the assumption that political collectives may be aptly described as *group agents* (e.g., List and Pettit 2011). The question of group or collective agency is much debated in the literature, and not everyone agrees that suitably organized groups may qualify as agents in more than a metaphorical sense. While acknowledging this disagreement, it should be clear that talk of a political collective's sovereignty cannot get off the ground unless we assume that certain collectives are in principle fit for sovereignty, namely agents. (Under any plausible definition, sovereignty cannot be an attribute of a non-agential system.) Sceptics about group agency, then, will find little of appeal in the chapter.

Second, I can imagine some readers finding the trilemma setup perplexing. These readers may doubt that there could be violations of a reasonably just collective's sovereignty that do not undermine individuals' interests.[1] The moment a reasonably just collective's sovereignty is violated, so the concern goes, individuals' interests in *self-determination* are thereby also set back. I will have more to say about this in the rest of the chapter, but for now let me note that a gap exists between individual and collective self-determination. While group sovereignty violations automatically undermine *collective* self-determination, it is not obvious that they equally undermine the self-determination of individuals, especially as most people's membership in political collectives—including reasonably just ones—is not voluntary. Claim (iii) in our trilemma, therefore, cannot be criticized for being *obviously* implausible. Challenging that claim requires some philosophical work, precisely the philosophical work offered by the views discussed in Section 5, and by the agency-respect view. And for those who can easily anticipate what that work is, the trilemma setup can still serve as a useful way of organizing the logical space occupied by different views on the wrong of sovereignty violations.

1. Defining Sovereignty

I begin by offering a general characterization of sovereignty. I first elucidate the concept of sovereignty in relation to individuals and then turn to its collective analogue. There are, of course, significant differences between the two. But, as I hope to show, the two also have much in common and there are explanatory advantages to discussing them in parallel (see, e.g., Feinberg 1986: Ch. 3).

1.1 Individual sovereignty

What is it to be sovereign? For any given domain of issues, the sovereign is whoever has *ultimate decision-making power* relative to it. When I have ultimate decision-making power, my "say so" has normative implications for others: they are

---

[1] Thanks to Peter Dietsch for raising this objection.

both bound by my word and under an obligation not to interfere with me. For instance, in a traditional patriarchal family, the eldest man is sovereign over family affairs: his decisions are binding on other family members, and outsiders should not interfere with them. Alternatively, at least in liberal-democratic societies, people are sovereign over whom they marry and associate with. It is up to them to make decisions within these personal domains, free from outside interference.

So far, I have characterized *de facto sovereignty*: the way the world is (or can be), as a matter of social fact, with respect to the allocation of ultimate decision-making power among individuals. This should be distinguished from *justified sovereignty*, which concerns who, from a moral point of view, ought to have the final say over which domains: what allocation of decision-making power is justified. While existing socio-legal arrangements certainly contribute to determining agents' de facto sovereignty, they may or may not be justified.

For instance, in a patriarchal society, a husband may be de facto sovereign over decisions concerning his family unit, yet this state of affairs is unjustified. He and his wife ought to have equal sovereignty over family matters: their joint decisions should be binding. Similarly, morality requires that each individual should have the final say over whom to marry, but in societies where arranged marriages are customary, the assignment of de facto sovereignty over personal relationships deviates from the morally mandated one.

How sovereignty should precisely be allocated is a complex question, which calls for separate treatment. Still, by and large, liberals hold that individual sovereignty should be distributed so as to give everyone a roughly equal sphere of agency, within which each may pursue their commitments, unhindered from interference (Rawls 1999a; Ripstein 2009).[2] This is precisely the function of rights, at least for those theories that define rights as involving particular normative powers (recall our discussion in Chapter 4). As H. L. A. Hart famously put it, a right-holder is a "small-scale sovereign" (Hart 1982: 183). Within the domain protected by our rights, it is up to each of us to make binding decisions.[3] When I ask you to leave my apartment, I thereby exercise my personal sovereignty. If you refuse to leave, you violate my sovereignty: my say so puts you under an obligation to leave, yet you fail to act on your obligation.

---

[2] Individual justified sovereignty is always circumscribed to whatever degree of sovereignty is consistent with the equal sovereignty of others. Preventing a criminal from stabbing an innocent passer-by is not a violation of the criminal's justified sovereignty, since it is not, morally speaking, up to the criminal to decide whether to stab another person.

[3] From this perspective, even well-intentioned paternalistic interventions, forcing us to act contrary to our judgements, count as problematic sovereignty violations. A case in point would be a government micromanaging its citizens' diet. The government's intervention may be well intentioned and improve citizens' health. Still, it should be up to each of them to decide what they eat. It's their, and not the state's, business.

Whether we are talking about de facto or justified sovereignty, we should acknowledge that not all entities are fit for it. Since sovereignty is the power to make binding decisions, only entities *capable of making decisions* may possess it (Feinberg 1986: 48). For instance, babies cannot be holders of sovereignty because they lack the relevant decision-making capacities. The more children acquire those capacities as they grow up, the greater their sphere of sovereignty ought to become. A five-year-old may not have justified sovereignty over whether to cross the road. But she may well have justified sovereignty relative to what picture she should draw on her mother's birthday card. Forcing her to draw a particular picture against her will may thus be wrong. Adults with full mental capacities, by contrast, qualify for full justified sovereignty: there are several domains within which they ought to be considered the final arbiters of their and others' actions. The set of legal rights typically ascribed to individuals within liberal democracies reflects this fact.

The idea of sovereignty, then, applies to "autonomous agents": agents with the requisite deliberative capacities. So far, I have been looking at individuals. But similar considerations can be extended to any entity that qualifies as an autonomous agent. This includes collectives in general and *political collectives* in particular. For simplicity's sake, from now on I shall be speaking of states. The argument in the chapter, though, is meant to apply to any political collective, including indigenous tribes and non-state-like entities, provided it displays the relevant decision-making abilities and group-agential features.

1.2 Corporate sovereignty

I characterized sovereignty as involving ultimate decision-making power over a given domain. This is precisely the notion of sovereignty invoked in international law to describe the normative status of states. There, states are said to be sovereign in that they hold "supreme authority within a territory" (Besson 2012; Philpott 2020). To have supreme authority is to have ultimate decision-making power, in the sense of one's pronouncements being binding. And the qualification "within a territory" designates the specific domain within which this authority is exercised: that is, over the individuals residing within the territory. This is sometimes referred to as "internal sovereignty". As in the case of individuals, state sovereignty entails independence from external interference, that is, interference on the part of outsiders, typically other states. This is often referred to as "external sovereignty" (Philpott 2020).

States' *de facto sovereignty* denotes states' actual power to make binding decisions. For example, states (typically) have de facto sovereignty over the treaties they sign, over the portion of the national budget they invest in national defence vs social services, over the particular electoral systems they implement, over the

184 EXPLAINING THE WRONG OF SOVEREIGNTY VIOLATIONS

laws that apply within their territories, over their immigration policies, and so forth (van der Vyver 2013). They may, of course, decide to temporarily give up sovereignty in some of these areas—e.g., by joining institutions such as the WTO or the EU—just as individuals may authorize third parties to make decisions on their behalf (Donnelly 2014: 233). Still, their ability to transfer their sovereignty is fully consistent with their sovereign status.

States' *justified sovereignty*, by contrast, denotes the ultimate decision-making power that states ought to have. Here, disagreement rages between advocates of the state system and cosmopolitan scholars who insist that such a system should be transcended in favour of new forms of political organization. Some argue that ultimate decision making-power should be horizontally or vertically dispersed among different non-state units, while others favour a more centralized global political structure akin to a world state (see, e.g., Cabrera 2004; Pogge 1992; Ulaş 2014).

For present purposes, I shall assume a widely accepted, somewhat reformist liberal perspective, according to which states' sovereignty can be justified so long as states (i) adequately protect the fundamental rights of their members (i.e., they are internally reasonably just), (ii) respect the sovereignty of other reasonably just states, and (iii) honour other international obligations of assistance, non-harm, and rectification (cf., Rawls 1999b). While the fulfilment of these principles may require the creation of some supra-national institutional entities, especially against the background of heavy interdependence, it does not imply dismantling state sovereignty (Ronzoni 2009; Valentini 2011). From now on, I shall call a state that meets these demands of domestic and international justice a "reasonably just state".

Just like with individuals, the extent of a state's sovereignty may well depend on its capacities to govern itself, to be a genuinely autonomous agent. A quasi state or a failed state may have much less de facto (as well as justified) sovereignty than a well-functioning one, precisely because and to the extent that it lacks the requisite capacities. Similarly, like children in the individual case, some collectives may have the potential of becoming sovereign, without that potential being yet actualized. This may be the case of national minorities within existing states who, if given the chance, would be able to constitute themselves into functioning political communities of their own.

So far, I have discussed individual and state sovereignty in parallel, but there is a significant difference between the two. While individual sovereignty is constrained by external considerations alone, that is, by the imperative to respect the sovereignty of other agents, state sovereignty is further constrained by respect for the sovereignty of *individual members* (Feinberg 1986: 50). This is why we typically regard proportionate interference with states' internal affairs as legitimate when the states in question severely harm their own populations. Think, here, of humanitarian intervention and the broader doctrine of the "responsibility to protect" (e.g., Pattison 2010).

More generally, whether a state's sovereign status places duties of non-interference on other entities depends on how said state's actions impact individual members and outsiders. Morally speaking, state sovereignty is meant to serve individuals' legitimate interests. Exercises of state sovereignty are thus morally acceptable whenever they serve or, at least, do not undermine those interests, but not otherwise. As we shall shortly see, this aspect of state sovereignty generates a philosophically interesting puzzle in cases of *pure sovereignty violations*. It is to these cases that I now turn.

2. The Sovereignty-Violation Trilemma

Sovereignty violations—by which, from now on, I mean violations of *justified sovereignty*—are often accompanied by wrongful harm, both when the targets are individuals and when the targets are states. Consider, first, an individual being robbed of her property. Theft is a paradigmatic example of individual sovereignty violation: it involves taking someone's property without her consent. The owner, qua sovereign over her property, ought to have the ultimate say over what happens to it. The thief ignores the owner's sovereignty, "usurping" her dominion. But theft of this kind is also a clear instance of wrongful harm: by taking what is yours, I typically make you worse off. Its wrongness is therefore easy to explain.

Like violations of individuals' sovereignty, sovereignty violations of reasonably just collectives are nearly always accompanied by serious harms befalling individuals. Recall the examples of colonialism, annexations, and wars of aggression offered in the introduction to this chapter. In these cases, too, explaining the wrong of sovereignty violations poses no particular philosophical challenge. We only need to point to the wrongful harm suffered by individuals.

That said, there are possible scenarios in which sovereignty violations are not accompanied by any obvious individual-level harm. These are instances of what I labelled "pure sovereignty violations". In earlier parts of the book, we already encountered one individual-level example of such violations: the *Barbeque* scenario. There, the Rossi family harmlessly uses your barbeque set without authorization. A case like *Barbeque* constitutes an instance of harmless individual sovereignty violation and, as I argued in Chapter 3, explaining its wrongness requires appeal to the moral normativity of socially constructed norms. Examples of seemingly harmless, but intuitively wrongful, sovereignty violations can also be found at the collective level. I have already mentioned the case of an immigrant (suppose not one in severe need) harmlessly violating a state's sovereignty by illegally entering its territory and settling there. Here are three further, larger-scale cases of this sort, where our intuitions about harmless sovereignty violations being wrongful are arguably even stronger. Two of them are drawn from the existing literature. The third is my own.

186 EXPLAINING THE WRONG OF SOVEREIGNTY VIOLATIONS

North America: "Suppose that both Canada and the United States are legitimate states. Now imagine that the United States annexes Canada against the will of the Canadian people, 90 percent of whom oppose the annexation. Nonetheless, the annexation goes peacefully and the Canadians acquiesce in their new status as citizens of the United States. Also imagine that the Canadians enjoy better protection of their human rights than they did before the annexation and that there is no loss in human rights protection in the rest of the United States or in respect for human rights elsewhere" (Altman and Wellman 2009: 14).

Scandinavia: Denmark and Sweden are both reasonably just states. "Suppose that Denmark is annexed by Sweden. Although not identical, the two countries' political values are very similar. Perhaps the laws post-takeover would even be largely the same as they would have been had Denmark remained independent" (Stilz 2019: 132). The human-rights record of the "enlarged Sweden" is as good as it previously was.

Europe: It's 2040. The UK is no longer part of the EU. Scotland has gained independence from the UK. The EU has tightened its governing structure, becoming a better-integrated political union—closer to a federal state, though not quite there yet—with some elements of common taxation and policing. Scottish politicians are preparing for a referendum, where the people will be asked whether they wish Scotland to apply to join the EU again. The vast majority of the population, one can reliably predict, will vote in favour of rejoining the EU: they are committed to the European project. In an unprecedented act of anticipation, the EU "annexes" Scotland prior to the referendum, treating it as bound by EU obligations, but also giving Scotland the privileges enjoyed by other EU countries.

All three cases are instances of unilateral annexation, hence paradigmatic examples of sovereignty violations. It should be up to each reasonably just state to decide whether to remain independent, merge with another political unit, or become a member of a supra-national entity. The three cases, however, do not involve any of the wrongs typically associated with such annexations.

In *North America*, although the annexation is contrary to the will of the majority of Canadians, nothing bad happens and, in fact, Canadians are even better off from the perspective of their human rights post-annexation. To that extent, they would seem to have no legitimate complaint: surely, human rights trump one's associative preferences.[4] Regarding *Scandinavia*, not only are the Danes no worse off from the perspective of their fundamental rights, but the laws they are subjected to after being incorporated by Sweden are, ex hypothesi, about the same as

---

[4] In fact, it is far from obvious how not accommodating an associative preference could automatically count as wrongful. Freedom of association is limited by all sorts of considerations.

the laws that would have existed had Denmark continued to be independent. What legitimate complaint could they have against the annexation, then?

In response, one might invoke national affiliation: Danes wish only to associate with other Danes. It is doubtful that national affiliation so conceived picks out *legitimate* interests: the sorts of interests that morality protects. After all, the scenario assumes that Danes and Swedes share the same culture, values, and priorities, so much so that the annexation makes virtually no difference to the laws and policies governing them. A preference for associating with one's fellow nationals, in turn, seems legitimate to the extent that it is a preference for sharing a political community with people whose values and priorities are in keeping with one's own. Other nationalist preferences, to do with ethnicity or presumed lineage—for instance—are morally suspicious, and it is far from clear that we have a legitimate interest in their fulfilment, especially in non-intimate associative contexts.

Furthermore, explanations appealing to national associative preferences are of limited help, since they cannot account for what seems morally problematic about our third case: *Europe*. There, the Scots get what they want—they become part of the EU—and more swiftly than if they had followed the standard application process. Their associative wishes are not frustrated, but fulfilled. Again, what complaint could they have?

These three cases present us with violations of states' sovereignty that do not involve obvious setbacks in individuals' legitimate interests. In fact, individuals are either just as well off, or even better off than they would have been had no annexation taken place. This is the sense in which they depict putative *pure sovereignty violations*: violations of a collective's sovereignty that do not result in individual-level unjustified harm. Yet, intuitively, the violations in question are wrongful. Members of Canada, Scotland, and Denmark would seem entitled to complain. This, I should add, is also assumed by the authors who originally developed the first two scenarios.

The puzzle presented by cases such as these can be neatly captured by a trilemma. We can distinguish different views about the wrong of sovereignty violations depending on which proposition in the trilemma they give up. Let us call this the "sovereignty trilemma".

(i) *Normative individualism*: There is no pro tanto wrong without setbacks in the legitimate interests of individuals.
(ii) *Just collectives' sovereign rights*: Violations of a reasonably just political collective's sovereignty are always pro tanto wrong.
(iii) *Independence between collective and individual violations*: Violations of a reasonably just political collective's sovereignty need not set back individuals' legitimate interests.

The first proposition points to the widely held view that only individuals are ultimate units of moral concern, such that wrongs need to be explained by violations suffered by individuals (see, e.g., Waldron 1987). These wrongs involve setbacks in their interests. But not any setback will amount to wrongdoing. If you open a restaurant next to mine, and lure a few customers away from me, you set back my interests, but you do not wrong me. I do not have *legitimate* interests in monopolizing my clientele. What interests are legitimate is, of course, a complex question, which we luckily need not settle here. In the scenarios I shall be discussing, the individual interests involved are either clearly legitimate or clearly illegitimate.

The second proposition asserts the wrongfulness of violating the sovereignty of reasonably just collectives: collectives that respect their members' and outsiders' rights. This proposition reflects the common-sense view that once states are reasonably just, their sovereignty ought to be honoured. The third and final proposition claims that violations of a reasonably just collective's sovereignty need not always involve setbacks of individuals' legitimate interests. The third proposition is prima facie supported by the examples I have offered, which do not involve any obvious setback in individuals' legitimate interests.

The trilemma provides a systematic way of distinguishing between different perspectives on the nature of the wrong of a collective's sovereignty violations. Some approaches may wish to relax the first proposition, others the second, while others—in fact, the majority—give up the third. In what follows, I consider each approach in turn. Unsurprisingly, I will devote most of my attention to approaches that relax the third proposition.

3. Giving Up Normative Individualism

One possibility is to abandon the first proposition, and thus give up the idea that individuals are ultimate units of moral concern. The plausibility of this option partly depends on whether entities that are not individuals—in our case, political collectives—also bear the properties that justify attribution of ultimate moral status. One of the most popular candidate properties is phenomenal consciousness.[5]

A phenomenally conscious agent is an entity for whom there is something that it is like to be that entity (Nagel 1984). To be phenomenally conscious is to have first-personal experiences, such as suffering, feeling pain and pleasure, being moved by emotions, and so forth. Phenomenally conscious agents are loci of subjectivity and this is what grounds their ultimate moral status (Jaworska and Tannenbaum 2013: sec. 5.3).

---

[5] On some accounts, phenomenal consciousness may be necessary but not sufficient for possessing ultimate moral status. For example, one may hold that in addition to consciousness, particularly sophisticated cognitive capacities are required, in which case most human beings would count as having ultimate moral status, but many non-human animals would not.

It is beyond doubt that individuals—at least in normal circumstances—possess phenomenal consciousness. Collectives, by contrast, even ones that count as group agents, are unlikely candidates for phenomenal consciousness.[6] This is generally acknowledged even by those who have offered strong defences of collective agency (List 2018).[7] It would thus be somewhat mysterious why we should regard them as *ultimate* units of moral concern. Of course, they may matter instrumentally, but not for their own sake. After all, why should we be concerned about the fate of entities that cannot experience anything? In the same way in which we do not treat tables and chairs as ultimate units of moral concern, we should not accord that status to collectives if, like tables and chairs, they lack consciousness. For these reasons, I take giving up normative individualism to be a rather unsatisfactory option. In fact, I am not aware of scholars in the literature who follow this path.

One important clarification before we proceed. Normative individualism is consistent with holding that certain groups should be accorded privileged moral status, and that their members have special obligations vis-à-vis one another. For example, a proponent of so-called nationalism—in political ethics—grants special moral status to national groups, but this does not entail that she abandons normative individualism. What the nationalist does is claim that members of national groups (via their states) have special responsibilities towards one another that do not hold among strangers (see, e.g., Miller 1995). So, while nationalists place a great deal of importance on groups, they do not thereby abandon normative individualism as understood here.

4. Giving Up the Wrong of Sovereignty Violations

Another option is to deny that all instances of sovereignty violations of a reasonably just state are morally problematic. Those who favour this way out of the trilemma will deny that in *North America*, *Scandinavia*, and *Europe* any wrongdoing occurs. Our intuitions, they might say, track real-world violations, which typically involve serious wrongdoing: this is why the annexations in the examples offered intuitively come across as wrongful. But, upon reflection, they are morally impeccable.

Proponents of this escape route may, for example, take the view that the value of a political collective rests entirely on its being instrumental to the realization of *justice* for individuals. Provided justice—including basic rights—is realized, which collective governs which individuals does not matter.

---

[6] They may, however, possess "consciousness as awareness", namely a particular cognitive state. What they lack is first-personal experience (List 2018: 299ff.).
[7] But see Schwitzgebel (2015).

By analogy, suppose the value of a food processor rests entirely on its ability to satisfactorily blend and mix various types of foods. Suppose, further, that the Kenwood and Phillips food processors are equally good at this. This being so, it really does not matter whether what you get is a Kenwood or a Phillips machine. By the same token, so long as individuals have their rights respected, whether they are governed by the institutions of the United States, Sweden, or the European Union does not matter. No legitimate interest of theirs is undermined in the examples of unilateral annexations offered above.[8]

Of course, in the real world, violations of sovereignty are typically accompanied by violence and harm. This is why, in the real world, we are better off holding on to a blanket rule requiring respect for the sovereignty of reasonably just states. But, at least philosophically, if the value of a state resides entirely in its ability to deliver justice, holding justice-facts constant, changes in state-identity should be of no moral concern.[9]

While this instrumentalist view has some plausibility, it does run counter to the widespread intuition that changes in state identity do matter, even when they do not affect the justice of a political community. In fact, if they involve sovereignty violations, they seem to matter *even when* the population ultimately welcomes them. This is precisely what happens in *Europe*. To be sure, the instrumentalist has a response available: our intuitions track real-world cases, which are accompanied by serious harms to individuals. But before completely discounting those intuitions as surreptitiously influenced by real-world assumptions, we should at least consider whether there are other views that can help us make sense of them.

5. Contesting That Individuals' Legitimate Interests Are Not Undermined

Several theorists focus on the third proposition in our trilemma and point to ways in which even seemingly harmless sovereignty violations are in fact accompanied by setbacks of individuals' legitimate interests. In what follows, I consider two variants of this position, which I call the "membership view" and the "autonomy view".

5.1 The membership view

Andrew Altman and Christopher Wellman argue that a political group has a right to self-determination provided it has the ability to, and does, respect human

---

[8] For instance, those who subscribe to purely instrumentalist accounts of the value of democracy would seem bound to accept this conclusion. See, e.g., Arneson (2004).

[9] I thank Cécile Fabre for discussion.

rights to an adequate degree (Altman and Wellman 2009: 13). Their view, they argue, can account for our intuitions in a case like *North America*, which they in fact introduce. Since Canada adequately protects human rights, say Altman and Wellman, it has a right to self-determination, and the peaceful unilateral takeover on the part of the US is wrongful because it violates that right.

Before continuing, let me make one brief side-point in connection with this case. Since, in this manifestly hypothetical scenario, the US is better at protecting human rights than Canada, it is not obvious that the scenario *unambiguously* triggers the intuitions Altman and Wellman are after: i.e., intuitions about the wrongness of the annexation. To eliminate confounding factors, then, from now on I assume that the human-rights record pre- and post-annexation is identical.

Altman and Wellman believe that the right to self-determination belongs to the group as a whole and is not "reducible to the moral rights of the individuals who constitute the collectivity" (Altman and Wellman 2009: 37). At the same time, since they subscribe to normative individualism, they emphasize that their view does not presuppose ascribing ultimate value to collectives. This is because even if violations of collective self-determination do not result in violations of individual rights to self-determination, they nonetheless involve *disrespecting individuals qua members of groups*.

Since, they argue, "a group's ability and willingness to govern in a satisfactory fashion is a collective achievement made possible only because of the actions and attitudes of the individuals within the group, it makes perfect sense that . . . respect is owed to these individuals qua members of this group" (Altman and Wellman 2009: 39). But how is the annexation envisaged in *North America* disrespectful? The disrespect, in their view, comes from the fact that the group is treated as unable to govern itself. Metaphorically put, the annexation conveys the message that the group is "a minor". And its members, qua members, have an interest in not being disrespected this way.

While this view is intuitively appealing, I am unconvinced that it can offer a robust enough explanation of the wrong of collective sovereignty violations.[10] To begin with, not all instances of sovereignty violations need to be so all-encompassing as to convey the message that the relevant group is unable to govern itself. For an analogy, consider the case of an individual. I may violate her sovereignty not just by taking de facto guardianship over her, but also by making unauthorized use of her possessions, by touching her without her consent, and so forth. Such sovereignty violations are a local affront to the individual's self-determination: part of being self-determining means being able to do what I want with my body and possessions.

---

[10] I should also mention, however, that it isn't obvious whether Altman and Wellman advance the view with this explicit ambition.

Similarly, a state's sovereignty can be violated not just through annexation or colonial domination, but also locally. A foreign power may steal classified information, or it may encourage illegal settlement of its own people within the state's territory. And as already mentioned, an immigrant entering a country without authorization is also violating that country's sovereignty: this is the equivalent of someone entering my apartment without being authorized. (Let me emphasize that we are considering sovereignty violations of states that are reasonably just, namely states that *both* are internally just *and* honour their duties of global justice, including by treating immigrants fairly.)

The type of disrespect Altman and Wellman appeal to, namely disrespect for one's ability to govern oneself, cannot plausibly explain why such sovereignty violations are wrongful. The foreign power stealing information and the illegal immigrant are not acting in a way that puts into question members' capacity for self-governance. All they are doing is sidestepping a state's governing power, by acting contrary to its will. To be sure, this is intuitively disrespectful, but not because it expresses the judgement that the target-states are "incapable of performing [certain] chores" (Altman and Wellman 2009: 40). The object of disrespect, here, is state sovereignty itself. But appeal to disrespect for state sovereignty cannot explain why sovereignty violations are wrong: it simply restates the intuition that they are.

Even setting these concerns aside, it remains unclear how disrespect for a collective translates into disrespect for individual members qua members. To see this, let us go back to *North America*. Recall that 90 per cent of Canada's population opposed the annexation on the part of the US. But if the annexation is disrespectful towards members qua members, this implies that *everyone* in Canada is disrespected by it, including the 10 per cent who in fact have their associative preferences fulfilled. Altman and Wellman, however, do not provide a clear explanation of why this is so. Furthermore, their emphasis on the fact that a large majority opposes the annexation intuitively ties the disrespect intuition to disregard for *individual preferences and wishes*, not to disrespect for members qua members.

This last consideration pushes us away from the membership view, in the direction of the autonomy view, to which I now turn.

5.2 The autonomy view

The autonomy view links collective self-determination to individual self-determination or autonomy: the ability to be self-governing. Two versions of this view are available, which I call the "outcome version" and the "political-project version".

The "outcome version" presupposes that the members of the relevant collectives are (i) united by political or cultural ties and (ii) able to participate freely in collective decision-making. When these conditions are met, collective self-determination is said to be conducive to individual self-government. Why? Because, on the assumption that we cannot plausibly do without political authority, participating in a decision-making process with others who share my values and priorities makes it more likely that the resulting *outcomes* will mirror my own preferences. This minimizes alien control and maximizes individuals' self-rule (see, e.g., Philpott 1995; Volmert 2010). Violations of collective sovereignty, on this view, are wrongful to the extent that they increase alien control for individuals. On this account, Canadians—or, at least, 90 per cent of them— would have a complaint because being governed by the United States would set back their individual self-determination, something in which they have a legitimate interest.

This line of argument is familiar, but its appeal is limited. First, it is unable to account for the wrong occurring in a case like *Scandinavia* where, ex hypothesi, the outcomes of collective decisions are virtually the same as what they would have been in the absence of annexation. Second, and more importantly, by locating the value of self-determination in the outcomes of collective decisions, this version of the autonomy view fails to explain the value of self-determination for individuals who belong to internally diverse democratic communities. As Allen Buchanan puts it: "it is simply false to say that an individual who participates in a democratic decision-making process is self-governing; he or she is governed by the majority" (Buchanan 1998: 17, cited in Altman and Wellman 2009: 17). In a pluralistic society, the outcomes of collective decisions are often at odds with many individuals' preferences. Outcome-based self-determination, then, cannot be what explains the wrongs of sovereignty violations, at least not reliably for many citizens.

A more promising account of how collective and individual self-determination (i.e., autonomy) relate to each other takes a different route. This involves acknowledging that individuals value membership in a political collective not solely based on considerations about the merits of political decision-making outcomes. Membership can be valuable even if the outcomes of collective decisions do not always accord with one's preferences.

To see this, imagine you are making a decision with your family, say, about where to go on holiday. The family has justified sovereignty over this matter. You vote for the mountains, but everyone else wants to go to the seaside. Suppose a third party intervenes, imposing a mountain holiday on the group. Even though the intervention results in your preferred option prevailing, you would presumably perceive this as a wrongful violation of your family's sovereignty (cf. Renzo 2019: 8). This suggests that the value of a group's sovereignty doesn't depend so much on the narrow alignment between group-decision outcomes and individuals' preferences, but on individuals' *broader commitment* to the group itself and its making decisions together: a commitment to a "family project".

194 EXPLAINING THE WRONG OF SOVEREIGNTY VIOLATIONS

This insight has been recently developed by Anna Stilz (2016).[11] In Stilz's view, the value of collective self-determination lies in individuals' interests in autonomy, namely in leading their lives according to their authentically endorsed goals and values. When those goals and values include cooperation in a joint political project with others, collective self-determination becomes indispensable for it. In particular, Stilz argues that "correspondence" is necessary for autonomy. Correspondence is achieved when a person "lives under an institution that she endorses, accepts, or believes to be justified or appropriate" (Stilz 2019: 107). This, however, does not require political outcomes to reflect individuals' preferences. As Stilz explains:

> [I]n a diverse political community, no individual's personal judgments can be mirrored by each-and-every political decision. Yet diversity of political opinions does not make correspondence impossible. There is a second-order sense in which an individual's judgments are often reflected in her governing institutions: namely, when she shares a commitment to a political enterprise and to certain values and procedures by which she believes that enterprise should be structured.   (Stilz 2019: 108)

When this happens, members affirm their group's institutions and see those institutions as "their own", not as alien impositions (Stilz 2016: 112).[12] Even peaceful violations of state sovereignty, therefore, can be wrongful to the extent that they frustrate the legitimate autonomy interests of citizens who are committed to the political project underpinned by that sovereignty (cf. Moore 2015; Renzo 2019). This is, in a nutshell, the "political-project version" of the autonomy view.

There is much that I find congenial in Stilz's view, and much that I have learnt from it. As will become apparent later in the chapter, the view has a good deal in common with the account I myself favour. Still, one might wonder whether, as currently formulated, the view fully captures the pro tanto wrong of pure sovereignty violations. In cases like *Scandinavia* and *European Union*, for instance, the relevant annexations do not obviously frustrate a majority of individuals' freely endorsed values and priorities. In the first case, the Danes become part of a cooperative enterprise that, when it comes to values and priorities, is virtually indistinguishable from what it would have been, had Denmark not been annexed by Sweden. In the second case, the Scottish find themselves members of an organization of which they genuinely wish to be members, thereby furthering a political project (that of the EU) to which they are committed. What Stilz calls "correspondence", one could argue, seems to be realized in both cases.

---

[11] Stilz uses examples structurally similar to the one I offered above, involving collective decisions within a university and a coffee shop.
[12] Affirming morally abhorrent institutions, Stilz rightly points out, is not valuable for individual subjects.

CONTESTING THAT INDIVIDUALS' LEGITIMATE INTERESTS   195

This conclusion would be too quick, however. Stilz herself introduces the example I have named *Scandinavia* and considers the concern I have just raised. This is how she responds to it.

> [C]orrespondence with shared political values is not sufficient for political autonomy. A participant in a group's shared will does not simply intend that values X, Y, and Z be realized. Instead, she intends that *we* pursue values X, Y, and Z *together*. In addition to shared values, then, a shared will includes a reference to a group engaged in institutionalized political cooperation. Sweden's takeover of Denmark fails to reflect this "*we*" dimension of a people's shared will, which involves being governed by *Danish* institutions... [N]ormally a shared political will involves not only a commitment to support certain institutions, but also a commitment to associate politically with a group of fellow citizens.
>
> (Stilz 2019: 132, original emphases)

Stilz then goes on to elaborate on this "we" dimension in the case of political communities. She relies on theories of joint intentions to explain how, even within large-scale organizations where members do not know each other personally, joint cooperative intentions are possible (Stilz 2016; see also Moore 2015: sec. 3.3). She compares the case of states with that of top-class US universities. For instance, she says, Princeton embraces roughly the same values as Harvard and Yale, but "it pursues them through a distinctive institutional structure that its members value and endorse" (Stilz 2019: 133). By analogy, members of Princeton University would find it objectionable if Harvard were unilaterally to incorporate Princeton.

I agree with Stilz that "being governed by Danish institutions" is a perfectly legitimate interest of the Danes *if* the term "Danish institutions" stands for institutions that include a certain set of values, procedures, and priorities. But if we assume that Swedish institutions are identical to Danish ones when it comes to values, procedures, and priorities, it becomes less obvious what legitimate autonomy interest of a Dane would be undermined by a sudden switch to Swedish institutions. Stilz's response, quoted above, points to how such a switch would involve a different, and in this case forced, associative profile. The Danes were pursuing a common political project *with other Danes* (a particular group of fellow citizens, a "we") and now they are forced to pursue an otherwise identical project, except for the fact that it's together with the Swedes. This, in turn, undermines a legitimate "we interest" of the Danes.

I worry that the "we interest" Stilz invokes to explain the wrong of *Scandinavia* tacitly relies on somewhat suspect nationalist considerations, considerations which Stilz herself wishes to avoid (Stilz 2019: sec. 5.6).[13] Let me explain. While we have

---

[13] For concerns along these lines see also Miller (2016) and especially Blake (2021).

legitimate associative interests in determining with whom we stand in intimate relations, the weight of these associative interests decreases the larger, more impersonal the associations become (S. Fine 2010). Take the case of two married couples: Fred and Wilma; Barney and Betty. Suppose the state of which they are citizens all of a sudden forced a swap upon them: Fred is now married to Betty, and Wilma to Barney. As it happens, all four share the same values and priorities. Still, it seems plain that the legitimate associative interests of all of them have been badly undermined. Given the intimacy of the association at stake, one has a legitimate interest in associating not just with someone who shares one's values and priorities, but with a particular individual. Fred can insist that his commitment is not just to pursuing a loving, egalitarian relationship with a partner, but *with Wilma in particular*. Why the forced couples' swap is wrongful is thus clear.

Now consider an analogous case, yet one involving a "population swap". Suppose I'm a Dane, I live in Denmark, and all of a sudden half of the Danish population (all people I didn't know personally) is replaced by Swedes. This, ex hypothesi, makes no difference to the policies and priorities the government will pursue. In what way would this population swap—itself a form of "forced association"—undermine a legitimate interest of mine? As a citizen of a liberal-democratic country, I have a legitimate interest in not being forced into an association with, say, conservative religious fundamentalists. Doing so would prevent the realization of what Stilz calls "correspondence", resulting in a likely shift in the values and priorities pursued by my government. But it is not clear how being forced into association with people who share my values and priorities, and whom I'll likely never meet anyway, undermines a legitimate associative interest of mine, *unless* we accept that we have a legitimate interest in pursuing a joint political project with people of a certain ethnicity or with a given historical background only. Note, ethnicity and historical background here aren't proxies for values or culture more broadly. The assumption throughout has been that the Swedish takeover of Denmark would result in the same values and policies as those that would be pursued by an independent Denmark. This means that whatever cultural specificities—e.g., language, customs—the Danes cherish wouldn't be threatened under the newly enlarged Sweden. And of course, whatever democratic procedures were in place prior to the annexation would continue to exist, but in the context of the enlarged Sweden. This is why I worry that, on the "political project" version of the autonomy view, the Swedish takeover can only count as wrongful if the "we-dimension" of the relevant political project is coloured by nationalist considerations.

Let us now turn to *Europe*. There, the Scots are not forced into a cooperative enterprise against their will with others they do not wish to associate with. To the contrary, they obtain what they want—their situation is the opposite of the Canadians'—and they do so even more quickly than they otherwise would have. It is precisely their wish to become part of the EU and be governed by EU institutions, together with other EU citizens.

It might be objected that, in the scenario just envisaged, the Scots have *not* committed to the European project yet. For that commitment to be properly formed, a referendum needs to happen.[14] But why is that? Suppose that the EU annexes Scotland *just a few hours* before the Scottish people are to vote in a referendum, and suppose it is clear—based on news coverage and campaigning—that the outcome will be a landslide victory for "rejoining". In this case, it is already common knowledge that "we, the Scottish people, intend to rejoin the EU" (cf. Stilz 2019: 108–9). The relevant commitment and joint cooperative intentions are already there. The fact that they haven't been officialized via a referendum seems like a purely formal detail.

Reflecting upon this description of the events, one might actually conclude that nothing wrong occurs in *Europe* and that, therefore, if this is the verdict of the political-project version of the autonomy view, that view is right. While I agree that the wrong in *Europe* is less egregious than the wrongs perpetrated in our two other cases, I still believe that Scotland would have grounds for complaint. To see this, consider the following analogy.

Suppose your good friend is a gym manager and asks you, hypothetically: "if I offered you a place at the gym for a discounted rate, would you take it?". You answer in the affirmative. On this basis, your friend demands that you pay him fifty dollars every month, "since you are now a gym member".

Here, your friend *follows your expressed wishes*, yet it seems that you would have reason to complain in the face of his "annexing you" to the gym, without something that counts as your consent. As we saw in Chapter 4, consent is governed by socially constructed norms, and can only be given in accordance with the requirements of those norms. In the case we are discussing, consent requires signing a contract in response to an actual proposal, not nodding in response to a hypothetical one. And the fact that you would have signed, had you been handed a contract, doesn't give rise to any obligations. As Dworkin famously argued, hypothetical consent does not bind (Dworkin 1975).

What is wrong, in this case, is that your sovereignty has been violated. To be sure, you may be happy with the status quo, and acquiesce with your newly acquired gym membership. The point is that you would have reason to feel slighted, to object to what your friend did. The case is entirely analogous to *Europe*. Scotland would have had to agree, via the relevant procedures, to becoming a member of the EU. The EU's unilateral takeover is therefore still wrongful, even if it does not prevent the Scottish people from participating in a cooperative political project—the EU—they wholeheartedly affirm.

This being so, while broadly on the right track the political project version of the autonomy view arguably still does not allow us to capture all those instances of sovereignty violations that strike us as intuitively wrongful. The reason lies in

---

[14] I am grateful to Annie Stilz and Peter Dietsch for pressing me on this.

the view's focus on individuals' commitment to pursuing a given *political project together with a group of others*. Reference to "a group of others" renders the view susceptible to a somewhat problematic nationalist reading (depending on how the relevant group is identified). And reference to the "pursuit of a political project" makes it tricky for the view to explain why sovereignty violations are problematic even in cases where they do not frustrate, but in fact track, people's commitments to a given political project (e.g., *Europe*).

Having said that, the political-project version of the autonomy view correctly focuses on individuals' commitments. But the commitments that matter—I shall argue in what follows—are not to a certain political project or to a specific set of fellow cooperators. Instead, they are commitments to the demands of existing socially constructed norms.[15]

6. The Agency-Respect View

In this section, I apply the agency-respect view to the problem of collective sovereignty violations. The view escapes the trilemma primarily by giving up the third proposition, suggesting that virtually all sovereignty violations of reasonably just political communities involve wrongdoing against individual members. To illustrate, I once again make use of our familiar grounding sequence. This time, our "action required" is respecting the sovereignty of a specific reasonably just political collective, which I call state X for simplicity's sake.

- Action required: You ought to respect the sovereignty of state X.
- By virtue of what ought I to respect the sovereignty of state X?
- Empirical fact: Because socially constructed norms—provided these are underpinned by people's authentic as well as permissible commitments, and respecting them is not too costly—require that you respect X's sovereignty.
- By virtue of what does the fact that respecting X's sovereignty is required by socially constructed norms—provided these are underpinned by people's authentic as well as permissible commitments, and respecting them is not too costly—ground my obligation to respect X's sovereignty?
- Target general moral principle: Because you have an obligation to respect people's commitments (i.e., "to give *agency respect* to people"), provided those commitments are authentic, morally permissible, and respecting them is not too costly.

---

[15] And while commitments to specific political projects may result in commitments to given socially constructed norms, insofar as those norms are regarded as constitutive of the projects in question, they need not. For example, one may be committed to joining the EU, but indifferent about the specific norms that happen to de facto regulate EU accession.

Many elements in the sequence should by now be familiar. Our target principle, in particular, should require little explanation, at least insofar as the rationale behind it has already been discussed at some length in Chapter 3 and again in Chapter 5. Furthermore, that principle echoes the fundamental normative rationale invoked by the autonomy view. This is the importance of respecting persons' agency. As Stilz explains, following other prominent accounts in the literature, autonomous persons have a right to lead their lives in accordance with their freely formed judgements and commitments (Stilz 2019: 105–6). Similarly, the agency-respect principle says that we ought to respect people's freely formed (i.e., authentic) commitments, provided such commitments are morally permissible and respecting them is compatible with leaving adequate scope for our own agency. From now on, I will thus take the agency-respect principle for granted.

More discussion is needed of the relevant empirical fact: that respect for sovereignty is mandated by existing socially constructed norms. First of all, let us clarify what counts as a lack of respect for state sovereignty. Violations of a state's sovereignty occur when the state's supreme authority relative to a given domain is disregarded. Disregarding this authority amounts to doing things within the state's area of jurisdiction that the state has not authorized. This is precisely what happens in the examples of unilateral annexation introduced in Section 2: the annexations take place without the state's consent or authorization. Similarly, a foreign drone being flown over a state's airspace without authorization or a migrant's illegal presence on a state's territory also count as sovereignty violations. Assuming just background conditions—clearly an unrealistic assumption in the world today—it should be up to the respective states to determine whether the drone or the migrant should enter their airspace or territory, in the same way in which it should be up to me whether you are allowed into my apartment. If you trespass, you violate my sovereignty. If the drone or the migrant trespasses into the state's area of jurisdiction, they violate its sovereignty.

In Chapter 4, we saw that what counts as the exercise of individuals' sovereignty—of their "rights as control"—is regulated by a complex set of socially constructed norms, which tell us when individuals have issued an order, when they have given consent, and so forth. Appropriately followed, these complex norms generate both permissions and obligations. The same broad line of reasoning applies, mutatis mutandis, to the case of collective agents, such as states. There are complex norms determining what counts as a state's consent, as a state's issuing an order, etc.

Those norms are of two kinds: *internal* and *external* (or international). First, there are the norms that make up the state's domestic decision-making processes. In the United Kingdom, for example, Parliament is sovereign, such that only acts of Parliament express the binding will of the collective. As was seen in the context of Brexit, for example, the 2016 referendum was not binding. Given how the UK system operates, only Parliament, not a majority of the people directly, can speak on the collective's behalf. Other political decision-making systems function differently. But provided these differences fall within the bounds of moral permissibility, what counts as an expression of sovereign power on the part of a given state depends on the content of its collective decision-making norms.

If the state in question is reasonably just, and if those norms exist by virtue of its members' genuine commitments, according to the agency-respect principle there is a strong prima facie case for respecting them. And if respect for them is not too costly, the prima facie case becomes a pro tanto obligation.

Note that, internally, the norm requiring respect for the sovereignty of a political collective is, essentially, the norm of the rule of law, which we encountered in the previous chapter. To the extent that the will of a political collective is expressed through law, respecting the law is tantamount to respecting a collective's sovereignty: its ultimate decision-making power relative to given domains. The law is "the voice" of the collective. Through law, the collective performs the speech acts that count as giving permissions and issuing obligations, in the same way in which a suitably positioned individual issues permissions and obligations through speaking or designated gestures.

In connection with this, let me open a brief parenthesis. Once we realize that violations of the law, seen as the binding will of the collective, are sovereignty violations, we can see how ubiquitous such violations are. From this perspective, the cases discussed in Chapter 2, and which have made appearances throughout the book—namely *Traffic Light*, *Barbeque*, and *Non-proceduralist President*—also qualify as instances of sovereignty violations. They all involve violations of the law, and thus acts that are contrary to the binding will of the political collective.

This realization gives further plausibility to the claim, discussed in an earlier chapter, that the harmless trespass described in *Barbeque* wrongs *both* the specific individual whose property is used without authorization *and* the community of norm-supporters as a whole. If we look at a political community as a collective agent, as we do in the context of sovereignty discussions, any legal violations amount to violations of the collective's binding will. If the law confers on you control rights over your property, when those rights are violated, your sovereignty, *but also the state's internal sovereignty*, are disrespected. Perhaps surprising at first, this conclusion seems to me just right, and an unavoidable implication of taking a group-agential stance with respect to collectives such as states.

Let me now return to our present discussion. Earlier I said that two kinds of norms determine how a state exercises its normative powers as a sovereign. So far, we have looked at state sovereignty from an *internal* perspective. But we can also look at it from an *external* one. Here, the norms structuring what respect for sovereignty amounts to are no longer domestic legal norms, but those of international law.

There is a well-understood norm, within the international system, which demands respect for state sovereignty, conditional on any given state's doing a good enough job at respecting individuals' and other states' rights (Besson 2013).[16] This is the norm of sovereign equality. Needless to say, in the state system as it is today the implementation of that norm is far from satisfactory. Global imbalances of power make the principle of sovereign equality more of a regulative ideal than an established reality. Differently put, in the current state system de facto sovereignty need not correspond to justified sovereignty. Consequently, not all de facto sovereignty violations can automatically count as wrongful.

But let us suppose—as we have been doing all along—that we are in a better version of the state system, one where states are reasonably just and well behaved, and where international law is squarely within the limits of morality. In such a system, disrespect for state sovereignty would count as wrongful not only when it would involve violating a community's *internal norms*, but also when it would involve violating *international law*.

Given the agency-respect principle, provided the international sovereignty norm is justified, it is genuinely endorsed by states (hence, indirectly, by their citizens), and respecting it is not unreasonably costly, that norm too places pro tanto obligations on us. This explains why a violation of sovereignty—specifically of the norms of international law that require respect for sovereignty—wrongs not merely the particular target state, *but the international community as a whole*, whose commitments sustain the international sovereignty norm. In the same way in which a crime is said to wrong the state, and not merely the individual victim, so too violations of international sovereignty norms wrong the international community as a whole, not only the members of the target state who support the domestic rule of law.

One might object that the commitments of the international community are the commitments of states and that, therefore, violating them is not of ultimate moral significance. States, per se, are not of ultimate significance, only individuals are. This is a correct observation. Yet, it is plausible to presume that the commitments of states are, at least to some extent, undergirded by the commitments of their individual members. It is agency respect for them which explains the moral normativity of the international sovereignty norm. If individuals are committed to their state, and their state is committed to the sovereignty norm, agency respect still gives that norm moral normativity. As I have mentioned in Chapter 3, commitments to norms can be either direct or indirect. In this case, we would be faced with indirect commitments.

To sum up, state sovereignty, namely states' right to be the ultimate decision-makers within a given domain, is constituted by two sets of socially constructed

---

[16] This is an oversimplification, especially since intervention is only regarded as legitimate in the most egregious cases of genocide or crimes against humanity. Still, as Donnelly explains, in the international arena, oppressive or otherwise deeply unjust states tend to become increasingly isolated, acquiring "pariah" status and being prevented from sharing the benefits of participation in the international community (Donnelly 2014: 234).

norms. First, there is the domestic norm of the rule of law, which requires respect for the state's will, as expressed in its legal pronouncements (internal sovereignty). Second, there is the international norm of sovereign equality, which requires non-interference in states' internal affairs, provided states meet some relevant conditions (external sovereignty). To the extent that these norms are under-pinned by authentic and permissible commitments, and to the extent that respecting them is not too costly, they generate pro tanto obligations on agency-respect grounds. On the agency-respect view, this explains when and why it is wrong to violate a state's sovereignty.

With this theoretical background in hand, in the next section I return to our three cases of alleged pure sovereignty violations.

7. Back to Our Three Cases

The agency-respect view helps us explain the wrongdoing occurring in *North America*, *Scandinavia*, and *Europe*. Let us start with our first case, in which the US unilaterally but peacefully annexes Canada, and governs Canada justly, but where 90 per cent of Canadians in fact oppose the annexation. The agency-respect view will deem this annexation at least pro tanto wrong, because it exhibits complete disregard for the collective decision-making procedures that structure the state of Canada and for international sovereignty norms. On the assumption that the rules constituting those procedures, and the international law of state sovereignty, are underpinned by authentic and morally permissible commitments, this unilat-eral annexation is morally problematic, at least in one respect.

The agency-respect view, however, also allows us to make sense of our some-what ambivalent reactions to the original version of this case, which stipulated an improvement in human-rights protection post annexation. Our verdict about whether the annexation is all-things-considered wrong will depend on (i) the extent to which human-rights protection improves post-annexation, and (ii) how we balance considerations of agency respect with considerations of human-rights protection. Unless the improvements are merely trivial, it is unlikely that agency respect will trump human-rights protection. Still, the agency-respect view allows us to detect in what way the annexation is pro tanto, though not all-things-considered, problematic: it is agency-disrespectful against those members of Canada who are committed to the rules structuring their collective decision-making process, as well as to the international community who is committed to the sovereignty norm more broadly.

Now let us turn to *Scandinavia*. Unlike the autonomy view, the agency-respect view allows us to explain why the unilateral annexation of Denmark on Sweden's part would be problematic, even if the Danes would be subjected to the same norms as they would be in the absence of the annexation. Once again, the reason is that the unilateral annexation in question is agency-disrespectful towards those who are committed to the norms making up Denmark's collective decision-making processes as well as to international sovereignty norms. The same goes for *Europe*. While the EU's "annexation" of Scotland happens to match the cooperative intentions of the Scottish people, it still involves disrespect for their sovereignty, and thus a disregard for both their internal legal norms and international ones. To that extent, the annexation is wrongful. What matters here, it is crucial to emphasize, are not the associative intentions of individuals, but their commitments to a set of socially constructed norms.

The agency-respect view successfully addresses the last two cases which, I have argued, the political-project version of the autonomy view has difficulties accommodating. But how is this possible, given the similarities between the two views? What gives the agency-respect view an explanatory advantage, compared to the autonomy view, is its being more capacious with respect to the commitments that call for respect. Both Stilz's view and my own are ultimately grounded in respect for persons' commitments as expressions of their autonomous agency. But while Stilz focuses on commitments to particular associative political projects, the commitments that matter, in my case, are *to socially constructed norms*. Those commitments, in turn, might be motivated by a variety of different considerations. Some such considerations may include the desire to jointly pursue a particular political project, whereby the relevant norms are crucial to the pursuit of that project, but they need not.

For example, one might be committed to decision-making in accordance with legal procedures—hence to respect for the sovereignty of reasonably just states—because one believes in the ideal of the rule of law. Or one may be committed to the particular rules structuring one's political association because one believes that they are, overall, best placed to deliver good outcomes. Or one may be committed to those rules in light of the values they promote and embody. Alternatively, one may be committed to the international norm of sovereign equality because one believes it incorporates centuries of human wisdom. It is respect for those commitments, provided these are permissible and authentic, that triggers demands of agency respect. By focusing on differently motivated commitments to existing norms, rather than on commitments to political projects, the agency-respect view can account for more instances of intuitively wrongful sovereignty violations than its alternatives.

8. Concerns

No doubt readers will have several questions about the agency-respect view as applied to the puzzle of sovereignty violations. Two of them are particularly relevant to the present discussion. The first concerns a matter that was already raised

8.1 Sovereignty for minorities?

in Chapters 3 and 5, namely the implications of the view for those who lack a commitment to existing norms, specifically for minorities and, in this context, national minorities. The second disputes the idea that people have genuine commitments to legal norms, and thereby casts doubt on the applicability of the agency-respect view to real-world political collectives. I now elaborate on, and address, each concern in turn.

8.1 Sovereignty for minorities?

Consider the following scenario, implicit in one of the cases I introduced earlier. Post-Brexit, the Scottish people no longer wish to be part of the United Kingdom: the values reflected in UK laws are at odds with their commitments and priorities. Scotland asks Westminster for an independence referendum. Westminster, however, does not give the go-ahead. The Scottish then proceed to hold an illegal referendum, where an overwhelming majority votes in favour of independence. A few days later, the Scottish Parliament declares independence, and Scotland unilaterally secedes from the United Kingdom. What would the agency-respect view say in the face of this scenario?

I assume that, in the eyes of many people, what the Scottish did was permissible. Yet readers may worry that the agency-respect view fails to vindicate this verdict. By seceding illegally, the Scottish violate the sovereignty of the United Kingdom, which—*let us suppose*—is a reasonably just state: a democratic state that protects human rights to a good enough degree. And doesn't the agency-respect view imply that such violations are always wrongful, as per proposition (ii) in our original trilemma?

As it turns out, it does not. The agency-respect view, therefore, also leaves room for challenging the second proposition in our puzzle. This is because, according to principle *P*, agency respect places demands on us *only provided that* respecting others' authentic commitments does not impose unreasonable burdens on our own agency. In the situation we have envisaged, assuming Scotland is in a position to establish itself as a reasonably just state, it is unreasonable for the United Kingdom not to allow it to secede, since continued membership of the United Kingdom would place too high a burden on the agency of the Scottish people.

To go back to language introduced in Chapter 3, this is one of those cases in which communities should be able to create different "normative worlds", constituted by different webs of socially constructed norms. The ideal of equal respect for persons' agency is best realized, in a case like this, if Scotland secedes. On this matter, the agency-respect view is fully in line with Stilz's autonomy-based one, according to which a right to independence should be given to:

> groups who have shared political commitments that are (i) consistent with the provision of basic justice for others, (ii) who possess or can create a territorially

organized structure of representation, and (iii) whose dissent can be feasibly addressed, at reasonable cost, by granting them separate political institutions.

(Stilz 2019: 116)

If the right is not given with the agreement of the original sovereign—i.e., if attempting to settle the matter without violating its sovereignty proves impossible— then unilateral secession cannot be deemed wrongful *on sovereignty-violation grounds*. That said, the agency-respect view does not give carte blanche to any minority to constitute itself into an independent community, whether with or without the original sovereign's consent.

Like Stilz's view, the agency-respect view confers this right on a potential normative community only to the extent that it can feasibly make itself into a reasonably just one. Unilateral secessions that would foreseeably not give rise to new, just sovereigns would be ruled out by the agency-respect view because contrary to basic constraints of morality. Similarly, while the agency-respect view does not condemn sovereignty violations per se when they are necessary to fulfil the reasonable agency-respect claims of a community, it does not imply that such communities are automatically justified in seceding. If secession is likely, for instance, to result in violence and much wrongdoing—civil war, at the limit—undertaking it would be wrongful for independent moral reasons.

These qualifications mean that, inevitably, some minorities will be unable to permissibly create political communities of their own, governed by norms that accurately reflect their commitments. As I have already noted in previous chapters, this isn't just an unpalatable implication of the agency-respect view. It is an inevitable fact of living in a complex, pluralistic world. The agency-respect view, however, has the resources to acknowledge this regrettable state of affairs, and to argue for respect and accommodation of permissible minority claims, even when such accommodation cannot lead to minorities creating self-governing communities. The same reasons that require minorities to be respectful of the agency-respect claims of majorities also call for majorities' sensitivity to minority claims. As I explained in Chapter 3, from the perspective of agency respect minority claims are just as legitimate as those of majorities. The reasons why we ought to respect them, provided the norms supported by majorities are morally permissible and do not impose excessive burdens on our agency, have much to do with epistemic and practical limitations, which make it impossible for each of us to respond to every single person's agency-respect claims.

8.2 Does sovereignty ever really matter?

Readers may worry that, since hardly anyone has any authentic commitments to domestic legal norms or to the international norm of sovereign equality, on the agency-respect view sovereignty hardly ever matters. This is because states are coercive entities, so *even if* people are committed to the norms making them up, we cannot regard those commitments as authentic. This being so, the agency-respect view fails to vindicate the wrong of sovereignty violations.

It is true that, on the agency-respect view, sovereignty matters independently of its repercussions on the material interests of individuals only so long as sovereignty norms are underpinned by *authentic* commitments. So, without those commitments, the agency-respect view cannot lend sovereignty any moral normativity. However, jumping from the coercive nature of the state to the conclusion that people's commitments to "their own norms" are not authentic seems far too quick. After all, all of our commitments are in some way or other affected by circumstances, and even those commitments violations of which would result in sanctions can be genuinely endorsed. Recall the example, offered in an earlier chapter, of my commitment to not murdering people being authentic even if murder is severely punished.

An authentic commitment is not one formed by altogether independent, "unencumbered selves", to use Sandel's (1984) expression. Instead, we can take commitments to be authentic when they are formed under adequately free conditions, such that their holders would likely not repudiate them upon reflection (cf. Stilz 2019: 105ff.). When faced with people who live in reasonably just states, and who therefore are adequately free and have the resources to reflect on what norms they adhere to, we can expect their commitments to be authentic, unless we have clear evidence to the contrary. In those circumstances, the agency-respect view will lend moral normativity to states' sovereignty. (This is a matter to which I shall return in the book's Conclusion.)

Which collectives satisfy these conditions in the real world is a tricky question. To be sure, oppressive collectives, such as North Korea, lack the background conditions under which we can expect their members' commitments to count as authentic. Other collectives will partially satisfy the relevant background conditions, and it is going to be a judgement call whether their members' commitments can count as freely formed, and therefore as authentic. Furthermore, as I have mentioned earlier, both domestic and international sovereignty norms fall short of what justice requires, in ways that arguably put into question their moral normativity *under present circumstances*.

Taken together, these considerations do support the objector's concern that the implications of the agency-respect view for sovereignty violations in the real world are somewhat limited. But this, it seems to me, is no bug or problematic deficiency of the view. After all, the aim of the view is to explain when and why socially constructed norms have moral normativity such that they place pro tanto moral obligations on us. But if it turns out that influential existing norms are unjust or not genuinely endorsed, then we should not lament the fact that the agency-respect view lends them no moral normativity. The limited implications of the view for the real world are a consequence of the deficiencies of the world itself, not of the view.

9. Conclusion

In this chapter, I have brought the agency-respect view to bear on a puzzle that has attracted the attention of political philosophers in the recent past. The puzzle is to explain how seemingly harmless violations of the sovereignty of political collectives can be wrongful, given that such collectives themselves lack independent moral standing. Explaining their wrongness thus requires identifying legitimate interests of individuals that are set back by such sovereignty violations. I have looked at two prominent views that purport to identify the relevant interests: the membership view and the autonomy view. I have found some lacunae in both of them, while acknowledging that the autonomy view, at least in its political-project version, is highly instructive and on the right track. I have then turned to the agency-respect view—which affirms a legitimate interest in having our authentic and permissible commitments respected—and explained how it can help us account for those intuitively wrongful instances of sovereignty violations that competing views cannot explain. In particular, those violations are wrongful to the extent that they involve disrespect for persons' commitments both to the internal norms structuring a collective's decision-making (the rule of law) and to the international norms protecting state sovereignty (sovereign equality). In doing so, the agency-respect view also explains why sovereignty violations wrong not only the members of those collectives, but also the international community more generally.

Morality and Socially Constructed Norms. Laura Valentini, Oxford University Press. © Laura Valentini 2023.
DOI: 10.1093/9780191938115.003.0007

Conclusion

I completed the first draft of this book's Conclusion in the spring of 2020.[1] At the time, I (like most others) was in social isolation, in the midst of the Coronavirus pandemic. The pandemic raised (and still raises) countless ethical questions: about the just distribution of scarce medical resources, about individual responsibility for public health, about how to balance deaths caused by the virus versus deaths caused by the economic downturn triggered by lockdowns, and many more. But the pandemic was also an occasion to reflect on the moral normativity of socially constructed norms. To tackle Coronavirus, such new norms were legislated or spontaneously emerged from the bottom up. Governments all over the world introduced strict prohibitions, enforcing social isolation and forbidding citizens from leaving their homes unless this was done to acquire basic necessities. At the same time, new salutation practices replacing the handshake developed, such as elbow bumps.

In this concluding chapter, I shall examine the implications of the agency-respect view for our obligations to do as these newly established norms required, and in part still require. (It is now late 2022, and Covid-19 remains a concern.) This will allow me to review the main claims of the book and its limitations. I do so in four steps. First, I reiterate the distinction between obligations to act in conformity with norms and obligations of obedience. Second, I briefly go over the book's account of the ground of obligations of obedience: the agency-respect principle. Third, I consider the question of who is wronged by failures to obey socially constructed norms. Fourth, I explain in what sense the agency-respect principle supports the old saying "When in Rome do as the Romans do" and steers a middle course between the concerns of liberal universalists and communitarians.

1. Conformity, Obedience, and the Deflationary View

There are, often, countless reasons for doing what socially constructed norms require. Some are prudential, but others are moral, and weighty enough to give us

---

[1] Yes, quite a bit of time has elapsed between the first full draft and the final manuscript, but Covid, a second child, and a move to a different country happened in the meantime. I know this isn't of scholarly interest, but I thought I'd mention it, just in case readers are curious.

pro tanto obligations. Those obligations, in turn, can be of two kinds: *to obey norms* and to *act in conformity with them*. The former are obligations to engage in the behaviour prescribed by a norm grounded in the fact that the norm prescribes it. They are obligations to act "because the norm says so". The latter are obligations to engage in the behaviour prescribed by a norm, but are not grounded in the fact that the norm prescribes it. Instead, the substantive, norm-independent virtues of the particular actions prescribed explain their obligatoriness.

For example, recall the discussion of traffic rules, in Chapter 2. The reason why we should follow them, I suggested, is first and foremost that doing so minimizes the risk of harm to self and others. Stopping at a red light is morally obligatory primarily because, in circumstances of widespread compliance with traffic regulations, doing so is safe. A similar line of reasoning applies to the social distancing norms introduced in response to the Coronavirus pandemic. People should keep at a safe distance (or even isolate) not so much because there is a norm requiring it. They should keep at a safe distance, first and foremost, because doing so slows down the rate of contagion and saves lives. And even if, by flouting social isolation and distancing norms, one were not endangering others—say, because one isn't infected, so would not risk spreading the virus—one would still act wrongly, free riding on their cooperation. In sum, social distancing in the midst of a pandemic is morally obligatory primarily because it is safe and fair, not because it is socially mandated.

Accepting this conclusion, and the broader thought that morality often enjoins us to act in conformity with socially constructed norms, is compatible with endorsing what I have called a *deflationary view* about the moral normativity of such norms. On this view, what might at first look like obligations to obey socially constructed norms are, ultimately, just duties to act in conformity with them. We should do what socially constructed norms require because the behaviour they mandate happens to match the demands of some independent moral principle. On the deflationary view, the idea that "we should do what a norm requires because it is required by a norm" is a dangerous illusion: dangerous because it has the potential of breeding uncritical conformism, if not subjection to potentially troublesome norms.

In the book, I have argued against the deflationary view, insisting that we have obligations not only to act in conformity with socially constructed norms but also to obey them. In particular, I have shown that a familiar moral principle lends moral normativity to those norms. This principle does not pick out the behaviour prescribed by socially constructed norms as independently morally mandated. Instead, it lends moral significance to the *very fact that* the behaviour is prescribed by socially constructed norms. This is what I have called the agency-respect principle.

210   CONCLUSION

2. Agency Respect

The principle says the following.

The agency-respect principle: one has a pro tanto obligation to respect people's commitments (i.e., "to give *agency respect* to people"), provided those commitments are authentic, morally permissible, and respecting them is not too costly.

Coupled with the fact, discussed in Chapter 1, that socially constructed norms are partly constituted by people's public commitments to their requirements functioning as general standards of behaviour, this principle grounds an obligation *to obey* such norms. On the agency-respect view, we ought to do as socially constructed norms require not because their requirements are independently morally mandated. It is not the content of those requirements that explains their bindingness; it is the fact that those requirements are expressions of, and supported by, permissible and genuine exercises of agency: commitments. Those exercises of agency, in turn, are the constituents of socially constructed norms.

As just stated, the agency-respect principle includes three limiting conditions. It gives rise to obligations to respect others' agency provided: (i) this is not too costly to us, (ii) their commitments are morally permissible, and (iii) those commitments are authentic. When one or more of conditions (i), (ii), and (iii) are not met, socially constructed norms lack moral normativity. Too see this, let us consider the implications of the agency-respect principle in relation to the social distancing norms introduced in the context of the pandemic. Does respect for the agency of those committed to such norms play a part in explaining why we should practice social distancing?

Answering in the affirmative would be counterintuitive. Even if, in the context of a pandemic, the social distancing norm appears fully morally permissible, it has certainly never crossed my mind that the reason I should practice social distancing or isolation is respect for those who are committed to the corresponding norms. Thankfully, the agency-respect view does not have this implication. Practicing social distancing, especially in the form of social isolation, out of respect for others' commitments would manifestly be too burdensome for one's own agency. The reasonable costs condition—condition (i)—would not be satisfied. Social isolation significantly hinders the pursuit of our most important ends and goals. To that extent, the agency-respect view does not consider a social-isolation norm a candidate for possession of moral normativity. We ought to isolate socially in order to save lives, not in order to respect those who are committed to this norm, whoever they might be.

However, what would the view imply if several people were publicly committed to the social distancing norm not directly, but indirectly, insofar as it is a *legal norm*? Their commitment to the norm would be derivative of their broader commitment to the rule of law. In this case, two scenarios open themselves up, in line with what was discussed in Chapter 5. First, suppose that the legal system of which the norm is a part is a deeply unjust one. In such a case, the agency-respect view would not vindicate an obligation to "obey the relevant norm because it is the law", since the moral permissibility condition—namely condition (ii)—would not be satisfied. People's commitments to the bindingness of law qua law would not be worthy of respect.

Second, suppose the norm is part of a reasonably just legal system. In that case, people's commitments *to that system* would indeed call for agency respect in general, but once again, given the burdens placed on most people's agency by such a norm, respect for one's fellow citizens' commitment to the rule of law would likely not suffice to generate agency-respect obligations. Recall how, in Chapters 3 and 5, we reached a similar conclusion in relation to women sincerely committed to wearing a full-face veil, but who are legally prohibited from doing so. Given the agency-costs of abiding by the prohibition, agency-respect for other people's commitment to the rule of law cannot make that prohibition morally binding on religious women. Different considerations, however, to do with reciprocity and public safety, arguably can. In the present case too, breaching the social distancing norm would not be wrongful on agency-respect grounds—though it would be on other, fair-play and reciprocity-based ones.[2]

These conclusions, I hope, are plausible enough. But a deeper worry may be lingering in readers' minds. This concerns condition (iii) in the agency-respect principle, which makes the moral normativity of socially constructed norms conditional on these norms being underpinned by genuine, that is *authentic*, commitments. Can the commitments underpinning socially constructed norms ever be authentic? This recurrent worry, which I briefly mentioned and addressed in the preceding chapters, is one that arises also in relation to the Covid-19 pandemic. The social distancing measures introduced by governments around the world were backed by the threat of the state's coercive force. Those who failed to respect the relevant measures risked fines if not imprisonment. And even those norms that were not legally enforced were often backed by social sanctions, such as public disapproval or shaming. How can we then conclude that any such norm is an expression of their supporters' *genuine* agency?

---

[2] Note that our conclusion would be different if social distancing norms had to do with something like "respect for personal space" and abiding by them wouldn't be too costly to us. For instance, Italians often interact with each other in ways that would involve problematic invasions of personal space if judged by the norms prevalent in other contexts (e.g., Britain). Typically, respect for such personal-space norms—concerning, e.g., when it is appropriate to hug someone, give them a pat on the back or a kiss on the cheeks, at what distance people should stand from one another, etc.—isn't too costly even for those who do not independently endorse them. Moreover, since these norms are by and large morally permissible, they tend to place agency-respect obligations on their addressees (of course, provided the commitments underpinning them are authentic).

212 CONCLUSION

This is an important worry, but one that should not be overstated. Who we are is always also the product of "alien forces" operating on us. My beliefs, preferences, and commitments are dependent on my upbringing. I was brought up as an only child in Milan in the 1980s and 90s. Had I been brought up in, say, India, one of several siblings, my beliefs, preferences, and commitments would likely differ. From this, however, it would seem excessive to conclude that no action I perform, no commitment I have, is truly mine. Such a conclusion would invalidate all talk of agency and responsibility. If no action is genuinely mine, then I cannot plausibly be held responsible for it. While such scepticism about responsibility and agency may be an apt topic for discussion in the context of debates about free will and moral luck, this is not the place to entertain it (see, e.g., Nagel 1979). I am thus assuming that the objector is not worried about the existence of "authentic agency" simpliciter, but about whether commitments to the demands of socially constructed norms *specifically* can be plausible candidates as expressions of authentic agency.

To answer this concern, we need to say a little more about what authentic agency requires. As John Christman explains, two families of conditions typically figure among such requirements: *competence conditions* and *authenticity conditions*. The former are conditions for agency simpliciter, and involve one's capacity for rational action and deliberation, coupled with the absence of psychological impairments such as psychoses and compulsions. The latter require that "desires, values or other springs of action are truly the agent's own" and not the result of alien forces (Christman 2007: 4). Commitments to socially constructed norms are looked at with suspicion insofar as they allegedly fail to meet this "authenticity" condition, because those norms always operate as external, coercive, manipulative influences undermining one's independence.

But again, it is difficult to see how wholehearted scepticism about the authenticity of commitments to socially constructed norms in particular could be compatible with optimism about the possibility of authentic agency in general. After all, our entire existence is shaped by encounters with such norms: within our families, our workplaces, our circles of friends, our societies, and so forth. While it is true that those norms are vehicles of power, the fact that our beliefs and commitments are shaped by power does not render them automatically inauthentic. As Bernard Williams puts it, we "should accept that a belief is not necessarily discredited just because it is caused through the power of someone" (Williams 2002: 226). The same goes for commitments.

Consider, for instance, school pupils. Many of them attend classes not out of their own choosing, but due to parental or state coercion. School attendance, in turn, is likely to expose them to ideas and information that will shape their beliefs, values, and commitments. Even so, it would seem implausible to suggest that, *just because* someone's going to school was the product of someone else's exercise of power—indeed, of norms requiring school attendance—school-induced beliefs and commitments are *never* authentic or genuine (Williams 2002: 226). While in some cases, namely when schooling involves brainwashing or ideological inculcation, we have reason to be suspicious of the resulting beliefs and commitments, in other cases, we should not be.

The challenge is to distinguish between cases in which suspicion is warranted from cases in which it is not. Operationalizing this distinction requires devising an appropriate "authenticity test".[3] While, as I have acknowledged in Chapter 3, several possibilities are available, I find John Christman's counterfactual test particularly illuminating and thus worth elaborating upon. On Christman's view, a commitment of a particular agent A is authentic when, were A to reflect upon the historical process that led her to develop that commitment, A would not feel *alienated* from it. That is, A would not repudiate the commitment, she would not feel negatively towards it, and would not perceive it as an unwelcome constraint on her agency (Christman 2007: 12).

This test allows us to rule out problematically coerced commitments while vindicating the possibility that socially constructed norms are often the object of authentic commitments. First, the test does not require A to engage in the relevant process of reflection. A may never actually reflect on her commitments and still those commitments would qualify as appropriate expressions of her agency, provided the non-alienation condition is counterfactually met. For our commitments to socially constructed norms to count as authentic we do not have to actually scrutinize and reflect upon them. Unreflective, automatic endorsement may well suffice, provided the right counterfactual attitudes hold.

Second, according to this test, the fact that a commitment has been caused by some exercise of power or coercion does not, per se, invalidate its authenticity. Take my commitment to not harming innocent others. As already remarked in previous chapters, this commitment has been formed during my upbringing and is reinforced by coercive law. Still, when reflecting upon it, I do not feel alienated from it: I fully embrace it, even if I know that when I developed it I was subject to certain non-voluntary influences.

Third, authentic commitments require non-alienation rather than wholehearted endorsement or approval. Consider, for instance, Julia's commitment to queuing up at the bus stop. Suppose that, upon reflection, Julia realizes that her acceptance of the queuing norm has been mostly due to social pressure. Still, she continues to

---

[3] Williams himself develops a version of such a test, applied to the domain of political legitimacy specifically, relying on what he calls the "Critical Theory Principle". According to this principle, "the acceptance of a justification does not count [as legitimating] if the acceptance itself is produced by the coercive power which is supposedly being justified" (Williams 2005: 6). The principle captures one of the core concerns of so-called critical theorists: it seeks to reveal false consciousness and curb the legitimating force of acceptance in those cases where acceptance is itself the product of oppression. On Williams' view, if our commitment to a particular political regime is a product of the regime's own exercise of coercive power, then that commitment has to be questioned. While Williams' critical theory principle may be useful when trying to devise an authenticity test for "political acceptance", it is not ideally suited when what we are trying to establish is whether one's beliefs and commitments to socially constructed norms are authentic.

214   CONCLUSION

feel perfectly okay about it. She does not enthusiastically endorse it, but is happy to go along with it, and to treat the queuing requirement as a general standard of behaviour. On Christman's test, so long as she is not *alienated* from it, her commitment qualifies as authentic, despite being bland and certainly not central to who Julia is.

In sum, the fact that commitments to socially constructed norms are often unreflective and accompanied by social—if not state—coercion does not automatically invalidate their authenticity. It does, however, highlight the need for careful contextual and interpretive analysis aimed at determining whether, in any given instance, commitments do express the genuine agency of those who hold them, and hence call for agency respect. This is all the more so in circumstances characterized by imbalances of power, where norms appear at least prima facie oppressive.

For an illustration, consider a woman who has been brought up in a conservative Muslim family and has, since childhood, been wearing the veil. Reflecting— either hypothetically or de facto—upon her childhood, upbringing, and the forces in play there, she may come to one of two conclusions. She may find the veil an unwelcome constraint on her freedom, a symbol of male dominance over women, and therefore feel alienated from it. Alternatively, she may embrace the veil, while acknowledging its history. She may, upon reflection, find it a useful instrument of identity affirmation and self-expression. In the former case, the woman's commitment to the veil would count as inauthentic, while in the latter it would count as authentic, despite a background of certain non-voluntary influences (cf. the highly instructive discussion in Laborde 2006).

As this example all too briefly illustrates, taking seriously the agency-respect principle and applying it to specific contexts calls for sensitivity to concerns that have been central to critical social theory. It requires trying to ascertain the authenticity of people's commitments to norms, without taking the demands of those norms for granted. And it requires avoiding imperialistically imposing one's own perspective on others, and dismissing their commitments as "inauthentic" as soon as they strike us as unpalatable. In the present book, I have not carried out the careful, psychologically and historically informed contextual analysis needed to ascertain whether specific socially constructed norms are worthy of respect. But I have offered a framework that hopefully makes it clear why this type of analysis is necessary for a correct appraisal of the moral demands applying to us.

3. Who Is Wronged by Breaches of Socially Constructed Norms?

The agency-respect principle, I have argued, lends moral normativity to socially constructed norms. Provided the three aforementioned conditions are satisfied,

WHO IS WRONGED BY BREACHES OF SOCIALLY CONSTRUCTED NORMS? 215

violations of those norms in any given context are at least pro tanto wrong. As we saw in Chapters 3 and 4, this raises the question of *who stands to be wronged by such violations*. Philosophical defences of practice-generated obligations routinely incur into the so-called wrong reasons problem (Scanlon 1990: 221–2). Often, disrespect for practice-based norms intuitively wrongs specific individuals, but equally often, the justification for the moral force of those norms traces back to reasons that have little to do with those individuals themselves.

Take, for instance, the fair-play justification for doing as the law requires, according to which breaches of law are problematic because they amount to free riding on others' cooperation. Now consider two possible breaches of law: flouting mandatory social distancing and entering a private residence without authorization. Intuitively, we may want to say that the first breach wrongs the community as a whole, while the second wrongs the owner of the residence specifically. However, a fair-play account seems committed to the arguably problematic conclusion that no particular individual is wronged in either case, and that both breaches of law are wrongful in that they involve taking advantage of others' compliance with the law, without reciprocation. Both breaches, that is, wrong the community as a whole.

The same difficulty, it might be thought, plagues the agency-respect view insofar as it traces the moral normativity of socially constructed norms to agency respect *for norm-supporters*. Contrary to first appearances, the agency-respect view has the resources to address this concern. To see this, we need to recall the suggestion—advanced in Chapter 4—that there are two understandings of rights and, correspondingly, of wrongings: "rights as inviolability" and "rights as control". The former designate duties grounded in others' important interests. The latter designate one's normative powers to control others' duties: demand- and waiver-powers. Acknowledgement of both types of rights—and wrongings—allows the agency-respect view to make sense of the ways in which some norm-breaches wrong both norm-supporters in general *and* certain individuals in particular.

First, since we have an interest in agency respect, on the agency-respect view, by flouting socially constructed norms that possess moral normativity, we breach the rights as inviolability of norm-supporters. To that extent, we wrong them. Here, my view converges with the fair-play account. Second, some socially constructed norms confer rights as control on individuals. Property and queuing norms, for instance, are a case in point. To own property is to control others' duties in relation to that property. Similarly, to occupy a particular spot in the queue is to have normative control over that spot: one may insist on keeping one's spot or offer it to someone else.

The agency-respect view can explain why, by breaching queuing or property norms, we also distinctively wrong *particular* individuals—not merely norm-supporters—insofar as we ignore their rights as control. To be sure, part of the moral weight of those rights—especially in cases where their existence is not independently

216   CONCLUSION

morally mandated—traces back to agency respect for norm-supporters, but it is precisely respect for them that, in turn, requires us to live by the rules of the normative world they have created. If, in that world, those in the queue and property owners count as right-holders—in the control sense—who are distinctively wronged by the breach, then, on the agency-respect view, this is precisely how they ought to be regarded.

In sum, from the perspective of the agency-respect view, whenever morally permissible power-conferring norms are violated, there are two sets of agents who stand to be wronged. On the one hand, all those who support the norms ("the community") stand to be wronged in the inviolability sense. On the other hand, the specific individuals who are granted control rights by the norms stand to be wronged in the control sense. In this way, the agency-respect view captures the plausible thought that, by breaching socially constructed norms, we disrespect the community who upholds them, *without* ignoring the special position of particular individuals in relation to those breaches.

4. When in Rome Do as the Romans Do

The agency-respect view, briefly summarized in the previous sections, is anchored in a familiar, liberal universalist principle, requiring respect for individual agency. At the same time, by understanding agency as embedded in rich social contexts and shaped by particular commitments, the view also accommodates important communitarian insights.[4] It grounds respect for norms, hence, to a large extent, respect for culture, in respect for the individual.

Still, a view of this kind is not without tensions, which I wish to acknowledge in conclusion. To do so, I once again take an example inspired by the Covid-19 pandemic. Consider the new, informal greeting norms that have emerged in response to the Coronavirus, such as the elbow-bump. These norms are meant to allow people to salute each other in ways less likely to spread germs than the familiar handshake. But suppose that, once the pandemic is over, while most societies return to their pre-pandemic greetings, Italians continue to adopt the elbow-bump as their new form of salutation. There is no specific public-health reason for doing so anymore—or, at any rate, not a particularly pressing one—and the greeting is a little awkward. Still, according to the agency-respect view, in such a situation, in the context of Italy, even one who is not particularly keen on elbow-bumping should greet others this way. But why? Why should those who would rather shake hands, or bow, or hug, or whatever, go along with the majority norm? Of course, the example here is trivial, but the point it illustrates is an important one. Since we live in pluralistic societies, ones where not everyone will share commitments to the same socially constructed norms, it looks like the agency-respect

---

[4] For a view that, in a structurally somewhat similar way, accommodates communitarian concerns within a liberal framework, see Kymlicka (1995).

view inevitably sacrifices the interests of the individual to those of the majority. It can thus hardly claim a liberal-individualist pedigree.

As I explained in Chapters 3, 5, and 6, there is something to this concern. But the concern arises not because of deficiencies inherent in the agency-respect view, but because of the complexity and "imperfection" of the world in which we live. On the agency-respect view, "when in Rome, we should do as the Romans do" not because the mere fact that a majority of people in context C ("Rome") accept a particular norm makes that norm more "morally valid" than an equally permissible alternative, preferred by a minority. Instead, it is because acting in line with this old saying allows us to approximate the regulative ideal of fairly responding to everyone's agency-respect claims. And what is more, from an agency-respect perspective, we should only behave "as the Romans do" when doing so isn't excessively burdensome for our own agency.

That saying encapsulates a "rule of regulation", to use G. A. Cohen's (2003) expression, one that is justified in light of agency respect in conjunction with practical and epistemic considerations. Since it is virtually impossible to know everyone's commitments, especially if we are operating outside the circle of our near and dear, relying on the requirements of socially constructed norms is our best bet when trying to honour the demands of agency respect. This, unfortunately, puts the agency-respect claims of minorities somewhat at risk of being marginalized. Aware of this unavoidable limitation, as I argued in Chapter 5, our political systems should try to minimize this occurrence, by enforcing strong protections for individual and minority rights, as well as by giving minorities ample space for contesting the existing social set-up. Furthermore, as I argued in Chapter 6, if membership in a shared political community would excessively burden a minority's agency, secession—even unilateral secession—may well be in-principle justified on agency-respect grounds.[5] The agency-respect view, then, does not achieve a miraculous reconciliation of the claims of individuals and those of communities. But it does justify sensitivity to the demands of communities on individualistic grounds, in a way that makes us aware of the trade-offs we must face in pluralistic contexts.

All this being said, as I have already emphasized, the agency-respect view is a framework and cannot be used to algorithmically derive particular prescriptions. Those must be arrived at by further specifying the conditions of "permissibility", "reasonable costs", and "authenticity", and by taking into account complex contextual details, allowing us to ascertain whether those conditions are met. But I do hope that the framework can help orientate our practical reasoning, by giving socially constructed norms their due when we deliberate about what we ought, morally, to do.

Morality and Socially Constructed Norms. Laura Valentini, Oxford University Press. © Laura Valentini 2023.
DOI: 10.1093/9780191938115.003.0008

---

[5] Whether it would be all-things-considered permissible is a different matter.

References

Abizadeh, Arash. 2018. *Hobbes and the Two Faces of Ethics*. Cambridge: Cambridge University Press.

Adams, N. P. 2017. "In Defense of Content-Independence". *Legal Theory* 23 (3): 143–67.

Alexander, Larry. 1996. "The Moral Magic of Consent (II)". *Legal Theory* 2 (3): 165–74.

Alexander, Larry. 2014. "The Ontology of Consent". *Analytic Philosophy* 55 (1): 102–13.

Alston, William P. 1989. *Epistemic Justification: Essays in the Theory of Knowledge*. Ithaca, NY: Cornell University Press.

Altman, Andrew, and Christopher Heath Wellman. 2009. *A Liberal Theory of International Justice*. Oxford: Oxford University Press.

Anscombe, G. E. M. 1957. *Intention*. Cambridge, MA: Harvard University Press.

Anscombe, G. E. M. 1958. "Modern Moral Philosophy". *Philosophy* 33 (124): 1–19.

Anscombe, G. E. M. 1978. "Rules, Rights, and Promises". *Midwest Studies in Philosophy* 3 (1): 318–23.

Arneson, Richard J. 1982. "The Principle of Fairness and Free-Rider Problems". *Ethics* 92 (4): 616–33.

Arneson, Richard J. 2004. "Democracy Is not Intrinsically Just". In *Justice and Democracy*, edited by Keith Dowding, Robert E. Goodin, and Carole Pateman, 40–58. Cambridge: Cambridge University Press.

Asudeh, Ash. 2019. "Grammar and Meaning". In *The Oxford Handbook of English Grammar*, edited by Bas Aarts, Jill Bowie, and Gergana Popova, 523–53. Oxford: Oxford University Press.

Austin, J. L. 1962. *How to Do Things with Words: The William James Lectures Delivered at Harvard University in 1955*. Oxford: Oxford University Press.

Australian Electoral Commission. 2019. "A Short History of Federal Electoral Reform in Australia". https://www.aec.gov.au/Elections/history-of-electoral-reform.htm.

Bader, Ralf M. 2021. "De Facto Monopolies and the Justification of the State". In *The Routledge Handbook of Anarchy and Anarchist Thought*, edited by Gary Chartier and Chad Van Schoelandt, 152–62. New York: Routledge.

BBC News. 2001. "Germany's Anti-Nuclear Protesters", March 28, 2001. http://news.bbc.co.uk/1/hi/world/europe/1247676.stm.

Beitz, Charles R. 2009. *The Idea of Human Rights*. New York: Oxford University Press.

Besson, Samantha. 2012. "Sovereignty". In *The Max Planck Encyclopedia of Public International Law*, edited by Rüdiger Wolfrum, Vol. IX: 366–91. Oxford: Oxford University Press. https://opil.ouplaw.com/view/10.1093/law:epil/9780199231690/law-9780199231690-e1472.

Bicchieri, Cristina. 2006. *The Grammar of Society: The Nature and Dynamics of Social Norms*. New York: Cambridge University Press.

Bicchieri, Cristina, Richard C. Jeffrey, and Brian Skyrms, eds. 1997. *The Dynamics of Norms*. Cambridge: Cambridge University Press.

Blake, Michael. 2021. "Unwanted Compatriots: Alienation, Migration, and Political Autonomy". *Ethics & International Affairs* 35 (4): 491–501.

220 REFERENCES

Bolinger, Renée Jorgensen. 2019. "Moral Risk and Communicating Consent". *Philosophy & Public Affairs* 47 (2): 179–207.

Bratman, Michael E. 1981. "Intention and Means-End Reasoning". *The Philosophical Review* 90 (2): 252–65.

Bratman, Michael E. 1984. "Two Faces of Intention". *The Philosophical Review* 93 (3): 375–405.

Bratman, Michael E. 1987. *Intention, Plans, and Practical Reason*. Cambridge, MA: Harvard University Press.

Bratman, Michael E. 1989. "Intention and Personal Policies". *Philosophical Perspectives* 3: 443–69.

Bratman, Michael E. 1999. *Faces of Intention: Selected Essays on Intention and Agency*. New York: Cambridge University Press.

Brennan, Geoffrey, Lina Eriksson, Robert E. Goodin, and Nicholas Southwood. 2013. *Explaining Norms*. New York: Oxford University Press.

Brennan, Geoffrey, and Philip Pettit. 2004. *The Economy of Esteem: An Essay on Civil and Political Society*. New York: Oxford University Press.

Broome, John. 2013. *Rationality through Reasoning*. Oxford: John Wiley & Sons.

Brownlee, Kimberley. 2012. *Conscience and Conviction: The Case for Civil Disobedience*. Oxford: Oxford University Press.

Buchanan, Allen. 1998. "Democracy and Secession". In *National Self-Determination and Secession*, edited by Margaret Moore, 14–33. Oxford: Oxford University Press.

Burke, Mary A., and H. Peyton Young. 2011. "Social Norms". In *Handbook of Social Economics*, edited by Jess Benhabib, Alberto Bisin, and Matthew O. Jackson, Vol. 1A: 311–38. Amsterdam: Elsevier.

Buss, Sarah. 1999. "Appearing Respectful: The Moral Significance of Manners". *Ethics* 109 (4): 795–826.

Cabrera, Luis. 2004. *Political Theory of Global Justice: A Cosmopolitan Case for the World State*. London: Routledge.

Calhoun, Cheshire. 2009. "What Good Is Commitment?". *Ethics* 119 (4): 613–41.

Ceva, Emanuela. 2015. "Why Toleration Is Not the Appropriate Response to Dissenting Minorities' Claims". *European Journal of Philosophy* 23 (3): 633–51.

Chang, Ruth. 2009. "Voluntarist Reasons and the Sources of Normativity". In *Reasons for Action*, edited by David Sobel and Steven Wall, 243–71. New York: Cambridge University Press.

Chang, Ruth. 2013a. "Commitments, Reasons, and the Will". In *Oxford Studies in Metaethics, Vol. 8*, edited by Russ Shafer-Landau, 74–113. Oxford: Oxford University Press.

Chang, Ruth. 2013b. "Grounding Practical Normativity: Going Hybrid". *Philosophical Studies* 164 (1): 163–87.

Chang, Ruth. 2020. "Do We Have Normative Powers?". *Aristotelian Society Supplementary Volume* 94 (1): 275–300.

Chignell, Andrew. 2018. "The Ethics of Belief". In *The Stanford Encyclopedia of Philosophy*, edited by Edward N. Zalta. Metaphysics Research Lab, Stanford University. https://plato.stanford.edu/archives/spr2018/entries/ethics-belief/.

Chomsky, Noam. 1975. *The Logical Structure of Linguistic Theory*. New York: Springer.

Christiano, Thomas. 2008a. "Democracy". In *The Stanford Encyclopedia of Philosophy*, edited by Edward N. Zalta. Metaphysics Research Lab, Stanford University. http://plato.stanford.edu/archives/fall2008/entries/democracy/.

Christiano, Thomas. 2008b. *The Constitution of Equality: Democratic Authority and Its Limits*. Oxford: Oxford University Press.

REFERENCES   221

Christiano, Thomas. 2013. "Authority". In *The Stanford Encyclopedia of Philosophy*, edited by Edward N. Zalta. Metaphysics Research Lab, Stanford University. http://plato.stanford. edu/archives/spr2013/entries/authority/.

Christman, John. 2004. "Relational Autonomy, Liberal Individualism, and the Social Constitution of Selves". *Philosophical Studies* 117 (1–2): 143–64.

Christman, John. 2007. "Autonomy, History, and the Subject of Justice". *Social Theory and Practice* 33 (1): 1–26.

Cohen, G. A. 2003. "Facts and Principles". *Philosophy & Public Affairs* 31 (3): 211–45.

Cohen, G. A. 2009. *Why Not Socialism?* Princeton, NJ: Princeton University Press.

Cornell, Nicolas. 2015. "Wrongs, Rights, and Third Parties". *Philosophy & Public Affairs* 43 (2): 109–43.

Correia, Fabrice, and Benjamin Schnieder, eds. 2012. *Metaphysical Grounding: Understanding the Structure of Reality*. Cambridge: Cambridge University Press.

Crisp, Roger. 2018. "Prudential and Moral Reasons". In *The Oxford Handbook of Reasons and Normativity*, edited by Daniel Star, 800–20. New York: Oxford University Press.

Dagger, Richard. 2000. "Membership, Fair Play, and Political Obligation". *Political Studies* 48 (1): 104–17.

Dagger, Richard, and David Lefkowitz. 2014. "Political Obligation". In *The Stanford Encyclopedia of Philosophy*, edited by Edward N. Zalta. Metaphysics Research Lab, Stanford University. https://plato.stanford.edu/archives/fall2014/entries/political-obligation/.

Dahl, Robert A. 1989. *Democracy and Its Critics*. New Haven, CT: Yale University Press.

Daniels, Norman. 2013. "Reflective Equilibrium". In *The Stanford Encyclopedia of Philosophy*, edited by Edward N. Zalta. Metaphysics Research Lab, Stanford University. http://plato.stanford.edu/archives/win2013/entries/reflective-equilibrium/.

Darby, Derrick. 2009. *Rights, Race, and Recognition*. Cambridge: Cambridge University Press.

Darwall, Stephen. 1977. "Two Kinds of Respect". *Ethics* 88 (1): 36–49.

Darwall, Stephen. 2006. *The Second-Person Standpoint: Morality, Respect, and Accountability*. Cambridge, MA: Harvard University Press.

Darwall, Stephen. 2012. "Bipolar Obligation". In *Oxford Studies in Metaethics Vol. 7*, edited by Russ Shafer-Landau, 333–58. Oxford: Oxford University Press.

Darwall, Stephen. 2014. "Agreement Matters: Critical Notice on Derek Parfit, *On What Matters*". *Philosophical Review* 123 (1): 79–105.

Davis, Wayne A. 1984. "A Causal Theory of Intending". *American Philosophical Quarterly* 21 (1): 43–54.

Donnelly, Jack. 2014. "State Sovereignty and International Human Rights". *Ethics & International Affairs* 28 (2): 225–38.

Dougherty, Tom. 2015. "Yes Means Yes: Consent as Communication". *Philosophy & Public Affairs* 43 (3): 224–53.

Dworkin, Ronald. 1975. "The Original Position". In *Reading Rawls: Critical Studies on Rawls's A Theory of Justice*, edited by Norman Daniels, 16–52. Stanford, CA: Stanford University Press.

Dworkin, Ronald. 1985. *A Matter of Principle*. Cambridge, MA: Harvard University Press.

Dworkin, Ronald. 1986. *Law's Empire*. Cambridge, MA: Harvard University Press.

Dworkin, Ronald, Kathleen M. Sullivan, Laurence H. Tribe, David Cole, and Curtis Bradley. 2006. "On NSA Spying: A Letter to Congress". *The New York Review of Books*, February 9, 2006. https://www.nybooks.com/articles/2006/02/09/on-nsa-spying-a-letter-to-congress/.

Ebels-Duggan, Kyla. 2009. "Moral Community: Escaping the Ethical State of Nature". *Philosophers' Imprint* 9 (8): 1–19.

222 REFERENCES

Edmundson, William A. 2004. "State of the Art: The Duty to Obey the Law". *Legal Theory* 10 (04): 215–59.

Eidelson, Benjamin. 2013. "Treating People as Individuals". In *Philosophical Foundations of Discrimination Law*, edited by Deborah Hellman and Sophia Moreau, 203–27. New York: Oxford University Press.

Elster, Jon. 1989. "Social Norms and Economic Theory". *Journal of Economic Perspectives* 3 (4): 99–117.

Enoch, David. 2011. "Reason-Giving and the Law". In *Oxford Studies in Philosophy of Law 1*, edited by Leslie Green and Brian Leiter, 1–38. New York: Oxford University Press.

Feinberg, Joel. 1970. "The Nature and Value of Rights". *The Journal of Value Inquiry* 4 (4): 243–60.

Feinberg, Joel. 1986. *Harm to Self*. New York: Oxford University Press.

Fine, Kit. 2001. "The Question of Realism". *Philosophers' Imprint* 1 (1): 1–30.

Fine, Kit. 2012. "Guide to Ground". In *Metaphysical Grounding*, edited by Fabrice Correia and Benjamin Schnieder, 37–80. Cambridge: Cambridge University Press.

Fine, Sarah. 2010. "Freedom of Association Is Not the Answer". *Ethics* 120 (2): 338–56.

Foot, Philippa. 2001. "Natural Norms". In *Natural Goodness*. Oxford: Oxford University Press.

Fraassen, Bas C. van. 1980. *The Scientific Image*. Oxford: Clarendon Press.

Gardner, John. 2001. "Legal Positivism: 5½ Myths". *American Journal of Jurisprudence* 46 (1): 199–227.

Gaus, Gerald F. 2013. "Why the Conventionalist Needs the Social Contract". *Rationality, Markets, and Morals* 4: 71–87.

Gilbert, Margaret. 2006. *A Theory of Political Obligation: Membership, Commitment, and the Bonds of Society*. New York: Oxford University Press.

Gilbert, Margaret. 2018. *Rights and Demands: A Foundational Inquiry*. New York: Oxford University Press.

Green, Leslie. 2009. "Legal Positivism". In *The Stanford Encyclopedia of Philosophy*, edited by Edward N. Zalta. Metaphysics Research Lab, Stanford University. http://plato.stanford.edu/archives/fall2009/entries/legal-positivism/.

Green, Leslie. 2012. "Legal Obligation and Authority". In *The Stanford Encyclopedia of Philosophy*, edited by Edward N. Zalta. Metaphysics Research Lab, Stanford University. https://plato.stanford.edu/archives/win2012/entries/legal-obligation/.

Griffin, Christopher G. 2003. "Democracy as a Non–Instrumentally Just Procedure". *Journal of Political Philosophy* 11 (1): 111–21.

Grillo, Ralph, and Shah Prakash. 2012. "Reasons to Ban? The Anti-Burqa Movement in Western Europe". *MMG Working Papers* 12 (5): 1–44.

Guerrero, Alexander A. 2014. "Against Elections: The Lottocratic Alternative". *Philosophy & Public Affairs* 42 (2): 135–78.

Habib, Allen. 2022. "Promises". In *The Stanford Encyclopedia of Philosophy*, edited by Edward N. Zalta. Metaphysics Research Lab, Stanford University. https://plato.stanford.edu/archives/sum2022/entries/promises/.

Hart, H. L. A. 1955. "Are There Any Natural Rights?". *The Philosophical Review* 64 (2): 175–91.

Hart, H. L. A. 1961. *The Concept of Law*. Oxford: Clarendon Press.

Hart, H. L. A. 1963. *Law, Liberty, and Morality*. Stanford: Stanford University Press.

Hart, H. L. A. 1982. *Essays on Bentham: Studies in Jurisprudence and Political Theory*. Oxford: Clarendon Press.

Hayward, Tim. 2013. "On Prepositional Duties". *Ethics* 123 (2): 264–91.

Hershovitz, Scott. 2011. "The Role of Authority". *Philosophers' Imprint* 11 (7): 1–19.

Hershovitz, Scott. 2012. "The Authority of Law". In *The Routledge Companion to Philosophy of Law*, edited by Andrei Marmor, 65–75. New York: Routledge.

Heuer, Ulrike. 2012a. "Promising—Part 1". *Philosophy Compass* 7 (12): 832–41.

Heuer, Ulrike. 2012b. "Promising—Part 2". *Philosophy Compass* 7 (12): 842–51.

Hieronymi, Pamela. 2005. "The Wrong Kind of Reason". *The Journal of Philosophy* 102 (9): 437–57.

Hill, Thomas E. Jr. 2000. *Respect, Pluralism, and Justice. Kantian Perspectives*. New York: Oxford University Press.

Hohfeld, Wesley Newcomb. 1913. "Some Fundamental Legal Conceptions as Applied in Judicial Reasoning". *The Yale Law Journal* 23 (1): 16–59.

Horton, John. 2010. *Political Obligation*. 2nd ed. London: Palgrave Macmillan.

Hurd, Heidi M. 1996. "The Moral Magic of Consent". *Legal Theory* 2 (2): 121–46.

"IFES Election Guide". 2019. http://www.electionguide.org/countries/id/150/.

Interis, Matthew. 2011. "On Norms: A Typology with Discussion". *The American Journal of Economics and Sociology* 70 (2): 424–38.

Ismael, J. T. 2016. "Self-Constitution: The Making of the Self". In *How Physics Makes Us Free*, 193–215. New York: Oxford University Press.

Jaworska, Agnieszka, and Julie Tannenbaum. 2013. "The Grounds of Moral Status". In *The Stanford Encyclopedia of Philosophy*, edited by Edward N. Zalta. Metaphysics Research Lab, Stanford University. http://plato.stanford.edu/archives/sum2013/entries/grounds-moral-status/.

Kamm, Frances M. 2002. "Rights". In *The Oxford Handbook of Jurisprudence and Philosophy of Law*, edited by Jules L. Coleman, Kenneth E. Himma, and Scott J. Shapiro, 476–513. New York: Oxford University Press.

Kamm, Frances M. 2007. *Intricate Ethics: Rights, Responsibilities, and Permissible Harm*. New York: Oxford University Press.

Kant, Immanuel. 1999/1797. *Metaphysical Elements of Justice: Part I of The Metaphysics of Morals*. Translated by John Ladd. Indianapolis: Hackett Publishing.

Klosko, George. 1987. "Presumptive Benefit, Fairness, and Political Obligation". *Philosophy & Public Affairs* 16 (3): 241–59.

Klosko, George. 2007. "John Simmons on Political Obligation". *APA Newsletter on Philosophy and Law* 7 (1): 1–9.

Klosko, George. 2011. "Are Political Obligations Content Independent?". *Political Theory* 39 (4): 498–523.

Korsgaard, Christine M. 1986. "Skepticism about Practical Reason". *The Journal of Philosophy* 83 (1): 5–25.

Korsgaard, Christine M. 2009. *Self-Constitution: Agency, Identity, and Integrity*. New York: Oxford University Press.

Kramer, Matthew H. 2010. "Refining the Interest Theory of Rights". *American Journal of Jurisprudence* 55 (1): 31–9.

Kukla, Rebecca. 2014. "Performative Force, Convention, and Discursive Injustice". *Hypatia* 29 (2): 440–57.

Kymlicka, Will. 1995. *Multicultural Citizenship: A Liberal Theory of Minority Rights*. New York: Oxford University Press.

Laborde, Cécile. 2006. "Female Autonomy, Education and the Hijab". *Critical Review of International Social and Political Philosophy* 9 (3): 351–77.

Laborde, Cécile. 2015. "Religion in the Law: The Disaggregation Approach". *Law and Philosophy* 34 (6): 581–600.

224 REFERENCES

Langton, Rae. 1993. "Speech Acts and Unspeakable Acts". *Philosophy & Public Affairs* 22 (4): 293–330.

Lefkowitz, David. 2006. "The Duty to Obey the Law". *Philosophy Compass* 1 (6): 571–98.

Lefkowitz, David. 2007. "On a Moral Right to Civil Disobedience". *Ethics* 117 (2): 202–33.

Lewis, David. 2002/1969. *Convention: A Philosophical Study*. Oxford: John Wiley & Sons.

List, Christian. 2014. "Three Kinds of Collective Attitudes". *Erkenntnis* 79 (9): 1601–22.

List, Christian. 2018. "What Is It Like to Be a Group Agent?". *Noûs* 52 (2): 295–319.

List, Christian, and Philip Pettit. 2011. *Group Agency: The Possibility, Design, and Status of Corporate Agents*. Oxford: Oxford University Press.

List, Christian, and Laura Valentini. 2016. "The Methodology of Political Theory". In *Oxford Handbook of Philosophical Methodology*, edited by Herman Cappelen, Tamar Gendler, and John Hawthorne, 525–53. Oxford: Oxford University Press.

Lyons, David. 1998. "Moral Judgment, Historical Reality, and Civil Disobedience". *Philosophy & Public Affairs* 27 (1): 31–49.

Maher, Chauncey. 2007. "Review of Cristina Bicchieri, The Grammar of Society: The Nature and Dynamics of Social Norms". *Ethics* 118 (1): 140–3.

Marmor, Andrei. 2009. *Social Conventions: From Language to Law*. Princeton, NJ: Princeton University Press.

Marmor, Andrei. 2019. "What's Left of General Jurisprudence? On Law's Ontology and Content". *Jurisprudence* 10 (2): 151–70.

Marmor, Andrei, and Alexander Sarch. 2019. "The Nature of Law". In *The Stanford Encyclopedia of Philosophy*, edited by Edward N. Zalta. Metaphysics Research Lab, Stanford University. https://plato.stanford.edu/archives/fall2019/entries/lawphil-nature/.

Meyer, Lukas H., Thomas Pölzer, and Pranay Sanklecha. 2017. "Introduction to the Special Issue on Legitimate Expectations". *Moral Philosophy and Politics* 4 (2): 173–5.

Miller, David. 1995. *On Nationality*. Oxford: Oxford University Press.

Miller, David. 2016. "Neo-Kantian Theories of Self-Determination: A Critique". *Review of International Studies* 42 (5): 858–75.

Moore, Margaret. 2015. *A Political Theory of Territory*. New York: Oxford University Press.

Munger, Kristen, and Shelby J. Harris. 1989. "Effects of an Observer on Handwashing in a Public Restroom". *Perceptual and Motor Skills* 69 (3): 733–4.

Nagel, Thomas. 1979. "Moral Luck". In *Mortal Questions*, 24–38. Cambridge: Cambridge University Press.

Nagel, Thomas. 1984. "What Is It Like to Be a Bat?". *Philosophical Review* 83 (4): 435–50.

Nagel, Thomas. 1995. "Personal Rights and Public Space". *Philosophy & Public Affairs* 24 (2): 83–107.

Nieswandt, Katharina. 2016. "Do Rights Exist by Convention or by Nature?". *Topoi* 35 (1): 313–25.

Nieswandt, Katharina. 2017. "Anscombe on the Sources of Normativity". *Journal of Value Inquiry* 51 (1): 141–63.

Nieswandt, Katharina. 2018. "What Is Conventionalism about Moral Rights and Duties?". *Australasian Journal of Philosophy* 97 (1): 15–28.

Noggle, Robert. 1999. "Kantian Respect and Particular Persons". *Canadian Journal of Philosophy* 29 (3): 449–77.

Nozick, Robert. 1974. *Anarchy, State, and Utopia*. New York: Basic Books.

O'Brien, Lucy, and Matthew Soteriou. 2009. *Mental Actions*. New York: Oxford University Press.

O'Neill, Elizabeth. 2017. "Kinds of Norms". *Philosophy Compass* 12 (5): 1–15.

Owens, David. 2006. "A Simple Theory of Promising". *The Philosophical Review* 115 (1): 51–77.

Owens, David. 2012. *Shaping the Normative Landscape*. Oxford: Oxford University Press.

Owens, David. 2017. "Wrong by Convention". *Ethics* 127 (3): 553–75.

Owens, David. 2020. "The Roles of Rights". In *Civil Wrongs and Justice in Private Law*, edited by Paul B. Miller and John Oberdiek, 3–18. Oxford: Oxford University Press.

Owens, David. 2022. *Bound by Convention: Obligation and Social Rules*. Oxford, New York: Oxford University Press.

Pattison, James. 2010. *Humanitarian Intervention and the Responsibility to Protect: Who Should Intervene?* Oxford: Oxford University Press.

Perry, Stephen. 2006. "Hart on Social Rules and the Foundations of Law: Liberating the Internal Point of View". *Fordham Law Review* 75 (January): 1171–209.

Perry, Stephen. 2013. "Political Authority and Political Obligation". In *Oxford Studies in Philosophy of Law 2*, edited by Leslie Green and Brian Leiter, 1–74. New York: Oxford University Press.

Philpott, Daniel. 1995. "In Defense of Self-Determination". *Ethics* 105 (2): 352–85.

Philpott, Daniel. 2020. "Sovereignty". In *The Stanford Encyclopedia of Philosophy*, edited by Edward N. Zalta. Metaphysics Research Lab, Stanford University. https://plato.stanford.edu/archives/fall2020/entries/sovereignty/.

Pogge, Thomas. 1992. "Cosmopolitanism and Sovereignty". *Ethics* 103 (1): 48–75.

Prentice, Deborah A., and Dale T. Miller. 1993. "Pluralistic Ignorance and Alcohol Use on Campus: Some Consequences of Misperceiving the Social Norm". *Journal of Personality and Social Psychology* 64 (2): 243–56.

Quinn, Warren S. 1989. "Actions, Intentions, and Consequences: The Doctrine of Doing and Allowing". *The Philosophical Review* 98 (3): 287–312.

Rao, Anand S., and Michael P. Georgeff. 1995. "BDI Agents: From Theory to Practice". In *Proceedings of the First International Conference on Multi-Agent Systems (Icmas-95)*, edited by Victor R. Lesser and Les Gasser, 312–19. Cambridge, MA: MIT Press.

Rawls, John. 1996. *Political Liberalism*. New York: Columbia University Press.

Rawls, John. 1999a. *A Theory of Justice*. Oxford: Oxford University Press.

Rawls, John. 1999b. *The Law of Peoples: With 'The Idea of Public Reason Revisited'*. Cambridge, MA: Harvard University Press.

Raz, Joseph. 1972. "Voluntary Obligations and Normative Powers". *Proceedings of the Aristotelian Society, Supplementary Volumes* 46: 59–102.

Raz, Joseph. 1975. *Practical Reason and Norms*. New York: Oxford University Press.

Raz, Joseph. 1979. "Legitimate Authority". In *The Authority of Law*, 3–27. Oxford: Clarendon Press.

Raz, Joseph. 1985a. "Authority and Justification". *Philosophy & Public Affairs* 14 (1): 3–29.

Raz, Joseph. 1985b. "The Obligation to Obey: Revision and Tradition". *Notre Dame Journal of Law, Ethics & Public Policy* 1 (1): 139–55.

Raz, Joseph. 1986. *The Morality of Freedom*. Oxford: Clarendon Press.

Raz, Joseph. 2006. "The Problem of Authority: Revisiting the Service Conception". *Minnesota Law Review* 90: 1003–44.

Raz, Joseph. 2010. "Human Rights without Foundations". In *The Philosophy of International Law*, edited by Samantha Besson and John Tasioulas, 321–38. Oxford: Oxford University Press.

Renzo, Massimo. 2011. "State Legitimacy and Self-Defence". *Law and Philosophy* 30 (5): 575–601.

Renzo, Massimo. 2012. "Associative Responsibilities and Political Obligation". *The Philosophical Quarterly* 62 (246): 106–27.

Renzo, Massimo. 2019. "Why Colonialism Is Wrong". *Current Legal Problems* 72 (1): 347–73.

Renzo, Massimo. 2022. "Defective Normative Powers: The Case of Consent". *Journal of Practical Ethics* 10 (1): 49–77.

Ripstein, Arthur. 2006. "Beyond the Harm Principle". *Philosophy & Public Affairs* 34 (3): 215–45.

Ripstein, Arthur. 2009. *Force and Freedom*. Cambridge, MA: Harvard University Press.

Risen, James, and Eric Lichtblau. 2005. "Bush Lets U.S. Spy on Callers Without Courts". *The New York Times*, December 16, 2005. https://www.nytimes.com/2005/12/16/politics/bush-lets-us-spy-on-callers-without-courts.html.

Ronzoni, Miriam. 2009. "The Global Order: A Case of Background Injustice? A Practice-Dependent Account". *Philosophy & Public Affairs* 37 (3): 229–56.

Ronzoni, Miriam, and Laura Valentini. 2008. "On the Meta-Ethical Status of Constructivism: Reflections on G. A. Cohen's 'Facts and Principles'". *Politics, Philosophy & Economics* 7 (4): 403–22.

Rosati, Connie S. 2016. "Moral Motivation". In *The Stanford Encyclopedia of Philosophy*, edited by Edward N. Zalta. Metaphysics Research Lab, Stanford University. https://plato.stanford.edu/archives/win2016/entries/moral-motivation/.

Rosen, Gideon. 2010. "Metaphysical Dependence: Grounding and Reduction". In *Modality: Metaphysics, Logic, and Epistemology*, edited by Bob Hale and Aviv Hoffmann, 109–36. New York: Oxford University Press.

Sandel, M. J. 1984. "The Procedural Republic and the Unencumbered Self". *Political Theory* 12 (1): 81–96.

Sangiovanni, Andrea. 2008. "Justice and the Priority of Politics to Morality". *Journal of Political Philosophy* 16 (2): 137–64.

Sangiovanni, Andrea. 2016. "How Practices Matter". *Journal of Political Philosophy* 24 (1): 3–23.

Saunders, Ben. 2010. "Democracy, Political Equality, and Majority Rule". *Ethics* 121 (1): 148–77.

Sayre-McCord, Geoff. 2014. "Metaethics". In *The Stanford Encyclopedia of Philosophy*, edited by Edward N. Zalta. Metaphysics Research Lab, Stanford University. http://plato.stanford.edu/archives/sum2014/entries/metaethics/.

Scanlon, Thomas M. 1990. "Promises and Practices". *Philosophy & Public Affairs* 19 (3): 199–226.

Scanlon, Thomas M. 1998. *What We Owe to Each Other*. Cambridge, MA: Belknap Press of Harvard University Press.

Scanlon, Thomas M. 2013. "Reply to Leif Wenar". *Journal of Moral Philosophy* 10 (4): 400–5.

Schaffer, Jonathan. 2009. "On What Grounds What". In *Metaphysics: New Essays on the Foundations of Ontology*, edited by David Manley, David J. Chalmers, and Ryan Wasserman, 347–83. New York: Oxford University Press.

Schapiro, Tamar. 2012. "On the Relation Between Wanting and Willing". *Philosophical Issues* 22 (1): 334–50.

Scheffler, Samuel. 2011. "Valuing". In *Reasons and Recognition: Essays on the Philosophy of T. M. Scanlon*, edited by R. Jay Wallace, Rahul Kumar, and Samuel Freeman, 23–42. New York: Oxford University Press.

Schelling, Thomas C. 1960. *The Strategy of Conflict*. Cambridge, MA: Harvard University Press.

Schmitt, Bernd H., Laurette Dubé, and France Leclerc. 1992. "Intrusions into Waiting Lines: Does the Queue Constitute a Social System?". *Journal of Personality and Social Psychology* 63 (5): 806–15.

Schroeder, Tim. 2020. "Desire". In *The Stanford Encyclopedia of Philosophy*, edited by Edward N. Zalta. Metaphysics Research Lab, Stanford University. https://plato.stanford.edu/archives/sum2020/entries/desire/.

Schupbach, Jonah N., and Jan Sprenger. 2011. "The Logic of Explanatory Power". *Philosophy of Science* 78 (1): 105–27.

Schwitzgebel, Eric. 2015. "If Materialism Is True, the United States Is Probably Conscious". *Philosophical Studies* 172 (7): 1697–721.

Searle, John R. 1964. "How to Derive 'Ought' From 'Is' ". *Philosophical Review* 73 (1): 43–58.

Searle, John R. 1969. *Speech Acts: An Essay in the Philosophy of Language*. Cambridge: Cambridge University Press.

Searle, John R. 2006. "Social Ontology: Some Basic Principles". *Anthropological Theory* 6 (1): 12–29.

Setiya, Kieran. 2015. "Intention". In *The Stanford Encyclopedia of Philosophy*, edited by Edward N. Zalta. Metaphysics Research Lab, Stanford University. https://plato.stanford.edu/archives/sum2015/entries/intention/.

Shiffrin, Seana Valentine. 2008. "Promising, Intimate Relationships, and Conventionalism". *The Philosophical Review* 117 (4): 481–524.

Shoemaker, David. 2013. "Qualities of Will". *Social Philosophy and Policy* 30 (1–2): 95–120.

Simmons, A. John. 1976. "Tacit Consent and Political Obligation". *Philosophy & Public Affairs* 5 (3): 274–91.

Simmons, A. John. 1979. *Moral Principles and Political Obligations*. Princeton, NJ: Princeton University Press.

Simmons, A. John. 2009. "Philosophical Anarchism". SSRN Scholarly Paper ID 1344425. Rochester, NY: Social Science Research Network. https://papers.ssrn.com/abstract=1344425.

Simmons, A. John. 2013. "Democratic Authority and the Boundary Problem". *Ratio Juris* 26 (3): 326–57.

Skorupski, John. 2010. *The Domain of Reasons*. Oxford: Oxford University Press.

Skyrms, Brian. 1996. *Evolution of the Social Contract*. New York: Cambridge University Press.

Smith, M. B. E. 1973. "Is There a Prima Facie Obligation to Obey the Law?". *The Yale Law Journal* 82 (5): 950–76.

Smith, Michael. 1987. "The Humean Theory of Motivation". *Mind* 96 (381): 36–61.

Soper, Philip. 1989. "Legal Theory and the Claim of Authority". *Philosophy & Public Affairs* 18 (3): 209–37.

Sorensen, Roy. 2018. "Vagueness". In *The Stanford Encyclopedia of Philosophy*, edited by Edward N. Zalta. Metaphysics Research Lab, Stanford University. https://plato.stanford.edu/archives/sum2018/entries/vagueness/.

Southwood, Nicholas. 2011. "The Moral/Conventional Distinction". *Mind* 120 (479): 761–802.

Southwood, Nicholas, and Lina Eriksson. 2011. "Norms and Conventions". *Philosophical Explorations* 14 (2): 195–217.

Southwood, Nicholas, and Daniel Friedrich. 2009. "Promises beyond Assurance". *Philosophical Studies* 144 (2): 261–80.

Sreenivasan, Gopal. 2005. "A Hybrid Theory of Claim-Rights". *Oxford Journal of Legal Studies* 25 (2): 257–74.

REFERENCES

Steiner, Hillel. 2013. "Directed Duties and Inalienable Rights". *Ethics* 123 (2): 230–44.

Stilz, Anna. 2009. *Liberal Loyalty: Freedom, Obligation, and the State*. Princeton, NJ: Princeton University Press.

Stilz, Anna. 2011. "Nations, States, and Territory". *Ethics* 121 (3): 572–601.

Stilz, Anna. 2016. "The Value of Self-Determination". In *Oxford Studies in Political Philosophy, Vol. 2*, edited by David Sobel, Peter Vallentyne, and Steven Wall, 98–127. New York: Oxford University Press.

Stilz, Anna. 2019. *Territorial Sovereignty: A Philosophical Exploration*. New York: Oxford University Press.

Stoljar, Natalie. 2014. "Autonomy and Adaptive Preference Formation". In *Autonomy, Oppression, and Gender*, edited by Andrea Veltman and Mark Piper, 227–52. New York: Oxford University Press.

Strawson, Peter F. 1962. "Freedom and Resentment". *Proceedings of the British Academy* 48: 1–25.

Sugden, Robert. 2004. *The Economics of Rights, Co-operation, and Welfare*. 2nd ed. Basingstoke: Palgrave Macmillan.

Sumner, L. W. 1987. *The Moral Foundation of Rights*. Oxford: Clarendon Press.

Sunstein, Cass R. 1996. "Social Norms and Social Roles". *Columbia Law Review* 96 (4): 903–68.

Taylor, Charles. 1985. "What's Wrong with Negative Liberty". In *Philosophy and the Human Sciences, Vol. 2*, 211–29. Cambridge: Cambridge University Press.

Thompson, Michael. 2004. "What Is It to Wrong Someone? A Puzzle About Justice". In *Reason and Value: Themes from the Moral Philosophy of Joseph Raz*, edited by R. Jay Wallace, P. Pettit, S. Scheffler, and M. Smith, 333–84. New York: Clarendon Press.

Tuck, Richard. 1979. *Natural Rights Theories*. Cambridge: Cambridge University Press.

Turnbull, Colin. 1972. *Mountain People*. New York: Simon and Schuster.

Ulaş, Luke. 2014. *Realising Cosmopolitanism: The Role of a World State*. Doctoral Dissertation. London: LSE.

Ullmann-Margalit, Edna. 1977. *The Emergence of Norms*. Oxford: Clarendon Press.

Valentini, Laura. 2011. *Justice in a Globalized World: A Normative Framework*. Oxford: Oxford University Press.

Valentini, Laura. 2013. "Justice, Disagreement and Democracy". *British Journal of Political Science* 43 (01): 177–99.

Valentini, Laura. 2015. "On the Distinctive Procedural Wrong of Colonialism". *Philosophy & Public Affairs* 43 (4): 312–31.

Valentini, Laura. 2018. "The Content Independence of Political Obligation: What It Is and How to Test It". *Legal Theory* 24 (2): 135–57.

Valentini, Laura. 2021. "Respect for Persons and the Moral Force of Socially Constructed Norms". *Noûs* 55 (2): 385–408.

Van Duffel, Siegfried. 2012. "The Nature of Rights Debate Rests on a Mistake". *Pacific Philosophical Quarterly* 93 (1): 104–23.

Velleman, J. David. 1989. *Practical Reflection*. Princeton, NJ: Princeton University Press.

Velleman, J. David. 1997. "How to Share an Intention". *Philosophy and Phenomenological Research* 57 (1): 29–50.

Volmert, Andrew. 2010. "Indigenous Self-Determination and Freedom from Rule". *The Good Society* 19 (2): 53–9.

Vossen, Bas van der. 2011. "Associative Political Obligations". *Philosophy Compass* 6 (7): 477–87.

REFERENCES   229

Vyver, Johan van der. 2013. "Sovereignty". In *Oxford Handbook of International Human Rights Law*, edited by Dinah Shelton, 379–400. New York: Oxford University Press.

Waldron, Jeremy. 1981. "A Right to Do Wrong". *Ethics* 92 (1): 21–39.

Waldron, Jeremy. 1987. "Theoretical Foundations of Liberalism". *The Philosophical Quarterly* 37 (147): 127–50.

Waldron, Jeremy. 1993. "Special Ties and Natural Duties". *Philosophy & Public Affairs* 22 (1): 3–30.

Waldron, Jeremy. 1999. *Law and Disagreement*. Oxford: Clarendon Press.

Waldron, Jeremy. 2020. "The Rule of Law". In *The Stanford Encyclopedia of Philosophy*, edited by Edward N. Zalta. Metaphysics Research Lab, Stanford University. https://plato.stanford.edu/archives/sum2020/entries/rule-of-law/.

Walzer, Michael. 1987. *Interpretation and Social Criticism*. Cambridge, MA: Harvard University Press.

Watson, Gary. 2009. "Promises, Reasons, and Normative Powers". In *Reasons for Action*, edited by David Sobel and Steven Wall. New York: Cambridge University Press.

Wellman, Christopher Heath. 2001. "Toward a Liberal Theory of Political Obligation". *Ethics* 111 (4): 735–59.

Wenar, Leif. 2013. "The Nature of Claim-Rights". *Ethics* 123 (2): 202–29.

Williams, Bernard. 2002. *Truth and Truthfulness: An Essay in Genealogy*. Princeton, NJ: Princeton University Press.

Williams, Bernard. 2005. *In the Beginning Was the Deed: Realism and Moralism in Political Argument*. Princeton, NJ: Princeton University Press.

Wolff, Robert Paul. 1970. *In Defense of Anarchism*. London: Harper.

Young, H. Peyton. 2015. "The Evolution of Social Norms". *Annual Review of Economics* 7 (1): 359–87.

Ypi, Lea. 2013. "What's Wrong with Colonialism". *Philosophy & Public Affairs* 41 (2): 158–91.

Index

Note: Figures are indicated by an italic "*f*", and notes are indicated by "n." following the page number.

Because the index has been created to work across multiple formats, indexed terms for which a page range is given (e.g., 52–53, 66–70, etc.) may occasionally appear only on some, but not all, of the pages within the range.

acceptance 22–3, 28–30, 51, 63, 73–4, 213 n.3
  of norms 9, 43, 109–10, 213–14
  of requirements 9, 23–5, 37, 94
  of rights and obligations 131 n.17
  of rules 23, 26–9, 36–7, 44–5
accountability 17–18, 20–1, 29–30, 32–3, 87, 126–8, 135–6, 137 n.23, 139
action-guiding attitudes 23–5, 27, 30, 30*f*, 34–6, 38–40, 74
aesthetic norms 48–50
agency burdens 99–100, 114–16, 174
agency respect 11, 14–15, 88–95, 96 n.15, 97–9, 101–4, 113–14, 116–17, 119–20, 122–3, 132, 144–5, 147–9, 167–8, 171–2, 198, 201, 203, 210–11, 214
  principle 9–11, 88–95, 101–2, 105–10, 167, 169, 173–4, 199, 208–11, 214–15
  view 9–10, 14–15, 81–118, 100 n.18, 150–2, 166–81, 198–207, 210, 215–17
agential-investment account 9, 18–19, 22–39, 30*f*, 51
Alternative Voting (AV) 154, 165–6, 170–1
Altman, Andrew 14–15, 179, 186, 190–3
ambitions 15, 26, 191 n.10
anarchism 150 n.3, 176–7
anarchists 5, 13–14, 150–1, 154, 156, 171–3, 175, 178
annexation 14–15, 45, 179, 185–7, 189–94, 196–7, 199, 202–3
associative
  contexts 187
  intentions 202–3
  interests 195–6
  obligations 14, 111
  political projects 203
  preferences 186–7, 192
  profile 195
  views 151, 157, 162–3, 169–70
attitudes 21, 23–5, 29, 32, 35–8, 43, 44 n.27, 45, 74, 76–8, 87, 95, 96 n.15, 169, 175, 191, *see also* moral reactive attitudes, normative attitudes, propositional attitudes, reactive attitudes

authority 3–4, 13–14, 71, 126, 133–4, 138, 140, 142–3, 146–9, 152, 154–5, 157–8, 158 n.10, 163–4, 166–7, 170, 183, 192–3, 199
  de facto 138
  interests 70, 72 n.25
  legitimate 146–7, 152–3, 158 n.11
  of law 3–4, 150, 152, 154–7, 175, 177
autonomous
  agency 200
  agents 118, 141, 143, 144 n.27, 183–4
  end-setters 89, 99
  persons 199
autonomy 10, 14–15, 89–91, 95, 106, 135–6, 138–9, 175, 180, 193–5, 204
autonomy view 190, 192–9, 202–4, 207

Barbeque 46–7, 58 n.9, 58, 64–5, 72, 85–6, 103–5, 144–5, 155, 185, 200
Belief–Desire–Intention (BDI) 35
Bicchieri, Cristina 1 n.1, 17, 19, 23, 27, 32, 35 n.21, 36–7
bindingness 63, 68, 76, 150–1, 154–5, 164, 210–11, *see also* moral bindingness
blame 1, 18, 30, 44–5, 47–8, 52–3, 74–5, 86, 126–8, 137, 155–6
Bratman, Michael 25, 35, 40 n.25, 40–2, 77–8
Brennan, Geoffrey 17, 19–21, 27–30, 32, 35–8, 43–4, 46
burdens 10, 91–2, 97, 99–101, 107, 109 n.27, 114–16, 118, 162, 169, 173–4, 180, 204–5, 210–11, 217

Calhoun, Cheshire 25–6, 89–90
Canada 156, 186–7, 190–2, 202
Chang, Ruth 22 n.9, 25 n.14, 26, 89–90, 112, 152 n.5
Christman, John 95, 212–14
civil disobedience 151–3, 172–5, 178
coercion 10, 45, 48, 90–1, 94–5, 169, 211–14, 213 n.3
cognitive dissonance 32–3
cognitive states 23, 37, 189 n.6
cognitivism 33–4

232 INDEX

collective
  achievement 191
  agency 180–1, 189
  agents 199–200
  analogue 181
  binding will 14–15, 200
  decision-making 105, 192–3, 199–200,
    202–3, 207
  decisions 164, 175, 193, 194 n.11
  level 185
  self-determination 162, 181, 191–4
  violations 187, 191, 198
  see also sovereignty
collectives 176–7, 179–80, 183–5, 188–9, 191–2,
  200, 203–4, 206
colonialism 12–14, 45–6, 121–4, 147, 150,
  152–4, 161, 163, 172–3, 179, 185, 192
commitments
  and intentions 25 n.14
  authentic 10, 90–1, 94–5, 97–8, 101, 148, 199,
    204–6, 211, 213–14
  impermissible 91–2, 98–9, 100 n.18
  joint 52–3, 75–80, 82 n.4, 84, 101–2
  permissible 9–11, 14–15, 92–3, 104, 118, 168,
    172, 178, 198, 201–2, 207
communitarians 5, 208, 216
conformism 23, 32–3, 95, 209
conformity 99–100, 150 n.3, 158 n.11, 208
  with norms 45, 73–4, 114–15, 208–9
  with rules 35 n.21, 75–6
  with the law 13–14, 150–1, 153–4, 157, 161,
    169–70, 178
consent 12–14, 47, 58, 59 n.10, 70–4, 122–6,
  127 n.11, 128–31, 128 n.13, 134–44,
  137 nn.22, 23, 139 n.24, 143 n.26,
  159 n.13, 162–3, 166 n.24, 180, 185, 191,
  197, 199, 205
content-independence 54, 152–4, 163–4, 177
  obligations 54–5, 154, 157–9, 159 n.14, 164,
    169, 176–8, 194
control 12, 26, 40, 48, 70, 89, 100, 121–2, 125–6,
  129, 144, 146, 148, 192–3, 215, *see also*
  rights as control
conventionalism 21, 43–4, 52–3, 65–9, 79,
  84, 119
conventionalist 68–9
  grounding sequence 67
  principle 66–7, 84
  view 65–9, 79–80
coordination 57 n.7, 114, 146, 154, 158–60
  practices 63
  problems 17, 20–1, 41
Coronavirus/Covid-19 93, 208–9, 211, 216–17
critical theory principle 213 n.3

Darwall, Stephen 30, 89, 93, 127, 135
decision-making 3, 112, 165–7, 169–72, 181–4,
  193, 199–203, *see also* collective
  decision-making
decisions 26, 75, 89–90, 93, 95–6, 105, 107,
  163–4, 169–70, 193–4, *see also* binding
  decisions, collective decisions
deflationary grounding sequence 61–2, 156
deflationary view 52–62, 64–5, 69, 71, 79–80,
  85–6, 97, 113, 150, 156, 158, 178, 208–9
demanding 12, 36–7, 42, 72, 82, 105–10, 124–6,
  128, 133, 136–8, 168
democracies 163–5, 183
democracy 163 n.19, 163–5, 170, 190 n.8
democratic
  approaches 151
  decisions 163–4, 169–70, 193
  laws 13–14, 158 n.11, 163–4, 173
  majoritarianism 165
  procedures 165–6, 170–1, 196
  regulative ideal 175
  societies 105, 110, 182
  theory 163–7, 169–72
Denmark/Danes 186–7, 194–6, 202–3
deontic/deontological
  attributes 147–8
  interests 70, 72
  operators 20, 35 n.21, 131, 131 n.17
  orientation 12–13
  powers 131 n.17
  rules 20 n.4
  value 70
desiderata 1–2, 7–10, 18–19, 55 n.3, 83–6, 101,
  103, 105, 112, 121
desires 24–6, 31, 34–7, 35 n.21, 37 n.22, 38 n.23,
  39–40, 67–8, 133–4, 203, 212
directive norms 18–19, 43–4, 46–8, 51, 131–2
directives 157–8
dispositions 1 n.1, 9, 21 n.6, 26–7, 34 n.20,
  35 n.21, 37, 81
duty/duties 12, 43, 46 n.30, 49, 52, 58–9, 66,
  68–9, 73–4, 82 n.5, 82, 91–5, 97–8, 101–5,
  111–12, 120 n.1, 121–7, 131 n.17, 132, 134,
  138, 141–2, 144–7, 146 n.29, 149, 161, 215
  moral 48–9, 53, 60–1, 72
  natural 142, 146, 151
  natural-duty view 157, 161–2, 164, 169, 177
  natural-duty-of-justice view 161–2, 161 n.16,
    169–70
  of care 71–2
  of justice 13–14, 192
  of non-interference 126, 185
  parental 71–2
  practice-internal 65–9

INDEX 233

Election Official 166, 170–1, 177
elections/electoral systems 46–7, 165–6,
 183–4, 197
emotions 1, 3, 48, 74, 188
established practices 52–3, 62–5, 72 n.24,
 79–80
ethical
 commitments 106
 convictions 169
 domain 60
 perspectives 110
 principle 101
 questions 208
ethics 101, 189
 of belief 48 n.31
 of promising 7 n.8
 of secession 179
European Union (EU) 183–4, 186–7, 190, 194,
 196–7, 198 n.15
evidence 7–8, 16, 27–8, 31, 48, 57, 82, 85,
 103–5, 103 n.20, 136, 140–1, 206
expectations 35 n.21, 37, 58, 78, 120 n.1, *see also*
 legitimate expectations
explanatory
 adequacy 75
 gap 74, 79–80, 84–5
 power 7–8, 10–11, 55, 82–5, 101–3, 105, 151,
 156, 181

Feinberg, Joel 12–13, 120 n.1, 124 n.5, 142,
 181, 183–4
fit 7–9, 11, 16, 24, 32, 34, 38, 55–7, 75, 81–3,
 85–6, 101, 103, 105, 144 n.27
formal
 laws 130
 legal norms 1 n.1, 14, 114–15, 130–1, 150–1
 norms 1–4, 18–19, 43–6, 44 n.27, 48, 51,
 111–12, 167
 regulation 111
 sanctions 36, 39, 95

Gilbert, Margaret 75–9, 82 n.4, 84, 120 n.1,
 124 nn.5–7, 133 n.19
grounding relations 60–1
grounding sequence 61–7, 72–3, 76, 88, 104–5,
 156, 168, 198
groups 17, 21, 29, 37–8, 40, 44–5, 77–8, 115,
 132, 148, 165, 171–3, 189–91, 194–5,
 197–8, 204–5
 agency/agents 29, 180–1, 183, 189, 200
 sovereignty 181, 193
guilt 1–4, 17, 27–8, 31–3, 39, 42, 48–50,
 52–3, 66, 74–5, 124, 126–7, 130, 136,
 146–7, 166

Hart, H. L. A. 1 n.1, 12–13, 17, 19, 21 n.7, 21,
 26–8, 37–9, 41, 43, 45–6, 54, 81 n.2, 95,
 120 n.1, 124 n.5, 126, 131–2, 143, 153–4,
 159, 167–8, 182
human rights 12–13, 91, 119, 186–7, 190–1,
 202, 204
Humean
 account of motivation 25, 34
 belief–desire model 24 n.11, 35
Hume, David 65 n.18, 119

identity 89 n.11, 89–90, 92–3, 97–8, 111, 173–4,
 190, 214
informal
 norms 1, 7, 14, 18–19, 35–6, 43–6, 48, 51,
 111–12, 114–15, 117–18, 130–1, 150–1,
 216–17
 regulation 111
 sanctions 39, 95
injustice 1, 11, 109–10, 172
instrumentalism 158, 162 n.18, 163–4
instrumentalist
 accounts 163–4, 190 n.8
 approach 177
 views 151, 157–9, 158 n.11, 169, 190
integrity 42, 92–3, 105–6, 115, 121–2,
 169, 173–4
intentions 22, 24–5, 27, 35, 39–41, 74, 77–9, 121,
 123 n.3, 127–8, 133–8, 139 n.24, 170–1,
 195, 197, 202–3, *see also* robust intentions
international
 communications 58–9, 85 n.8, 155 n.6
 community 201–2, 207
 justice 184
 law 183, 200–2
 legal norms 202–3
 norms 199–200
 obligations 184
 sovereignty norms 14–15, 201–3, 205–7
 system 200–1
inviolability 146, 216, *see also* rights as inviolability

Japanese Tourist 113–14
joint commitments 52–3, 75–80, 82 n.4,
 84, 101–2
 grounding sequence 76
 obligation-generating 76–9
judgements 3, 8–9, 32, 37–9, 55–7, 85, 101, 103,
 105, 109 n.27, 110, 122–3, 148, 155–6,
 158 n.11, 158, 176–7, 182 n.3, 192, 199, 206,
 213, *see also* moral judgements
justice 13–14, 18, 52, 91, 109 n.27, 112, 153–4,
 161–2, 164, 169–70, 175–7, 184, 189–90,
 192, 204–6

234 INDEX

Kantian 101
  injunction 10
  particularism 89 n.11
Kant, Immanuel 89 n.11, 141–2
Klosko, George 13–14, 53–4, 151–2, 159,
    161, 177

Lefkowitz, David 13–14, 52, 150 n.1,
    161–2, 175
legal
  disobedience 104 n.21, 153, 168, 173–4,
    199–200
  mandates 153–4, 157–8, 162, 168, 176–7
  normativism/normativists 150–1, 154, 156,
    175–7, 179
  norms 1 n.1, 4, 8–9, 28–9, 35 n.21, 44 n.27,
    45–8, 59, 65 n.17, 104 n.21, 111–12,
    114–15, 130–1, 150–1, 154–6, 158, 167–71,
    176–7, 200, 202–6, 210–11
  obedience 160–1, 168
  obligations 52, 163, 173
  positivism/positivists 4 n.5, 45, 167–8
  see also obligation to obey the law
liberal
  conception 142
  democracies 183
  democratic country 196
  democratic societies 110, 181–2
  deontological dispositions 110
  ethics 9–10, 101
  framework 216 n.4
  pedigree 216–17
  perspective 184
  tenet 11
  theorists 106
  universalists 208, 216
liberals 5, 182
linguistic
  competence 49
  conventions 128–34
  norms 48–9
  power 134
List, Christian 16, 18 n.3, 25 n.12, 29, 32, 42 n.26,
    129 n.14, 147 n.31, 180–1, 189
local norms 2–3, 5–7, 55–7, 97, 102–3, 113–15,
    128 n.13, 144–5

membership 111–12, 162–3, 181, 193, 197,
    204, 217
membership view 190, 192, 207
membership-based
  obligations 111
  responsibilities 111
  views 180

moral
  binding/bindingness 5, 8, 18, 52, 55, 67–9,
    72–4, 81, 84, 111, 155–6, 169–70,
    173, 211
  force 2–5, 8, 11, 52–80, 101–2, 147–8,
    169, 214–15
  judgements 8, 11, 15–16, 55, 85
  normativity 1–13, 15, 18–19, 23, 29–30, 32–4,
    38–9, 45–6, 49–55, 57, 59 n.10, 60–3,
    65 nn.17, 18, 66–72, 75–86, 88, 97–8,
    101–4, 106, 108–13, 116–18, 141–2, 144–5,
    149, 156, 169, 176–8, 185, 201, 206,
    208–11, 214–15
  norms 19–22, 22 n.8, 45, 138, see also valid
    moral norms
  obligations 1, 3–5, 9–10, 13–14, 52, 55, 60–1,
    67 n.21, 74–7, 84, 106–7, 112, 117, 139 n.24,
    147–8, 152, 154, 168–9, 206
  permissibility 91, 108–10, 114, 169,
    199–200, 210–11
  powers 70, 74, 119–20, 126, 137–45, 148,
    150 n.2, 152
  reactive attitudes 35 n.21, 46, 48–52,
    68, 135–6
  rights 1–2, 12–13, 15, 52, 66, 119–49, 191
  status 5, 54–5, 65, 85, 91–3, 97–8, 120 n.1,
    122, 146, 155–6, 188–9

Nieswandt, Katharina 13, 65–9, 79, 84, 119
Noggle, Robert 82, 89, 89 n.11, 92–3
Non-proceduralist President 58–60, 64–5, 76–7,
    85–6, 103, 105, 155, 200
normative
  attitudes 17, 31, 37–9, 38 n.23, 50–1
  individualism 187–9, 191
  interests 52–3, 69–75, 79–80, 84–5, 101
  interests grounding sequence 72–3
  powers 12–13, 25 n.14, 70–1, 78 n.30, 119–21,
    123–42, 144 n.28, 144, 182, 200, 215
  premise 9
  worlds 86–9, 102, 148, 204, 215–16
normativity 20–1, 35 n.21, 73, 76, 129, 147, 150,
    168–9, see also moral normativity
norms
  evidence of 27–8, 48, 82
  existence of 1 n.1, 6–7, 9–10, 12–13, 18–23,
    20 n.5, 26–34, 35 n.21, 36–8, 41, 44–5,
    47–8, 51, 53–5, 59, 64–5, 71–4, 76, 81–2,
    94–8, 111, 113–17, 119–20, 122, 128–9,
    132–4, 136–7
North America 185–7, 189–92, 202, see also
    United States
North Korea 206
Nozick, Robert 159 n.14

INDEX

obligations, existence of 5, 69, 74–5, 122, 125, 150–2, 168–9
obligation to obey the law 1, 3, 5, 12–15, 52, 57 n.6, 59 n.10, 111–12, 150–9, 158 n.11, 161, 163–4, 169–70, 172–4, 176–8
ontological premise 9–10
Owens, David 12, 15 n.11, 44–5, 65 n.17, 69–72, 73 n.26, 74–5, 84–5, 102, 123 n.3, 126, 144–6, 147 n.30

people's commitments 10, 14, 82, 87–8, 88 n.9, 90–1, 94–7, 104–5, 114, 167–70, 172, 176–8, 197–8, 206, 210–11, 214
pluralistic
   ignorance 32–4, 46
   societies 106, 114–15, 171–4, 193, 216–17
   world 178, 205
power-conferring norms 12–13, 18–19, 20 n.5, 43, 46–8, 51, 119–20, 132, 141–5, 216
property 56, 71, 81, 131, 185, 200, 215
   laws 107–8
   norms 8–9, 58, 71, 73, 101–2, 104–5, 143–5, 215–16
   requirements 104–5, 129, 131–2
   rights 11, 58, 63, 71, 72 n.25, 84, 101–2, 107–8
   rules 84
   violations 84
propositional attitudes 23–4, 24 n.11

queuing/queues 1–2, 4, 9, 11, 17, 23, 26–7, 43, 49–50, 55–7, 63, 76–7, 79, 81–2, 94–5, 97–100, 102, 106–7, 109–10, 143–4, 147–8, 176, 213–16

Rawls, John 8 n.10, 13, 16, 85, 101, 109 n.27, 110, 142, 161, 172–3, 182, 184
reactive attitudes 1 n.2, 18–19, 33–4, 37, 48–51, 72, 74–5, 155, 168–9, *see also* moral reactive attitudes
reflective equilibrium 8 n.10, 16, 85
right-holders 11, 102 n.19, 102, 122, 125, 146, 182, 215–16
rights
   as control 13, 119–26, 128–9, 140–1, 143–9, 199–200, 215–16
   as inviolability 13, 119–23, 126, 145, 147, 149, 162 n.17, 215
   existence of 12–13, 119, 122–3, 148–9, 215–16
   natural 12–13, 119–20, 126
   moral 1–2, 12–13, 15, 52, 66, 119–49, 191
   legal 183
robust intentions 25–8, 30*f*, 34, 39, 89–90, 107

rule of law 14, 105, 150–1, 154–5, 160–1, 167–73, 176–8, 200–3, 207, 210–11

Scandinavia 172, 186–7, 189, 193–6, 202–3
Scanlon, T. M. 52–3, 62–4, 65 n.17, 66, 72 n.24, 78–80, 101, 114, 214–15
Scotland 157, 173–4, 186, 197, 204
Scottish people 187, 194, 196–7, 202–4
Searle, John R. 5 n.6, 60 n.13, 128–9, 131 n.17, 132 n.18
secession 179, 205, 217
slavery/slaves 1 n.1, 49, 90–1, 109–10, 122–3, 138–41, 143, 154
Southwood, Nic 6–7, 17 n.2, 22 n.8, 31 n.18, 41, 59 n.10, 98, 112
sovereign 126, 143, 181–5, 205
   equality 200–3, 205–7
   power 199–200
   rights 187
   state 141–2, 200
   status 183–5
   will 179
sovereignty 1–2, 12, 15, 121, 143, 181–5, 198, 206
   collective 14–15, 158, 179–81, 187–8, 191–3, 198, 200, 207
   corporate 183–5
   de facto 182–4
   individual 181–4, 199
   internal 183, 200–2
   justified 182 n.2, 182–5, 193, 200–1
   norms 14–15, 201–3, 205–7
sovereignty violations 14, 152, 179, 182 n.3, 185–7, 190, 192–3, 197–200, 203–7
   collective 180, 191–3, 198
   de facto 200–1
   individual 185
   pure 14–15, 179–80, 185, 187, 194, 202
   trilemma 180–1, 185–90, 198, 204
   wrong of 12, 179–207
speech acts 12, 128–34, 137, 200
Stilz, Anna 14–15, 99 n.17, 109 n.26, 112, 141–2, 161–2, 179, 186, 194–7, 199, 203–6
Sweden/Swedes 164, 186–7, 190, 194–6, 202–3

target general moral principle 62–4, 67, 73, 76, 88, 157
target grounding sequence 61–2, 156
taxation 23, 43, 63–4, 153–4, 159–64, 186
Traffic Light 57–8, 60, 64–5, 85–6, 103, 150, 155–6, 158–63, 176, 200

United Kingdom 2, 4, 55–6, 81–2, 97, 170, 186, 199–200, 204

236 INDEX

United States 76, 165–6, 173, 186, 190–2,
  195, 202
  civil rights movement 173
  Congress 58–9, 85 n.8, 155 n.6
  Constitution 59, 59 n.10, 77
  Foreign Intelligence Surveillance Act
    (FISA) 58–9, 77, 85 n.8, 155 n.6
  National Security Agency 58–9, 85 n.8, 155 n.6
  Presidents 58–60, 59 n.10, 77, 85 n.8,
    105, 155 n.6
  see also North America

Valentini, Laura 14, 16, 60 n.14, 81 n.1, 151–4,
  157 n.8, 159 n.12, 163–4, 165 n.20,
  179, 184
valid moral norms 1 n.1, 18–19, 21–2, 50–1

waiver power 125, 131–4, 138, 141–5, 215
Wellman, Christopher H. 14–15, 161 n.16, 179,
  186, 190–3
Williams, Bernard 212–13, 213 n.3
wrong reasons problem 67–8, 79–80, 101–2,
  214–15